TRIPLE ENTENDRE

TRIPLE ENTENDRE

Furniture Music, Muzak, Muzak-Plus

HERVÉ VANEL

UNIVERSITY OF ILLINOIS PRESS

Urbana, Chicago, and Springfield

© 2013 by the Board of Trustees
of the University of Illinois
All rights reserved
Manufactured in the United States of America
c 5 4 3 2 1

♾ This book is printed on acid-free paper.

Library of Congress Cataloging-in-Publication Data
Vanel, Hervé.
Triple entendre : furniture music, Muzak, Muzak-plus / Hervé Vanel.
pages   cm
Includes bibliographical references and index.
ISBN 978-0-252-03799-3 (cloth : alk. paper)
ISBN 978-0-252-09525-2 (E-book)
1. Environmental music—History and criticism.
2. Muzak (Trademark)
I. Title.
ML3920.V35   2013
781.5'3—dc23   2013017024

To Rebecca, with love.

To Victor Culbertson, for things might be done that haven't yet.

Contents

Preface: Cage Free   ix

Introduction   1

Chapter 1. Furniture Music: A Musical Irresolution by Erik Satie   10

Chapter 2. Muzak Incorporated   46

Chapter 3. Muzak-Plus and the Art of Participation   84

Conclusion: The Community to Come   126

Notes   135

References   181

Index   189

Preface
Cage Free

Rob Haskins once remarked that John Cage had always been "many things to many people—an extraordinarily prolific composer, performer, teacher, essayist, aesthetician, painter, and poet. He was known for his avid and often learned pursuit of subjects other than music, such as Zen Buddhism, Thoreau, mushrooms, and Marshall McLuhan. His musical output was no less diverse."[1] Cage also, suggests Daniel A. Herwitz, may have been many things to himself, and it remains daunting to distinguish clearly among the composer's many voices: "[They] both coagulate and contradict, leaving one unsure as to what one is hearing and thus how one should respond. Furthermore, Cage isn't simply a man of many selves; he specifically intends to conflate and confuse."[2] Many scholars have thus studied the work of this tutelary and versatile figure from a wide range of critical perspectives. The following inquiry is fully indebted to many incredibly sophisticated studies devoted to Cage by scholars like James Pritchett, Richard Kostelanetz, William Fetterman, David Patterson, Douglas Kahn, and more recently Branden W. Joseph, Julia Robinson, and Rebecca Y. Kim.[3] While it may, at times, conflict with existing interpretations, the purpose of the discussion in this volume is not to dispute their relevance. It would not only be impossible to resolve the contradictions that the large body of Cagean studies reflects, discusses, perpetuates, and sometimes accentuates. It would also be fundamentally useless to attempt to imprison the polysemic nature of his artistic trajectory into a single and fixed meaning. The following inquiry does not seek to subsume the extraordinary plurality of John Cage's art into one interpretative model; it is first and foremost concerned with the implications of the strange (and ultimately unrealized) concept of Muzak-plus, formulated by Cage in 1961. In this light, what follows is not a musicological study, and the figure of John Cage that is privileged is that of the artist-thinker, especially in its 1960s incarnation.

This volume, however, is not strictly devoted to Cage. In order to discuss the concept of Muzak-plus, it appeared necessary to examine its industrial counterpart, that is, the pervasive product known as Muzak. The existing body of literature devoted to this phenomenon may not be as vast as the one dedicated to Cage, but it is nonetheless significant. Joseph Lanza's *Elevator Music: A Surreal History of Muzak, Easy-Listening, and Other Moodsong* (1994) is certainly the most popular book on this controversial genre of music, but Stephen H. Barnes's 1988 study on the Muzak Corporation presents a more focused critical history of the major company that developed and distributed functional music. Jerri A. Husch's unpublished dissertation *Music of the Workplace: A Study of Muzak Culture* (1984) offers a notable foray into the study of Muzak as a tool for work management.[4] In addition, one cannot but mention the innumerable articles published on the subject from various points of view, including ethnomusicology, sociology, psychology, (pop) cultural studies, and marketing. Ultimately, all of those sources contribute to an understanding of Muzak. Still, probably the most fascinating literature on Muzak remains that produced or sanctioned by the company itself; unburdened by critical concerns and bolstered by an unashamed desire to subjugate, it exhibits Muzak's rhetoric in all its crudeness.

Muzak-plus undeniably responds to Muzak, but Erik Satie's earlier investigations into *musique d'ameublement* (furniture music) are inscribed as a watermark within Cage's concept. Satie is, no less than Cage, a complex personality. Here again, it would be impossible to consider part of Erik Satie's oeuvre without referring to the work of many experts, from Pierre-Daniel Templier, Rollo H. Myers, Robert Orledge, and Alan M. Gillmor, to Ornella Volta and Jean-Pierre Armengaud.[5] Although many of them have discussed *musique d'ameublement*, reaching various conclusions, this minor output of the composer's production remains nonetheless remarkably problematic. The issue becomes even thornier when it intersects with John Cage's aesthetics and/or Muzak.

It quickly appears, for instance, that furniture music and Muzak are bound to explain each other. Readers interested in this issue mostly face a double bind: Satie invented muzak, and muzak realized Satie's idea (whether unfaithfully or not). Oftentimes, rather interchangeably, the understanding of the first depends on a missing definition of the second. As it seems, many attempts to examine the influence of one concept from a single point of view—say, the legacy of Satie's work—end up mainly perplexing.

PREFACE   xi

In his 2009 study on Satie, for instance, Jean-Pierre Armengaud argues that furniture music is remembered only thanks to John Cage's understanding of its value as "a reflection upon the use of music as a means of improving man's environment and upon the functionality of music."[6] According to Armengaud, one must also admit that the challenge opened by furniture music positioned Satie as "the prophet of all marketing-oriented musics, capable of stimulating the work force as much as the spending of consumers."[7] At last, he argues, one may understand furniture music as a fully Dadaist and nihilistic gesture, as a "music" (i.e., from which Music is protected) whose not-so-subtle message could be thus summarized: "Down with music; long live the sounds that paint the world anew!"[8] Certainly, Armengaud's volume—published in 2009—benefited from its predecessors' efforts and relies on an indisputable and extraordinary knowledge of Erik Satie's life and work, which lies far beyond the reach of the present inquiry. Nevertheless, the scope of such versatile interpretations borders syllogism: Cage's music pursued the concept of furniture music; furniture music anticipated muzak; Cage's music follows muzak as a (Dadaist?) "means of improving man's environment."

Consideration of Satie and Muzak is certainly not absent from Cage's scholarship. Readers of Douglas Kahn's 1997 study "John Cage: Silence and Silencing"[9] may be familiar with many of the issues at stake in the following inquiry. While he does not refer to Muzak-plus, Kahn's lengthy and intricate discussion is undeniably wide-ranging. It is hard to follow the author, however, when he argues that as Cage was offering to "replace" Muzak with *musique d'ameublement*, he was "calling for a Muzak not-to-be-listened-to, [therefore] attempting to make Muzak more Muzakal."[10] Faced with a new adjective made out of a noun whose meaning is assumed, one can only wonder. Does the author imply that Muzak is meant to be listened to, or that it is listened to despite itself? Why would Satie's furniture music succeed in raising the level of inconspicuousness of Muzak, as the expression "more Muzakal" seems to imply? How could furniture music hypothetically succeed in not being listened to at that point when it failed in another instance (as we will be reminded in Chapter 1)? Seen through the lens of Cage's art and thinking, the concept of furniture music sometimes looks like an unchecked alibi. Satie's *Vexations*, for instance, whose performance was organized by Cage, is certainly a relevant piece to discuss in relation to furniture music. But does it represent an "epic of *musique d'ameublement*," as one biographer of Cage asserts?[11] The chapters devoted to Satie and Muzak will show, at least, that some of these questions do not deserve to be asked.

Visibly, the specific terms of the discussion—furniture music, Muzak, and Cage's subsequent reflection—remain ill defined. Consequently, the present study offers to articulate its inquiry in three sections devoted to each object of study, before concentrating, in relation to Cage, on the concept of Muzak-plus. Undeniably, Cage was interested in Satie's music. But when it comes to furniture music, what is known of this strange musical object remains vague. Moreover, it is quite easy and expected to think that an avant-garde composer like Cage did not like Muzak and was eager to criticize it. But what was he criticizing exactly? Muzak is commonly rejected as bad music, but it is also a much more complex apparatus whose objective may sometimes overlap with an ambitious artistic project. The chapters respectively devoted to furniture music and to Muzak are, first and foremost, responding to the necessity of approaching Cage's concept with a better understanding of these two essential points of reference. Clearly, one cannot pretend that Cage's formulation of Muzak-plus included every piece of information about one or the other. Nonetheless, it is possible to assume that the composer was not simply reacting to rumors (about furniture music or Muzak) and that his reflection was reasonably well informed. To a certain extent, this inquiry sprang from a simple desire to gain a more informed and multilateral point of view in order to discuss one of the composer's ideas.

From the outset, the significance of an unrealized concept such as Muzak-plus, formulated in the margins of an otherwise extraordinary body of work, may be questioned. Reviewing the remarkable study of Cage's music conducted by James Pritchett, Rob Haskins justly praised Pritchett for making "Cage's music—not his ideas—a central focus of study."[12] The present reflection, quite obviously, does not respond to this nonetheless legitimate concern. Considering the influence of Cage's ideas rather independently of his music, or at least without pretending to approach it from a musicological standpoint, may seem aberrant. An artist like Bruce Nauman, however, readily acknowledged that his interest in Cage's ideas was not dependent on hearing his music. As he remembered, "[you] could read [John Cage] and still get lots of useful information. In fact, in some ways it was more useful than hearing him."[13] Such a remark does not forbid listening to Cage's music, and bears no insult. After all, James Pritchett himself conceded that, in one notorious instance, Cage's music may have failed to realize his ideas. Considering *4'33"*, Pritchett indeed comes to the conclusion that, in the end, "Cage's understanding of silence could never be communicated directly through a piece of music of any kind, either with sounds or without them."[14] In this regard, while it will ultimately be suggested that Cage found some opportunities to design musical situations corresponding to the concept of Muzak-plus, the latter remains fundamentally prospective. As an idea, it anticipates the blurring of boundaries and the definition of unstable dynamics within a collective space. Its realization, however, is left to the imagination. For an art historian interested in a concept formulated by an avant-garde composer whose ideas were central to the development of performances and happenings in the 1960s, a concept such as Muzak-plus is relevant to understanding the complex relationships between art and life emerging at that time and still influencing the development of contemporary arts. Ultimately, this attempt to explore an artist's ambition does not intend to uncover his intentions in order to demonstrate how well implemented they may be in resulting artworks. It simply wishes to discuss, from a philosophical standpoint, the ambition of an artistic program whose utopian and prospective nature forces reflection upon the capacity of art to reform society. What could be more appropriate in this regard than an unrealized idea? The conclusion of this inquiry will hopefully offer some elements of an answer, but the existence of Muzak may already furnish an obvious one.

TRIPLE ENTENDRE

INTRODUCTION

> The music of the future? Surely beyond notes and based on sound. In reality, of course, the music of the future can only be the music of the present, but is, with rare exceptions, the music of the past.[1]
> —Edgard Varèse

In October 1961, to his own puzzlement, the avant-garde composer John Cage was commissioned by the artist and thinker Gyorgy Kepes to write an essay on the questions of module, rhythm, proportion, symmetry, beauty, balance, and so on.[2] Cage's piece was to contribute to the collective volume *Module, Proportion, Symmetry, Rhythm*, part of the "Vision + Value" series, finally published in 1966.[3] As he had done before,[4] Cage used his score for *Cartridge Music* (1960) as a tool and ended up designing his piece of writing following a set of directives such as: "from line 24 to line 57, tell a story that is relevant to proportion, discuss an idea about rhythm, follow this with an idea that has nothing to do with balance." In the final text, paragraphs are separated by empty spaces that were translated into silences when Cage delivered his piece as a lecture.[5] There, in between two paragraphs, Cage offers a peculiar vision of a future music. "There'll be centrally located pulverized Muzak-plus ('You cling to composition.') performed by listeners who do nothing more than go through the room."[6]

Cage's formulation of Muzak-plus remains, at first sight, rather elliptic. It is expressed in impersonal terms ("There'll be . . .") preventing the identification of Cage, or anyone else, as the composer. The future tense not only indicates a forthcoming phenomenon, it also induces its inevitability. Muzak-plus is described as being both contained ("centrally located") and perfectly volatile ("pulverized"), as if Muzak-plus were an emanation of sorts, consciously or inadvertently released by "performers-listeners." In between brackets, an unidentified voice opposes a conventional mode of making music to Muzak-plus, as if composition were getting in the way of a form of decomposition. The term *Muzak-plus* itself is meant, with some humor, to convey a sense of what this future music will be. Ringing like those advertising slogans promoting an old wine in a new bottle, Muzak-plus promises something "more" than muzak but not, one might think, something entirely other. Cage died in 1992, and none of his work bears the title of Muzak-plus; to this extent it is reasonable to think that it remained unrealized. But the idea persisted, and, among "things that might be done that haven't yet," one reads in Cage's "Diary: How to Improve the World (You Will Only Make Matters Worse) Continued 1973–1982," "The use of photoelectric eyes to scan the principal entrances and exits at Grand Central bringing about pulverization of Muzak."[7] What was Cage, with such persistence, expecting to pulverize? The general and common understanding of *Muzak* could not be clearer: It is "a registered trade name that has insinuated itself into people's minds as a generic noun signifying 'canned' or pre-recorded background music played in places of public resort."[8] Or again, as the company defined itself at the end of the 1970s: "Muzak is a company that provides functional music as a tool of management in environmental situations."[9] The term has nonetheless a double entendre: *muzak* (lower case) refers to the genre of background music in general, while *Muzak* (with a capital, as in Cage's remark above) refers specifically to the trademarked product. Generally speaking, however, both meanings easily convene in one common sentence: "Muzak is the single most reprehensible and destructive phenomenon in the history of music."[10]

Muzak may be to blame, but it is impossible to consider Cage's reference to Muzak outside of his lifelong interest in the work of the French composer Erik Satie and more specifically in *musique d'ameublement* [furniture music]. Designed by Satie in the late 1910s and early 1920s, such "music" (as it is often prudently labeled) would play in our houses "a role similar to light [and] heat."[11] Very few examples of such music by Satie exist, and, despite Cage's notorious efforts to promote the composer's achievements, they have long been regarded as marginal, eccentric, or "deliberately ludicrous"[12] experiments within a body of work of disputable quality. As the composer Lothar Klein remarked in 1966, Satie's work is "small and much of it is purposely awkward," and, in any case, it is "more discussed than performed."[13] Such lack of performance is quite understandable if one admits with Klein that, with furniture music, Satie had made a major yet embarrassing contribution to the twentieth century: "he invented Muzak."[14] "Clearly today's Muzak is yesterday's *Musique d'ameublement*," wrote another critic in the late 1970s. "The only difference is that now the idea works."[15]

John Cage's lifelong interest in the work of Erik Satie is a well-known matter.[16] Even though by the mid-1960s he had given away his collection of Satie's music,[17] numerous ephemera (scores, book clippings, catalogues, concert programs) related to the French composer subsist in his papers, including "I Love Satie" buttons, and many musical pieces by Cage—beyond *Cheap Imitation* (1969)—refer implicitly or explicitly to Satie.[18] While in Paris, in 1949, Cage spent countless hours researching Satie's music, hunting for unknown and unpublished scores.[19] His search included furniture music, even though he had been told that such pieces might never have existed.[20] Twenty years later, in 1969, Cage was still taken aback by the dearth of information available on furniture music and the general lack of interest in these uncanny pieces. The score of one of them, *Carrelage phonique*, was reproduced without a date in Cage's 1969 volume *Notations*, and *Tapisserie en fer forgé*, listed here as well, was similarly undated. But how many of such pieces had Satie written? How had he conceived them? After asking Darius Milhaud, Henri Sauget, and "all the people who'd written books on Satie" about them, Cage only concluded that, in the end, "[not] one of those people devoted to Satie took the matter seriously."[21] Yet, estimated Cage, furniture music—that is, "the concept of a music to which one did not have to listen"—may have been Satie's "most far-reaching discovery."[22] Located in an indeterminate future, the yet-to-come Muzak-plus thus echoes the omnipresent murmur of functional background music in contemporary society while nodding toward the "far-reaching" precedent of Satie's furniture music. It could thus be heard as a twisted response to the definition of the music of the future that the composer Edgard Varèse gave to Cage in 1947: "[It] can only be the music of the present, but is, with rare exceptions, the music of the past."[23]

Conversing about Satie with Cage and the musicologist Alan Gillmor in the early 1970s, Roger Shattuck[24] expressed a common dilemma. "I have to admit," said Shattuck, "that [as] much as I am ready to accept in aesthetic terms what Satie calls 'furniture musique,' . . . I nevertheless do a slow burn whenever I walk into an airport and have to listen to the canned muzak. When it comes from Satie it seems to be all right. But when it comes from the commercial establishment . . . it seems outrageous."[25] Hence, implies Shattuck's remark, furniture music and muzak are not fundamentally different, but, from the point of view of the esthete, it would be better if one could set them apart. Basically, background music sounds acceptable when it is formulated in the field of high culture but sounds intolerable when it emanates from a commercial venture. Cage sounds more relaxed about the issue. Answering Shattuck's concern, he does not hesitate to suggest that one could convince Muzak to "record the *musique d'ameublement* and use that."[26] Clearly, Cage's response is not prescriptive (i.e., not offering to replace Muzak with furniture music) but only intends, in the context of a debate, to question Shattuck's position. Indeed, one can always suppose that such use of Satie's music—or, following Shattuck's understanding, the use of any other "things of that *quality*"[27]—would drastically improve the standards of canned music. Still, finding reassurance in such criteria of judgment is only illusory. How could a conventional notion of "quality" respond to a kind of music to which—as Cage stresses—"we need not pay special attention"?[28] Logically, traditional standards do not apply. Cage himself was eager to separate furniture music and Muzak, but not necessarily on aesthetic grounds. When he did, it was by comparing their alleged social function. On the one hand, he estimated, Muzak simply "attempts to distract us from what we are doing," whereas on the other hand, "Satie's furniture music would like us to pay attention to whatever else we are doing."[29] In these terms, Satie's concept is meant to foster a form of self-awareness or to draw attention to existing collective dynamic, while Muzak is meant only to induce a state of general numbness.

Cage's distinction between Satie's concept and Muzak's product already clarifies why the artist may have been so eager to pulverize the latter. Muzak appeared, beyond doubt, as an instance of power in contemporary society. Cage himself demonstrated a clear awareness of the harsh implications of industrial background music when he identified it as music "for factory workers, or for chickens to force them to lay eggs."[30] Actually, Cage's criticism strictly mirrors the discourse of the company, whose vice president could state in all earnestness: "We do furnish Muzak in a few other kinds of places—like stables, to keep horses calm—but our primary function is the furnishing of environmental music in work areas."[31] Following this standard, the company clearly considered its product as responding to a "cultural universal," whose careful criteria of production made it suitable for transmission "twenty-four hours a day throughout the world."[32] Then again, if Muzak is simply understood as a form of "subliminal music" influencing "people's moods, to make them function better, or buy more," one could simply—as suggested in Klaus Maeck's 1984 movie *Decoder*—turn the motivation around: "Make people puke instead of feeling well, make people disobey instead of following, provoke riots."[33] The consequences of the proposal certainly do not lack appeal, but its logic paradoxically comforts the company in the promotion of its product's efficiency. After all, criticizing Muzak for its efficiency is as absurd as blaming teenagers' suicide on the influence of heavy metal music—as did the Parent Teacher Association in the 1990s—while ignoring that the source of the problem lies elsewhere.[34] Ultimately, the performative value of the company's promotional discourse is so strong that Muzak's claims about the effectiveness of its product, and notably its capacity to increase productivity, have been accepted uncritically even by its harshest opponents.[35]

The violence of the discourse that supports Muzak's achievement is in inverse proportion to the inconspicuousness of its implementation. At this juncture, the sheer banality of muzak, both as a brand and as a generic form of background music—that is, literally its ordinariness—makes it both a matter of contempt and an object of fear. While the aesthetic poverty of background music may elicit sheer disdain, its pervasiveness is dreaded as a powerful ideological apparatus. Of course, contrary to its principle, one may pay attention to background music, but always—and quite paradoxically—inadvertently. By all means, muzak constitutes a fully integrated form of "environmental music." For that matter, muzak might have been the most successful art form to emerge in the twentieth century or, more specifically, as Allan Kaprow once defined the function of experimental arts, the most efficient "introduction to right living."[36] Indeed, suggested Kaprow, once an artistic proposition has been welcomed as a component of our existence, "art can be bypassed for the main course," that is, life itself.[37] This conviction, said Kaprow in the late 1980s, remained the most important lesson to be gained from Cage's experiments.

Notoriously, art and muzak do not go well together. They do not belong to the same cultural spheres, and their functions, apparently, cannot be reconciled. Criticisms raised against muzak mostly qualify it as a corrupted form of music, attempting to regulate our lives inconspicuously. Then, against such corruption, it is tempting to emphasize the subversive power of art and to praise its capacity to mark out "a space of autonomy within the discourse of power."[38] Yet isn't this distinction nothing more than practical? By furnishing what Hal Foster calls our "world of total design" with an embedded soundtrack, muzak certainly contributed to the realization of the modernist dream that "high art would lose its autonomy in the general aesthetisation of life."[39] In the perspective of this dissolution, this study situates muzak in between its problematic and disputable anticipation in the work of the French composer Erik Satie (furniture music) and the response to muzak offered by John Cage (as Muzak-plus) in the aftermath of World War II.

It is not only the field of high culture that is suspicious of muzak. In turn, Muzak long resisted any association of its product with art.[40] Understandably, such amalgamation would only have weakened the perception of its product's functionality. Yet by the late 1960s, certainly inspired by the increasing role played by LP covers in marketing popular music, Muzak's promotional recordings relied on the visual impact of specifically designed artwork to convey the virtue of their product:

> To represent MUZAK's contemporary international sound, [Ray] Harrow selected an up-to-date abstract format, and rendered it in oils. He was particularly cautious to avoid painting in recognizable shapes. Instead, he took advantage of psychological findings that reveal how colors and shapes affect human behavior. He used these visual tools to evoke carefully calculated physiological and psychological effects, just as MUZAK uses sound.[41]

Despite Muzak's misguided sense of what constituted the most advanced art in the late 1960s, the association of their product with a pseudo-Pollock is telling (see figure 2.3). The related concept of "stimulus progression" was one of Muzak's strongest achievements. By rationalizing the use of all musical factors (tempo, orchestration, programming, duration, etc.) the company expected to modulate artfully the responses of listeners. It was this very ability that was presented as an artistic achievement. For the "artist-engineers" of Muzak, the collective social body constituted the ultimate musical instrument, recalling a metaphor used by Wassily Kandinsky in the early 1910s, "The soul is a piano with many strings," whose vibrations Muzak expected to master fully.[42] As for today, the company has reached an interesting compromise and does not hesitate to call "creative" the process leading to the crafting of specific "musical solutions": "What we call Audio Architecture is equal parts art and science."[43] Its art is perhaps to have escaped the attention of many studies devoted to the fascinating topic of "art and science," however regrettably.

For John Cage, Muzak's discourse, however preposterous, was not only objectionable. It also clarified the stakes of a competition in which both the arts and the products of industry were engaged. His comparative evaluation of furniture music and muzak may have stressed the possibility of separating one from the other, but by the same token it also indicated that they share a parallel if irreconcilable ambition. Introducing the collective of society to "right living" undeniably constituted the most coveted prize. "The gravest and most painful testimony of the modern world, the one that possibly involves all other testimonies to which this epoch must answer," wrote Jean-Luc Nancy, "is the testimony of the dissolution, the dislocation, or the conflagration of community."[44] Cage, among other artists involved in the emergence of happenings and performance-related art forms, not only attempted to prevent this collapse. By acknowledging the increasing power of functional music, the composer also recognized the need to circumvent the excessive and proselytizing grounds upon which many happenings of the 1960s, not unlike Muzak, attempted to outline those communitarian bounds.[45] Cage's efforts to redefine the condition of muzak can be seen as more than a *reaction* to a coercive instrument of social control. For the artist, it implied thinking actively of the collective foundations of a future form of living together. By examining the trajectory that goes from the formulation of furniture music by Erik Satie, through the development of industrial background music, to its redefinition in Cage's Muzak-plus, this study wishes to contribute to a broader reflection on the function of the artist in society.

Cage's politics constitute, nonetheless, a point of contention. It is widely accepted, as William Brooks observed, that every piece made by Cage after 1950 "was intended to further, one way or another, changes of mind and in society," and in this regard, he adds, the "range of strategies is astonishing."[46] On the one hand, Cage's compositional strategies, as much as the rejection of conventions that his art entails, seem to foster a sense of emancipation. The "performative freedoms, collaborative creative processes, and audience participation" that the composer promoted may, more or less readily, appear to be "consonant with the antiauthoritarian and democratizing movements" of the 1960s.[47] On the other hand, this superficial kinship should not conceal, in Yvonne Rainer's terms, the "goofy naivety" of the composer's politics. As she sees it, Cage's loyalty to the messianic discourse of Buckminster Fuller only leads the composer to a "total ignoring of worldwide struggles for liberation and the realities of imperialist politics."[48] In turn, by analyzing Cage's relation to silence from the standpoint of sound rather than music, Douglas Kahn sought to highlight the repressive dynamic of the composer's work and ideas. Recently, Sara Heimbecker condemned Cage's "dismissive" attitude toward countercultural tendencies such as "flower power" and "black power."[49] Remaining largely silent on these issues, argues Heimbecker, Cage simply appears to "give consent to the status quo."[50] *Qui tacet consentit . . .* Such criticisms corroborate Paul Virilio's observation that in today's society, silence has lost any capacity to express disapproval.[51] Reading them, one is also reminded of Meyer Schapiro's remark, in the late 1930s, when he observed: "The fact that a work of art has a politically radical content therefore does not assure its revolutionary value. Nor does a non-political content necessarily imply its irrelevance to revolutionary action."[52] Whether or not Cage is guilty according to current standards of artistic responsibility, shouldn't one rather (or at least also) question the capacity of an aesthetic denunciation of class struggles, apartheid, political repression, or again social injustice to take effect in society (i.e., to produce the desired reaction)? Should a politically engaged artwork, necessarily subject to interpretation, anticipate its effect? How does one step, in the field of art, from disputing the status quo to disturbing it?[53] Rather than being simply condemned on moral grounds, Cage's position could be used to examine the difficult relationship between art and politics.

William Brooks's discussion of the relationship between Cage's art and society articulates an internal tension. Although it is impossible to fully disregard Cage's concerns about "society and politics and about the relation of these to art," writes Brooks, it is nonetheless true that "Cage was rarely a 'political' artist in the usual sense; he resolutely avoided affiliations and causes."[54] While he forcefully defined himself as an anarchist, Cage failed, most of the time, to demonstrate his commitments to the topical issues of his time. Cage's comments may even appear crudely insensitive to those issues. Brooks recalls the artist's shocking answer to a composer who lamented that there was "too much pain in the world." Cage retorted bluntly: "I think there's just the right amount." Shall we conclude that Cage felt comfortable accepting a nonetheless revolting situation? Was he demonstrating once again a complete disdain for worldwide struggles? One could as well understand Cage's answer as an ironic way to question the very possibility of quantifying the pain in the world: Was the amount of pain yesterday more acceptable? Will it ever be "not enough"? In any case, is it really necessary to rally around a cause that is not debatable? Clearly, Cage saw no point in sanctioning a commonplace. The issue, suggests Brooks, is altogether elsewhere; it is located in Cage's sense of the articulation between past, present, and future:

> Cage says nothing about the amount of pain tomorrow, nor does he preclude efforts to reduce pain in the short or long term; he simply asserts that *at this moment,* this very *now* instant, the world *is* as it should be—not because it conforms to a judgment made yesterday about today, but because any effort to affect its condition tomorrow is futile unless its present state is accepted in full and without qualification.[55]

Cage's seemingly shocking estimation that there is actually the "right amount" of pain in the world is thus only understandable if, with Brooks, one agrees that Cage's social thought depends on a "reconception of time: not a continuum in which past flows into future through the present."[56] In other words, the artist neither evaluated the present against the past, nor did he envision the future as a better version of the present ("You will only make matters worse"). Rather than succeeding to anything, what is to come may rather embody a beginning from scratch. According to Brooks, Cage's chance-derived compositions implement such a dynamic, for in order to perform them, questions necessarily arise: "[Does] one approach the immediate future (the next musical event) with the same attitude, the same anxieties, that would be brought to the next event in a fully *intended* composition? Or is a certain insouciance about the outcome acceptable, if not inevitable? If all is acceptable, why shape the future at all?"[57] Cage's politics, according to Brooks, can be located in such an ethic of performance. Following this perspective, Branden W. Joseph also regards Cage's artistic program as being intrinsically political: "For Cage, form and politics seemed connected by the simple fact and to the degree that form was politics."[58] For instance, summarized Joseph, "the determinate passages from composer to score, score to performer, and performer to listener were understood as power relations."[59]

Ultimately, my inquiry in this volume remains fundamentally attached to the utopian dimension of Cage's thought. It is assumed—for instance—that the audience for which Cage may have designed Muzak-plus was an ideal one or, in other words, one that remains to come. To keep this conclusion in mind may be necessary to articulate the passage from the specific social context in which Muzak exists to the prospective ideal of society that permeates the discussion of Cage's project. Relying on the utopian dynamic that motivated an artist like Cage does not assume that his project was meant to outline a flawless political and social system designed to substitute itself for the existing one. Cage, it is true, was captivated by the technological, ecological prospect of a engineer-architect-poet like Buckminster Fuller and was confident that his all-encompassing vision could offer a technologically oriented and effective way to solve the problem of the distribution of the world's resources.[60] Like many others, Fuller's dream of a reconciled society has been criticized for its authoritarian dimension. Such criticism is surely deserved, but whether it turns out to be genuinely utopian or fully dystopian, any vision of the future can still serve, as it did Cage, as a point of reference—but not a past one—to evaluate the present. All creative gestures geared toward the future, however, do not have the retrieval of a golden age as their fundamental prospect. The conception of what Cage described as "musical situations" may point toward "desirable social circumstances"[61] and thus imply the projection of idealized conditions. But, as the last chapter will suggest, they do not *de facto* embody an immutable state of perfection.

CHAPTER 1

Furniture Music
A Musical Irresolution by Erik Satie

Musical Analphabet

That the French composer Erik Satie (1866–1925) could be considered—at least until the 1970s—as a "musical analphabet"[1] certainly motivated John Cage's respect for his art. If nothing else, his analphabetic status signaled the degree to which Satie had shaken the tradition of "serious music" and infuriated the guardians of its flame. Satie himself gladly upheld his reputation, introducing his 1912 *Memoirs of an Amnesiac* by saying, "Everybody will tell you that I am not a musician. This is correct."[2] Who else but such an analphabet could have posthumously received—more or less ironically— the questionable title of "father of muzak" for having coined, in the late 1910s, a genre that he called furniture music? By conceiving an unassuming music that would be "part of the noises of the environment," Satie could only vex established conventions that required, as Michael Nyman puts it, a piece of music, or any work of art for that matter, to "be interesting and dominating at all costs."[3]

It is true, however, that it may be difficult to take some of Satie's music entirely seriously. William Austin summarized quite aptly the kind of critical perplexity that part of his work may (still) trigger. One may indeed conclude that "1) Satie was cynically joking in a ponderous way; 2) he was deeply committed to a fantastic ideal, which he abandoned by 1900; 3) he served a subtler ideal, to which he remained faithful while protecting it with a shell of irony; 4) he was uncertainly groping his lonely way amid conflicting ideals."[4] Is *Vexations* (1893), for instance—a short piece consisting of four repetitive phrases to be repeated 840 times—really meant to be performed?

Vexations

ERIK SATIE

NOTE DE L'AUTEUR:
Pour se jouer 840 fois de suite ce motif, il sera bon de se préparer au préalable, et dans le plus grand silence, par des immobilités sérieuses

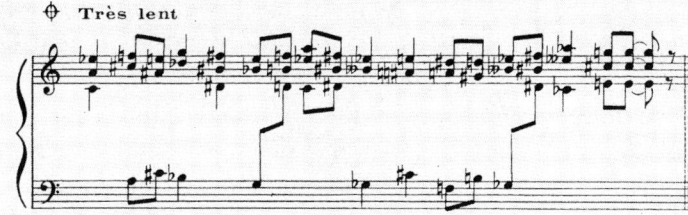

A ce signe il sera d'usage de présenter le thème de la Basse

Figure 1.1. Erik Satie, *Vexations* (1893). Indication: Tempo: Very Slow / At this sign, it will be proper to introduce the Bass theme. "Pour se jouer 840 fois de suite ce motif, il sera bon de se préparer au préalable, et dans le plus grand silence, par des immobilités sérieuses" (In order to play this motif 840 times in succession, it is recommended to prepare oneself in advance, and in the deepest silence, by means of serious immobility).

Even John Cage, who eventually organized a full performance of *Vexations* in 1963, taking turns with a team of pianists for eighteen hours and forty minutes, had not always been convinced that the piece should ever be performed. As a matter of fact, Cage had written five years earlier, "one could not endure a performance of *Vexations*... but why give it a thought?"[5] It seemed more reasonable not to give it any thought indeed, and at this point, at least, Cage considered the value of the piece to reside entirely in its concept. One could end up thinking of *Vexations* as a musical equivalent of some of Andy Warhol's (painfully long) movies. After all, as Warhol himself suggested, these films may be "better talked about than seen."[6] As its very title intimates, *Vexations* would thwart any conventional expectations of variations and comforting resolution.

Satie's pieces of furniture music (often assimilated with *Vexations* in the 1960s, and still today[7]) are each fundamentally based on a short musical fragment, to be repeated ad lib (at one's pleasure). As such, they are intrinsically monotonous and can retain the attention of the active listener for only a short span before boredom inevitably sets in. *Vexations*, as Robert Orledge noticed, was thus only one of Satie's "numerous ways to cheat the passage of time" through an "absence of any climax or movement towards a goal."[8] Furniture music is grounded on such principles, forever eluding resolution. Repetition, of course, is not an uncommon musical feature and does not necessarily deprive the listener of a conventional sense of linear, passing time. Yet, to this effect, as Theodor Adorno insisted, repetition is meaningful only if it elucidates differences and develops nuances. To make his point, Adorno relies on the famous example of the first movement of Beethoven's Fifth Symphony. After the "short and precise motif" has been presented and once it starts to be repeated, "it remains clearly recognizable as the same" throughout the movement. Yet, Adorno continues, "there is no mere repetition, but development: the melodic content of the basic rhythm, that is to say, the intervals which constitute it, change perpetually." Thus, balancing repetition and difference, "the richness prevents the simple from becoming primitive, while simplicity prevents richness from dissipation into mere details."[9] Such balance, concluded Adorno regretfully, was fully lost in a radio broadcast of the piece that compressed the successive stages to a point where the processual character of the work was lost and "the static repetition becomes purposeless: the material repeated is so simple that it requires no repetition to be understood."[10] Thereby broadcast into humdrum repetition, the only escape for the Fifth would be to turn itself into a piece of furniture music: something to be heard but not listened to.

Discarding, for now, this accidental contribution to Satie's concept, the small number of existing pieces of furniture music (five in total are known) still cannot justify the relative oblivion into which they have fallen after Satie's death. While a single piece—*Vexations*—has acquired a near-mythical/legendary status following Cage's performance, furniture music still stands for little more than a footnote in the exegesis of Satie's oeuvre, and by extension it does not bear much weight in the history of twentieth-century music and art. While not entirely ignored by scholars devoted to his oeuvre, furniture music is nonetheless discussed in frustratingly brief terms. Not concert-oriented music, and entirely lacking any clear temporal boundaries, such pieces stood no chance at becoming integral parts of anyone's general performance repertoire. More than *Vexations*, the pieces of furniture music possess an intrinsic and inherent marginality, which has prevented them from becoming "classic," even within the permissive landscape of experimental music. And finally, the question and by extension the definition of "functional music" remains a fundamentally uneasy one and, to this extent, a topic generally avoided by scholars. Satie, observed Wilfrid Mellers, may have composed "functional" or "circumstantial" music, which with its "intended banality" and refusal to express or illustrate anything "only serves as background 'music.'" Still, a music of that type—concluded Mellers—"has obviously no intrinsic value, but at a time when the emotional and intellectual life of the 'masses' is continually brought down by the low standard [infériorité] of the art they are offered, it was important to ask clairvoyantly the question of the 'emotional material of music' and of the quality of this material."[11] In other words, furniture music has no value (no function, no interest) beyond addressing critically the poverty of music "for the masses" by bringing such poverty of emotional content to an extreme degree. And this being said, the case of furniture music is closed.

As the musicologist Stephen Hinton puts it, the concept of "useful music" may appear either as a tautology (after all, music always has some use) or as an oxymoron: "if music has a specific use then it is not really music at all."[12] Mellers's appreciation exemplified this latest conviction, and the implicit understanding of art as an autonomous activity has rarely ceased to motivate, if not to dominate, the critical discourse.[13] As Hinton continues, "the shared and tacit assumption of music's autonomy had been unreflected; music had been considered autonomous, as it were ontologically."[14] The following study is, from a nonmusicological point of view, an attempt to grapple with both the challenges and the legacies of furniture music. Subsequent chapters examine the relationship of furniture music to industrial and functional music as they develop in the 1940s, as well as the influence of Satie's conceptions, in the second half of the twentieth century, on the artistic endeavors of John Cage, especially his attempts to formulate a "Muzak-plus."

Esoterik Satie

"It is important with Satie," once remarked Cage, "not to be put off by his surface."[15] The warning is indeed necessary for, as with Warhol, Satie's personal surface can be quite essential to the study of his compositions. Francis Picabia once described the composer as "a very susceptible man, arrogant, a real sad child, but one who is sometimes made optimistic by alcohol."[16] Also known as "the Velvet Gentleman" for his manner, in the 1890s, of confining his wardrobe to seven identical velvet suits, Satie was by all means a complexly self-fashioned, dandyish character. Whether or not one considers him a dandy from the top of his bowler hat down to his socks, his persona was part and parcel of his art. Satie might have defined himself as a *fantaisiste*,[17] but he was one of a serious kind. Bereft of most public and official recognition, he applied three times to l'Académie des Beaux-Arts in the 1890s, only—it seems—for the sake of being repeatedly rejected, a scenario that allowed him to express with some irony, in 1912, his "colossal chagrin" ["cela me fit grosse peine"].[18] But it is also clear that Satie genuinely resented negative criticism—to the point of deliberately misconstruing some critiques as praise.[19] His career is paradoxical and offbeat, very much in the image of a "gentle medieval musician lost in this century,"[20] as his friend Claude Debussy depicted him in 1892. On the one hand, Satie received delayed recognition in the 1910s for his earlier compositions, ones written without much formal training. On the other hand, his later work—composed after he received a diploma in counterpoint in 1908—was, to his consternation, mostly dismissed by a younger generation of musicians (known as "Les Six") who nonetheless adopted him as a "father" figure. The gap that Satie carefully maintained between his public life and his pitiable living conditions became manifest to his friends only when, after his death, they stepped foot for the first time into the composer's sanctuary in the suburbs of Paris.

> A narrow corridor, with a washbasin in it, led to the bedroom into which Satie had never allowed anyone, not even his concierge, to penetrate. It was with a feeling akin to awe that we approached it now. What a shock we had on opening the door! It seemed impossible that Satie had lived in such poverty. This man, whose faultlessly clean and correct dress made him look rather like a model

civil servant, had literally nothing worth a shilling to his name: a wretched bed, a table covered with the most unlikely objects, one chair and a half-empty wardrobe in which there were a dozen old-fashioned corduroy suits, brand-new and absolutely identical. In each corner of the room there were piles of old newspapers, old hats, and walking sticks. On the ancient, broken-down piano with its pedals tied up with string, there was a parcel whose postmark proved that it had been delivered several years before: he had merely torn a corner of the paper to see what it contained—a little picture, some New Year's present no doubt.... With his characteristic meticulous care, he had arranged in an old cigar-box more than four thousand little pieces of paper on which he had made curious drawings and written extravagant inscriptions.[21]

An extremely solitary and independent character, Satie merged in and out of disparate and conflicting artistic circles in the late 1910s and early 1920s. One can thus see him, in the last decade of his life, serving Jean Cocteau's neoclassical and nationalistic call for order supported by a "French music from France" ["une musique française de France"].[22] Conversely, he also appears in tune with the universal laws of purism promoted by Le Corbusier and Amédée Ozenfant; and he can be seen as echoing the aspirations of a painter like Fernand Léger to synchronize art with the rhythm of a mechanical world. Furthermore, he can be seen engaged in debates opposing a nascent surrealist spirit and Dadaist factions. Still, his readiness to collaborate with other artists was equaled by his capacity to mock them and turn them into enemies. One may think, as does Ornella Volta, that to a certain extent Satie subscribed or associated himself with a movement or party only to have the pleasure of leaving it loudly.[23] Regarding Cocteau, for instance, with whom he had notably collaborated on the controversial ballet *Parade* (1917), Satie would subsequently point out in the Dadaist publication *391* that the formerly outrageous poet was, by 1924, avoiding any scandal, becoming serious, and even "growing a belly (morally speaking, of course)."[24] To the end, Satie remained visibly eager to join whatever appeared to be the most insolent and potentially subversive artistic enterprise at any given time, trying his best to avoid a canonization he was nonetheless seeking. Leftist at heart, and opportunistically registered as a socialist after the assassination of Jean Jaurès in 1914, Satie nonetheless drew no correlation between progressive politics and advanced art. To the contrary, he remarked that "his dear communist friends . . . [were]—in Art—bafflingly Bourgeois."[25] In other words, Satie was well aware that a work's revolutionary content does not guarantee its revolutionary impact. Concomitantly, as the history of its premiere reveals, his innovative form of furniture music drastically failed to alter successfully the behavior of the listeners and consequently to fulfill its function.

Unfulfilled Promises

The only performance of furniture music during the composer's lifetime took place on March 8, 1920, at the Galerie Barbazanges in Paris. As furniture, the music was only one of several ingredients of a multifaceted soirée. Following the opening of an exhibition of children's drawings titled *Les belles promesses* [Pretty Promises], the audience was invited to hear music by Stravinsky and by members of the Groupe des Six.[26] The evening also included the staging of a (now lost) play by Max Jacob entitled *Ruffian toujours, truand jamais* (approximately: *Always Wicked, Never a Crook*). Satie had written, to be embedded within that play's two intermissions,[27] two pieces of furniture music, *Chez un 'bistrot'* ("At a 'Bar'"; first intermission) and *Un salon* ("A Living Room / Lounge"; second intermission).[28] As with all of Satie's pieces of furniture music, the titles appear to indicate a context, that is, the kind of space for which the musical fixture has been designed and where it is to be installed. Yet one can question Satie's contextual directives. The titles of the two pieces to be played during the evening at the Galerie Barbazanges refer neither to an art opening nor to a theater. Rather, the locations of a bar and a living room, as stipulated in the titles, correspond to the specific stage sets of two different acts within Max Jacob's play. It appears that Satie did not compose these pieces to furnish the event per se (i.e., the soirée) and enhance its atmosphere, but that he used the opportunity of stage settings indicated within the play to showcase his music in "real-life" situations of the everyday (i.e., a living room and a bar), and all this staged during two theatrical intermissions.

Still, the soirée itself remained the primary context for Satie's introduction of his concept of furniture music, and the audience, rather than the actors of the play, were meant to become the consumers of furniture music. To clarify the situation and prepare the audience, Pierre Bertin introduced the product (indeed, for sale) by speaking these words, which he had noted on the back of the program for another concert:

> We will also present today for the first time, thanks to Messieurs Erik Satie and Darius Milhaud,[29] and under M. Delgrange's direction, the *musique d'ameublement*, during the intermissions. We urge you to take no notice of it [*de ne pas lui attacher d'importance*] and to behave during the intermission as if it did not exist. This music, specially written for Max Jacob's play, claims to make a contribution to life in the same way as a private conversation, a painting of the gallery, or the chair in which you may or may not be seated. You will be trying it out. / MM. Erik Satie and Darius Milhaud will be at your disposal for any information and commissions.[30]

Part of the "furnishing" quality of the pieces thus depended on the specific circumstances of the event. Indeed, the orchestration of the two pieces, composed for piano duet, three clarinets, and a trombone, takes into consideration the instruments available following the six other musical numbers. The performers, as well, were the ones already engaged for other parts of the evening. As a first token of its deliberate unobtrusiveness, Satie's furniture music, like Cage's later *Living Room Music* (1940), was simply making use of what was around: the instruments and musicians used to perform numbers by Stravinsky, Milhaud, Poulenc, and others; the scene settings already conceived for the surrounding play by Jacob; and the context of the soirée itself, including the temporal boundaries laid in place by the "free time" of the two intermissions.

While the evening's other "traditional" musical performances used an onstage orchestra, for Satie's pieces, the three clarinets and the piano were placed into the four corners of the room. This distribution at once filled the space with sound and weakened any single visual or aural point of focus. Yet, despite the careful orchestration of what Volta calls a "musical décor," the performance failed miserably. Darius Milhaud, who assisted Satie in this endeavor, remembered that the warnings "not to pay any more attention to the ritornellos that would be played . . . than to the candelabra, the seats, or the balcony,"[31] to take no notice of the music and to "behave as if it did not exist,"[32] were all to no avail. Indeed, recalled Milhaud, "as soon as the music started up, the audience began to stream back to their seats. It was no use for Satie to shout: 'Go on talking! Walk about! Don't listen!' They listened [to the music] without speaking. The whole effect was spoiled."[33] Today's audience, fully immersed in a culture dominated by technologies of recording and broadcasting that have largely supplanted the traditional aesthetic contemplation induced by the concert hall, might be used to a form of "listening" that denotes "perceiving sound in either the active or the passive sense, or both."[34] But at the time of Satie and Milhaud, asking listeners to take no notice of the music sounded like an insurmountable contradiction.

At stake, however, is not only the resistance of an audience trained to signify their appreciation of music by adopting a respectful silence and assuming a static attitude understood to convey the appearance (at least) of "active" listening. Even today, giving all the visible signs that one is subjugated by a given artwork can function efficiently as a way to express one's appreciation and a means to communicate one's "understanding" of the work, even though in fact one may well be thinking of the grocery list. Quite certainly, the physical presence of an orchestra—no matter how small—could only be reminiscent of a traditional concert setting, even despite the performers' unconventional spatial distribution. While the highly repetitive nature of the music should have provided a quick hint of its low level of tolerability in terms of conventional listening, the simple and undeniable presence of the musicians proved to be a clear obstacle to Satie's design.

This problem was not a new one for American retailers, who had been trying to use music to promote sales since the 1880s. By the early 1910s, they had started to hide their hired orchestras from view, realizing that any visible musicians would distract customers from their purchases.[35] This solution, however, preceded the 1920s boom of broadcasting in the United States, and by the time Satie was promoting his furniture music in Paris, many American department stores were already equipped with their own radio stations (though music—mainly in the form of conservatory pieces and operatic selections—was, then, only a minor part of a more diverse programming effort that targeted housewives with the likes of cooking lessons and fashion talks).[36] It has nowadays become a given that "programmed music," largely understood as background and/or functional music, "requires the absolute separation of performer and audience." This definition has since been further fostered by recording industries.[37]

To a certain extent, Satie's concept of furniture music can be seen as (indirectly) competing with the commercial use of music. Indeed, rather than using potentially unsuitable selections from a classical repertoire to enhance sales (unsuitable, if nothing else, because such music is written to be listened to actively, not while shopping), Satie conceived of a genuinely functional music specifically designed both for its given setting and the activities associated with that setting. Ideally, a piece of Satie's furniture music, specifically written for a single venue, would solve the problem of using music as a means of "attracting" customers without "distracting" them from their duties as consumers. But the French composer was lagging behind the technological sophistication and experience of American retailing strategists in the functionalizing of music. Yet, if one is inclined to consider Satie as a Dadaist-minded artist, it is possible to understand the failure of the event as its actual success. Accordingly, a purposefully dysfunctional furniture music—one that reversed the hierarchy subduing an audience beneath the domination of the artwork—served to expose a set of weary conventions by orchestrating a clash between audience expectations and the musical output. Still, concluded Satie's collaborator Milhaud, the achievement of furniture music should not entirely be measured by the failure of its premiere. As a corrective, suggested Milhaud later on, such pieces could be "recorded and played over and over again," in order to further their integration.[38] No matter how innovative musically, the experiment demonstrated that Satie's product still needed some technological improvement to become effectively functional. Inasmuch as Cage considered that a performance of *Vexations* was ultimately necessary, the premiere of furniture music stresses a disjunction between the concept (of a music not meant to be noticed) and its realization (prompting the listeners to contribute unlooked-for duties of attention). Undeniably, the premiere of furniture music reveals a conflict between the composer's attempts to showcase his music—that is, to promote his product in order to attract commissions—and the need to make it inconspicuous in order to demonstrate its efficiency. In itself, this tension may explain an otherwise incomprehensible gap between the function of the two pieces (bistrot and salon) and the context of their performance (during an intermission, itself ostensibly a time of nonperformance).[39]

Musical Appliances

Strictly speaking, three sets of furniture music by Satie exist, and they reveal quite different specificities.[40] The first set,[41] from 1917, is composed for flute, clarinet, and strings, plus a trumpet for the first piece. The titles of the first two pieces—*Tapisserie en fer forgé* [Wrought-iron tapestry] and *Carrelage phonique* [Phonic tiling], identify the music as mock-decorative fixtures. Each piece consists primarily of a short musical phrase that, as a pattern, is to be repeated ad lib, or as the composer indicated for *Tenture de cabinet préfectoral*, "as often as one wants, but not more" ["à volonté, pas plus"]. The titles also provide examples of social circumstances for which the piece might be suited. The first and quite solemn motif, *Tapisserie en fer forgé*, could thus be played in the vestibule of the residence to welcome the guests at a reception [pour l'arrivée des invités (grande réception) / À jouer dans un vestibule]. *Carrelage phonique*, a more insistent and even slightly grating motif, could be played at a "lunch" or a wedding ceremony. As a piece of "tiling," this second motif calls for more extensive repetition and for a subdued interpretation (the movement is labeled "ordinaire") so that, in the end, it could be fully assimilated within the extant environment rather than attracting undue attention to itself.

The second set, from 1920 and labeled *Sons industriels* [Industrial sounds], was the one performed at the Galerie Barbazanges. The *Salon* piece is the most varied and accentuated motif, providing, it seems, a good background for multiple conversations. But more importantly, the motif quotes two popular pieces of the repertoire: first, the (tremendously popular) melody of "Connais-tu le pays, où fleurit l'oranger?" from Ambroise Thomas's *Mignon*

(1866) and then a variation on a brief passage of Saint-Saëns's *Danse macabre* (1872–74).[42] We can thus understand that part of the concept of furniture music relies on the recycling and quoting of popular tunes, discreetly appealing to the consumer's memory without being too intrusive. (As there are no footnotes in music, such "conversation" with popular refrains may very well be heard without being noticed.) The other piece ("Chez un 'bistrot'") is a short, upbeat, and slightly irritating tune, at least to an active listener who is not properly inebriated. To this extent, it is clear that "Chez un bistrot" can only take on its full meaning (that is, fulfill its function) in a very specific context, and perhaps with a drink in hand.

A last piece of furniture music for small orchestra from 1923, was commissioned by Mrs. Eugène Meyer Jr. of Washington, D.C. *Tenture de cabinet préfectoral* (approximately: Upholstery for a Governor's Office) was delivered by Satie to furnish the library of her residence. Again, as already noted regarding the relationship between the "salon" and "bistrot" compositions and the actual space and circumstances of their execution, the piece *Upholstery for a Governor's Office* hearkens to a more pompous and official setting than the one in which it was actually meant to be used. Yet the difference between a gubernatorial office and a domestic library may not be as great as it appears: both, in a way, call for a piece of background music that fits the pretentiousness of their ambience (an "eye-catching" piece, as Satie defined it).[43]

All in all, a few basic principles emerge that help to define Satie's concept of furniture music. Firstly, of course, there is the ad lib repetition of a short motif. Each piece of furniture music is therefore (theoretically, at least) never-ending. In accordance with this temporal elasticity, the "environmental" nature of furniture music was emphasized by the spatial distribution of the musicians in all corners of the room. If the temporal and spatial structure of furniture music appears quite clearly, its musical style is more difficult to pinpoint. This, clearly, is due to the intrinsic functionality of the music, which implies that the style of each composition is adapted to a specific style of situation. Still, this basic principle is already questioned within furniture music itself. In one case (the "Salon" piece) the fragmentary quotations of popular tunes offer the audience an unassuming reminiscence of familiar refrains. But here, the use of quotation is problematic and circular, because it transforms once-autonomous music into now-functional music, indicating a possible communication between two otherwise wholly distinct realms (autonomous music/functional music). Thus, as Hinton has noted, inasmuch as useful music could potentially be "listened to as—and thereby 'become'—autonomous music," likewise, "[a]utonomous music can . . . be 'functionalised,'" as has been powerfully demonstrated by the film industry, for example.[44] The use of musical quotation by Satie may thus appear to be at once a criticism of the "autonomy" of music and an inherent criticism of the concept of furniture music itself, if it is defined as a specific, irreducible genre. On the other hand, Satie is careful enough to stress this specificity through his titles, and sometimes offered additional notes as well (to the point of overstatement), thereby indicating the suitability of the music for a given architectural and social setting, though, as we have seen, these settings may refer to stage settings, or rooms other than the actual. In the end, the full or partial combination of these principles is meant to produce an entirely new kind of music—one not to be listened to.

Trapped in an Armchair

Within the literature devoted to Satie, two main interpretative tendencies, closely intertwined, have emerged in order to solve the problem of furniture music. The first one identifies the musical concept as a neoclassical equivalent, in the field of music, of the aims and endeavors of Henri Matisse's paintings. Roger Shattuck thus inaugurated the understanding of the "furnishing" component of Satie's music in the light of the painter's aspiration to create an art "analogous to a good armchair."[45] The trouble, however, is that such a decontextualized use of Matisse's words (from 1908) contributed to the drastic softening of the edge of the painter's aesthetic. For a long time, within the bulk of Matisse's exegesis, the regrettably powerful image of the armchair only helped to conceal the complexity of his art and especially to muffle the dissonances of its spatial organization.[46] Yet since Shattuck assimilated, quite freely, Satie's furniture music to Matisse's statement, the painter's words have often been introduced as the unequivocal source of Satie's idea. "As is well known," writes Robert Orledge, "Satie's concept of 'furniture music' derived from Matisse, who 'dreamed of an art without any distracting subject-matter which might be compared to a good armchair.'"[47] This is a disservice to Matisse, and to Satie. Orledge goes on to argue that "the term"—that is, "a good armchair"—"applies to much of Satie's music from 1916 onward."[48] All in all, suggests Orledge, Alfred Cortot's classification of Satie's piano works from 1916 to 1925 as "musique d'ameublement" may have been supported by the composer himself.[49] Undoubtedly, Shattuck's connection between Matisse's armchair and the furnishing component of Satie's music has been stretched to extremes. Ultimately, whatever elements possibly made Satie's music, or any music for that matter, comparable to a comfortable armchair for these authors remained unexplained. Did they consider the music relaxing in essence? If so, how could one explain the failure of Satie's premiere? Doesn't it, as the soirée at the Galerie Barbazanges revealed, depend on the listener's disposition?

Leading to a second interpretative trend, it has then been argued that it was because Satie was "tired of music's metaphysical pretensions" that he "sought to make music a commonplace pleasure."[50] Hence, echoing the armchair analogy, the composer Lothar Klein ventured, "Listening to music was to become like sitting on a comfortable sofa. The answer was musique d'ameublement or furniture music. Satie wanted 'to establish a music designed to satisfy useful needs. Furniture music fills the same role as light and heat. Furniture music for law offices, banks, etc.' The idea was not farfetched. Satie was completely twentieth-centuryized; he invented Muzak."[51] The dynamic that binds an individual artist to society at large is certainly difficult to fathom. Still, there is no excuse (even though Klein was writing in the mid-1960s) to suggest that an artist creates a certain type of work because s/he "tired" of another one. In the case of furniture music, at least, it is not up to an isolated artist to decide arbitrarily that a genre has worn off and to replace it with something "new." Certainly an artist may respond to or even anticipate a change that is, maybe too slowly but inevitably, taking place in society. Klein reflects a poor but widespread conception of the artist as driven only by his/her fancy, and an artist strangely in contradiction with Satie's noted ambition to satisfy useful needs (strangely equated to "commonplace pleasure"). Satie, in this light, would only have incidentally satisfied those needs, having invented Muzak despite himself. While the analogy is evocative of a soothing, unobtrusive art form integrated with the environment, Satie's ambition was arguably more complex. One can certainly use or misuse an armchair and even more so a sofa for many things for which it is not intended, but reducing furniture music (and by extension Muzak) to the function of a given piece of furniture is misleading. Furniture music is not meant simply to fit in the environment, nor is it necessarily meant to "relax" people. More specifically, furniture music is meant to contribute actively to the definition of the environment by creating a "vibration"—that is, an ambience or an atmosphere. Intrinsically modern and geared to the exigency of an industrial society, Satie's formulation of furniture music anticipated the status that industrial background music, more commonly called Muzak, strives to acquire in our society. As the president of Muzak Corporation (the pioneer and one of the leaders in background music) explained in the 1970s, his product aspired to fulfill a function in the surroundings that could be compared to "air-conditioning or the color of an office."[52]

Undeniably, one can easily draw connections between Satie's concept and the subsequent technology of Muzak. As for concluding that Satie "invented Muzak" per se, this only appears to be a commonplace, grounded in a set of superficial claims pervading most commentaries on furniture music. Satie, Joseph Lanza tells us in this regard, "affirmed his role as Muzak's true progenitor in a 1920 manifesto advocating musique d'ameublement ('furniture music')."[53] Using the loaded term "Manifesto," Lanza is, more than certainly, referring to Satie's 1917 draft for an unpublished promotional leaflet advertising furniture music for an event that ultimately fell through. Of course, it is not difficult to consider avant-garde manifestos as a means to promote artistic ideas. Likewise, Satie needed to convince the audience of the supremacy of his concept over other conventional genres of music. But a manifesto would have introduced it wrongly as an experimental form of advanced art (and one soon to be supplanted), not as a commercial product. Regardless of any nuances, Lanza feels free to conclude that "furniture music, far from being just another smug Dadaist hoax, was Satie's serious attempt to facilitate the simultaneous rise of canned music and movie soundtrack."[54] In the instance of "canned music," at least, it appears pointless to speculate on the composer's intention to foster the ascent of something he had never heard of. Nonetheless, Lanza's insistence on Satie's seriousness helps offset the numerous hasty judgments long cast over "background music" as "boring," "dehumanized," "vapid," "cheesy."[55] Nevertheless, in an attempt to define the genre, the same author cannot help but depict it in terms of "an artfully contrived regimen of unobtrusive harmonies and pitches, metronomic repetition; melodic segments that overlap into a tonal wash; a concatenation of hypnotic violins, harps, celestes, and other instruments connoting inherited concepts of how heaven sounds," and so on.[56] In other words, the general critical attitude against Muzak, based on moral ("dehumanized") or aesthetic ("cheesy") grounds and so quickly dismissed by Lanza, promptly enough reenters his own discourse through the back door.

Interestingly, the very first correlation drawn between furniture music and the development of functional music applied to daily life was, it seems, not motivated by any aesthetic judgment and was deprived of moral connotations. It was formulated in 1953 by Darius Milhaud, who had collaborated with Satie during the only public performance of the composer's furniture music. Milhaud perceived in the pervasive use of background music the confirmation that Satie's experimentation and insights in this domain responded to a "need." If one were to question the validity of the concept, "the future was to prove that Satie was right," Milhaud suggested. Indeed, he had noticed, people were nowadays commonly "reading and working to the sound of the radio," and "in all public places, large stores and restaurants the customers are drenched in an unending flood of music. In America cafeterias are equipped with a sufficient number of machines for each client to be able, for the modest sum of 5 cents, to furnish his own solitude with music or supply a background for his conversation with his guest. Is this not 'musique d'ameublement,' heard, but not listened to?"[57] While he remained a "serious" composer—that is, one who did not write functional music—Milhaud's collaboration with Satie apparently led him to appreciate the paradoxical concept of music not meant to be listened to. Whether one likes it or not, modern life seems to require such music to regulate and organize itself.

Following Darius Milhaud's insight, the opportunity is rarely missed to introduce the concept of furniture music as conceptual forerunner of muzak and—why not?—to give the composer the honorific and ironic title of "father of Muzak."[58] Roger Shattuck noted that, since Satie's unsuccessful experiment, "jukeboxes, radios, television, music while you work, canned music, audiotherapy—a whole race of creatures—have sprung into existence to fill the aural background of our lives the way interior decoration fills the visual background."[59] Is this to say that such an outcome was explicitly or implicitly imbedded in Satie's project? More prudently, David Toop argues that "the notion of music as a utilitarian and unobtrusive background to other activities was predicted with typical wit in 1920 by Erik Satie with his Musique d'ameublement, or 'furniture music.'"[60] Furniture music thus is not a force initiating Muzak, but only something anticipating critically (thanks to the composer's "typical wit") its inevitable occurrence. The composer is essentially credited with a concept, and Muzak with its regrettable implementation. When one sees Erik Satie, suggests Robert Orledge, as "a man of ideas"—that is, as a conceptual artist—it is possible to regard the composer as "a precursor of virtually everything from neoclassicism to minimalism (and even muzak)."[61] In reality, when establishing a link between Satie and Muzak, chronological precedence is not really the issue. What matters more to scholars is that a highly despised form of commercial and industrial music could have originated in the field of "serious" music—whether or not this latest term (serious) serves well the composer's notable wit. That is why, in this academic struggle to define the relationship between furniture music and Muzak, the doubt will always persist as to whether or not Satie intended his concept to be implemented in the terms of contemporary background music. We simply can't know. In the end, it always remains possible to absolve Satie from all responsibility, either by insisting on his Dadaist inclination (the ironic gesture) or on his conceptual nature (safe in the realm of ideas).

Such debate, however, might simply be situated on the wrong plane. The problem is not whether Satie facilitated the rise of canned music or not, and it goes beyond the question of the aesthetic quality of any music conceived as background. From a different point of view, the issue appears to be twofold. First, as the following remarks will suggest, the challenge of furniture music is less in inventing a genre than in reforming an existing tradition and adapting it to the present time. Second, by conceiving furniture music, which is a form of functional music, Satie addresses the broader and crucial issue of his time: the function of the artist in society. What the concept of furniture music questions, both seriously and with relative irony, is an existing competition between the fine arts and the products of industry, and the ambition of artists to contribute actively to the shaping of modern society.

Everyday Life's Music

Satie's 1921 definition of l'Esprit Nouveau as "essentially a return to the classical form—with a modern sensibility"[62] may well aid our understanding of furniture music. In Jean Cocteau's famous postwar notes on music, written after the 1917 scandal of his ballet *Parade*, Satie's music—and this may include his furniture music[63]—is presented as a salutary reaction to the degenerating influence of German instrumental music, which culminated with Wagner. "No more clouds, waves, fish tanks, floats and perfumes at night, we need an earthbound music: AN EVERYDAY LIFE'S MUSIC."[64] On the one hand, asserted Cocteau, avoiding Wagner's (or Debussy's) vagueness requires a return to the primacy of the melodic line as opposed to colorful harmonic blurs. On the other hand, Cocteau's call for an "everyday life's music" refers notably to his post-Futurist attempt in the ballet *Parade* to assimilate the liveliness of the "music hall, circus and American Negro orchestras," which Cocteau stressed "are not art but only inspire the arts."[65] In this context, Cocteau clearly regarded Satie's score for the ballet as a form of functional music supporting his attempt to assimilate the music of "everyday life" within a theatrical art form. Introducing the score of the four-hands piano reduction of the music, published in 1917, George Auric accordingly asserts that Satie's score was conceived to "serve as a musical background to a foreground of drums and scenic noises."[66] As Cocteau saw it, indeed, "the score of PARADE was to be used as a musical background to suggestive noises, such as sirens, typewriters, dynamos."[67] Cocteau's idea for *Parade* only reiterated the more aggressive proposal put forth few years earlier by the futurist Luigi Russolo, in his 1913 manifesto for the *Art of Noise*. Indeed, Russolo explained, this musical [r]evolution, undertaken within the futurist general synchronization of the arts with modern life,

> is paralleled by the multiplication of the machines, which collaborate with man on every front. Not only in the roaring atmosphere of major cities, but in the country too, which until yesterday was totally silent, the machine today has created such a variety and rivalry of noises that pure sound, in its exiguity and monotony, no longer arouses any emotion. . . . The ear of an eighteenth-century man could never have endured the discordant intensity of certain chords produced by our orchestras. . . . To our ears, on the other hand, they sound pleasant, since our hearing has already been educated by modern life, so teeming with variegated noises. Our ears, however are not content with them, and ask for an abundance of acoustic emotions. . . . [Musical sound] is too limited in its qualitative variety of tones. The most complex orchestras boil down to four or five types of instrument, varying in timbre: instruments played by bow or plucking, by blowing into metal or wood, and by percussion. And so modern music goes round in this small circle, struggling in vain to create new ranges of tones. This limited circle of pure sounds must be broken, and the infinite variety of "noise-sound" conquered.[68]

Compared with Russolo's radical attempt—most notably in *Risveglio di una citta, per intonarumori* (1913)—to shape an entirely new family of sound (such as rumbles, explosions, crashes, hisses, grumbles, gurgles, screeches, buzzes, groans),[69] Cocteau's struggle to introduce a few mechanical, industrial sounds within *Parade* is certainly rather tame. Still, the influence of American jazz on the poet and numerous musicians of the time, integrated in *Parade* via ragtime, denotes an interest for a type of music notoriously perceived as being in direct synchronization with the modern industrial soundscape. "With its cowbells, auto horns, calliopes, rattles, dinner gong, kitchen utensils, cymbals, scream, crashes, clanging and monotonous rhythm," noted the African American writer Joel A. Rogers in 1925, jazz "bears all the marks of a nerve-strung, strident, mechanized civilization."[70] Cocteau's appreciation of such music, heard in the context of bars and nightclubs, prompted him to assimilate the "barman" as a band member who, "surrounded by the accessories for making resonant noises, banging, and whistling, composes cocktails to swallow . . . all this resulting in a furor of sound."[71] Even though for European artists the Parisian urban soundscape of the time might not have been as exhilarating (i.e., noisy) as the American one, they clearly drew their inspiration from it and shaped their ideal accordingly.[72]

Musically speaking, however, Cocteau's endeavor differed from Russolo's efforts to create an art of noise, which had necessitated entirely new instruments. The framework of *Parade* was intended, from Cocteau's point of view, at least, to test the capacity of a musical composition to take into account certain nonmusical noises, offering them an efficient backdrop to become fully expressive. Cocteau was so infatuated with this idea that he even put in Satie's mouth the following claim: "I composed . . . a background to certain noises that Cocteau considered indispensable to outline the mood of his characters."[73] There is no reason, however, to accept uncompromisingly Cocteau's appreciation of Satie's score for *Parade*. First, as Ornella Volta recently remarked, Satie purposefully reserved, within the score, interstitial silences to be filled with the sound effects, thereby making a clear distinction between his music and the sound effect.[74] Listening to a performance of *Parade* from 2000,[75] including all of the sound effects desired by Cocteau, the "distinction" between music and noise is certainly clear, but this does not mean that they are as strictly independent as Volta suggests. There is clearly some legitimacy in Cocteau's exaggerated claim, a claim to which Volta, as a contemporary critic reluctant to reduce Satie's score to a mere "background," responds with expected suspicion.

Satie's score for *Parade* is certainly not furniture music per se, but collaborating with Cocteau nonetheless implied that his composition would take the noises into account. This does not necessarily imply the wholesale integration of the noises within the music, but it requires—at least—that they would not be perceived as disruptive of the musical performance. Integrating noises within a ballet inspired by the traditions of the music hall and circus, Cocteau insisted that the arts must look outside of themselves. On the one hand, popular arts provided a source of regeneration for the fine arts, gearing them to the beat of modern life (loud, fast, hectic . . .). On the other hand, the fine arts presented themselves as a means of organizing and articulating (visually and sonically) the disjointed language of modern industrial life. The responsibility of the artist in this regard was perfectly expressed by Fernand Léger: "Let us [. . .] look, with our eyes wide open, at contemporary life as it rolls along, shifts and brims over beside us. / Let us try to dam it up, to channel it, organize it artistically. / An enormous task, but one that can be accomplished."[76]

Only by accomplishing such a task could the Arts (with a capital A) expect to reduce an existing fracture between a fast-paced, rapidly changing society and its members, still incapable of registering and processing (other than as noises and confusion) the sensory impressions that modern life violently imposed upon them. To this end, the message that *Parade* was sending to artists was thus spelled out in Cocteau's *Le Coq et l'arlequin* in these terms:

"DO NOT MAKE ART AFTER ART."[77] With these words, Cocteau positioned himself, and a group of composers related to Erik Satie, against the supremacy of "absolute music," which had acquired paradigmatic significance in all forms of musical thought in the nineteenth and early twentieth centuries.[78] In 1813, E. T. A. Hoffmann famously defined what music ought to be to respond to a romantic sensibility:

> When we speak of music as an independent art, should we not always restrict our meaning to instrumental music, which, scorning every aid, every admixture of another art (the art of poetry), gives pure expression to music's specific nature, recognizable in this form alone? It is the most romantic of all the arts—one might almost say, the only genuinely romantic one—for its sole subject is the infinite.[79]

What at the time must have seemed a "challenging paradox," wrote Carl Dahlhaus in 1978, has since been "eroded to a commonplace that determines the day-to-day use of music without our being aware of it, let alone doubting it."[80] For the romantic generation, a musical work—and any artwork following this model—was "not only perceived as a 'world in itself' but . . . also conceived as such."[81] Thus, as Stephen Hinton stressed, by emancipating itself from any function, "[not] only did music not serve religion, it became itself the focal point of a 'Kunstreligion.'"[82] Paradoxically, Hinton's invaluable study on the emergence of a form of "useful" or "functional" music in the 1920s suggests that one of the strongest echoes of Cocteau's germanophobic aesthetic and loudest calls for an "everyday life's music" was to be found in the German *Gebrauchsmusik*. It is during the Weimar Republic that musicologists, composers, and critics started to question the assumption that music was ontologically autonomous.[83] As a challenge to late nineteenth-century aesthetics of art for art's sake, the term *Gebrauchsmusik*, or "utility music"—*Gebrauch* meaning "use" or "application"—started to circulate to refer to a tradition of music more inclined than concert-oriented music to be a part of everyday life.

While the term had already been coined a few years earlier, in 1923 the musicologist Heinrich Besseler (1900–1969) developed the concept of *Gebrauchsmusik* to the level of a general theory.[84] Contrary to the dominant idea, he argued, musical life had not always been reduced to "concert-determined" music—music written for and performed in the concert hall. Besseler's interest thus focused on "fundamentally different approaches to music where the . . . essentially concert-determined characteristics were missing." In this context, he wrote in 1926: "Perfection of reproduction would count as inessential, the listeners would not constitute a limitless crowd taking in what is performed in passive devotion, but would approach the music as a genuine community of like-minded individuals with an active attitude and in active expectation. Such art would therefore always correspond to a concrete need, it would not have to find its public but would grow out of it. Such an art is *Gebrauchsmusik*."[85] Thus, as Hinton points out, *Gebrauchsmusik* is (strictly speaking) not art: "As music that grows out of the community, it does not belong to a separate musical life led in the concert hall but is much more an integral part of life as such."[86] In this tradition, wrote Besseler, the appreciation of music does not involve contemplative listening but participation, "whether through playing, dancing or singing along; in general, through use." Following this line of thought, the composer Paul Hindemith developed his music in accordance to the pedagogical and social tendencies of a contemporary *Gebrauchsmusik*. Hence, as he wrote in 1930: "In the last few years I have almost completely turned away from concert music and have written virtually only music of a pedagogic or social tendency: for amateurs, for children, for the radio, mechanical instruments etc. I hold this type of composition to be more important than writing for concert purposes because the latter is almost just a technical exercise for the musician contributing little to the further development of music. I must therefore view concerts as a purely business matter."[87] Is there, as Ornella Volta suggests, any correlation between Satie's concept and *Gebrauchsmusik*?[88] One could argue, for instance, that they both render the concert setting obsolete. Both genres, it seems, are meant to escape the conventions of concert music and to engage the "listeners" in a different relationship to the musical material. It would be impossible, or at the very least a complete nonsense, to play Satie's furniture music in a concert hall in front of a passive audience. One could also say that both *Gebrauchsmusik* and furniture music stress—albeit very differently—that a social imperative should be at the inception of music. Ultimately, what led Volta to associate *Gebrauchsmusik* with furniture music may be that both constitute a direct or indirect attack against the romantic ideal of *l'art pour l'art*—art as an autonomous, self-sufficient, and self-fulfilling activity. The connection is nevertheless fortuitous, and it is impossible to follow Volta's suggestion that *Gebrauchsmusik* prolongs the idea that music should be heard but not listened to.[89] The level of involvement or engagement that *Gebrauchsmusik* requires from its audience is not comparable to the state of distraction that furniture music induces. One could nonetheless understand that the requirement to "pay no attention" to furniture music, if unaffectedly fulfilled by the audience, constitutes the ultimate level of participation, that is, reaching a perfect merging of art and life.

The Sphere of Agreeable Arts

In many ways, the concept of functional music, and by extension that of furniture music, is only an aberration in a tradition dominated by the ideal of absolute music. At the same time, whenever one turns to earlier periods in order to examine a different tradition, it seems reasonable to admit that such inquiry into the past of functional music is inevitably inflected by our acquaintance with Muzak in its contemporary incarnation. There is no doubt, indeed, that Muzak has influenced the way older music has been evaluated. According to the musicologist Hans Lenneberg, the notion that music could be conceived as a "background to other activities" is not that new. Hence, he writes, as much as "[we] know that Bach's French overtures were entertainment music, dinner music, in fact, . . . the Watermusic was apparently played to King George—who may have regarded it as so much Muzac [*sic*]—during both crossings of the Thames."[90] In such a view, Muzak appears both to pursue a tradition of functional music—albeit a democratized one—and to serve merely as a modern means of understanding a past tradition.

Muzak, however, has not always been a required referent for discussions of the function of music in the seventeenth and eighteenth centuries. Such a function, suggested Ruth Halle Rowen in the late 1940s, can simply be said to be the product of "the location at which music is performed" and "the style of the music itself."[91] Thus, she observed: "[the] early 17th-century musician recognized three functions, namely: the service of the church, theatrical entertainment, and private chamber practice." Here the word *chamber* mostly designates the "administration of the princely residence,"[92] and, pursues Rowen, although the term *chamber music* has "acquired a host of qualifying characteristics through the centuries, it is obvious that it derived its name from its function. As an appendage to the two secular functions of theater and chamber, there was also musique de table, music played at mealtime to entertain the nobility."[93]

This last genre, known especially through the popular set of *Tafelmusik* published by Telemann in 1733, caught the attention of Kant, who observed in his *Critique of Judgment* (*Kritik der Urteilskraft*, 1790) how strange and remarkable a concept it was. "It is meant to act on the mind merely as an agreeable noise fostering a cheerful spirit which, without anyone paying the least attention to the composition, promotes free conversation of each with his neighbor."[94] To be truly successful, no doubt, table music had to be written to and for its very purpose, and used as such. That is why *Tafelmusik* is not, in Kant's terms, to be considered fine art, but part of the "agreeable arts." As such, it has only "mere enjoyment" for its object, providing carefree and fleeting pleasure. *Tafelmusik* would thus be conceived to facilitate whatever could make a social gathering a pleasant yet forgettable time: the "art of conversation, jest, laughter, gaiety, simple-minded entertainment, irresponsible gossip around the table, the art of serving,"[95] and so on. Agreeable arts, in Kant's view, have "no further interest than that of making the time pass by unheeded" [§44]. Contrary to the fine arts, agreeable arts are "only given out for the entertainment of the moment, and not as a lasting matter to be made the subject of reflection or repetition" [§44]. Ultimately, one could not find beauty in agreeable arts, for they do not possess this finality without purpose ["*Zweckmäßigkeit ohne Zweck*"] that characterizes only the fine arts.[96] In itself, Kant's judgment does not rule out functional music from the vast and highly hierarchical field of artistic production, but simply defines it as an inferior kind of production. Functional music can exist only under the constraint of the service it is supposed to render, and its final purpose is to fulfill its task—no more, no less. Music written for a purpose necessarily falls, in this regard, into the lower category of mercenary arts—in the sense that its reception is the occasion of a consummated exchange.[97] It would be misleading, in other words, to listen to table music in a contemplative, reflective way and expect to find in it the kind of beauty that is the fruit only of free arts. Such was already the position of Charles-Henri Blainville, who stressed in his 1754 remarks on *L'Esprit de l'art musical* the strict separation between different musical genres. "We have theater music, chamber music, and table music. These are three species which we know how to distinguish very well; and we even agree that what would be very proper to one, either in composition or execution, would be very ridiculous in another."[98] Yet, noted Blainville regretfully, "we have come to confuse these types by usage. We perform operas in the chamber: we sing that type of air at the table; and for our theaters, we also compose airs which should only be reserved for our social amusements."[99] It was, in a sense, a similar confusion of genres and an ensuing lack of efficiency in its function that prompted Satie, according to the memory of the painter Fernand Léger, to conceive furniture music. As Léger remembered it, Satie shared his conviction during lunch at a restaurant, surrounded by a few friends. The company, upset by "a noisy and unbearable music," felt forced to leave the establishment. And it was following this unfortunate turn of events that Satie observed out loud: "A *musique d'ameublement* remains to be conceived, that is to say a kind of music that is a part of ambient noises and that takes them into account."[100] While no date is attached to the anecdote, the episode would logically precede the first known example of furniture music written by Satie in 1917. More importantly, Léger's memory suggests that, no matter how innovative, furniture music can also be regarded as a fairly conservative concept. It reacts against a confusion of genres to ensure, in consequence, that only a music written as a functional background could be used for this very purpose.[101]

Léger's interest in the concept of furniture music is not surprising. Among his contemporaries, the painter had an especially acute sense of the need to reevaluate the function of the arts in the early twentieth century: "The situation at the present moment is tragic enough," wrote Léger in the early 1920s. "The artist is 'in competition' with the useful object, which is sometimes beautiful; or at least fascinating. He must create as well or better."[102] It is such awareness of a competition, and a related attempt at creating a modern, highly specialized industrial product, that Satie echoed in the above-mentioned letter to Cocteau [c. 1920], defining the concept of furniture music:

> "Furniture Music" is essentially industrial. It is the habit—the custom—to play music in occasions where music has nothing to do with it. There, one plays "waltzes," Operatic "Fantasies" & other similar things, written for another purpose. / As for ourselves, we want to establish a kind of music designed to satisfy "useful" needs. Art has no part in such needs. "Furniture Music" creates vibrations; it has no other goal; it plays a role similar to light, heat—& comfort in every possible way.[103]

It is thus not the lack of music in the background that bothered Satie, but the lack of specialization of music played as a background to other activities. Adorno's account of his experience of "background music" in the mid-1930s reached a similar conclusion while refraining from suggesting any remedy. Effectively, as Adorno wrote in 1934, the sound of the customers shouting, "'Waiter! The bill!' while they strike the glass with their spoon," has become part of "the sound of cafe music."[104] Adorno was less than favorable toward the concept of "background music" that simply "keeps the customers company—the tired ones with their stimulating drink, the busy ones at their negotiations, even the newspaper readers; even the flirts, if there still are any." Yet his commentary reveals how the concept of "background music" could appear to be as revolting as successful to a "true" music lover like him:

> The first characteristic of background music is that you don't have to listen to it . . . It seeps into the murmur of the conversations. If an unfortunate tenor bellows out his Italian canzonettas, we experience him as intrusive. The silence lasts only the couple of seconds until the next order is taken. Art connoisseurs who go "Shhh!"—here they are implacably exposed as comical. / In piano passages

the music wants to disappear altogether. Then you can hear the clatter of spoons and cups, mingled with the glockenspiel, maybe the high notes of the piano; the phrases of the cello fall away, lost. In forte passages, the music climbs like a rocket. Its arcs glisten over the listeners until they sit there, abandoned once more, in the gray of their cigarette puffs. They are not an audience. Scarcely ever will one of them comment on the quality of the music that is offered. Nor are they in a musical mood. The music scarcely touches their inner stirrings. Rather: it is an objective event among, above them.[105]

Adorno was notoriously not favorable toward any form of useful music. Still, what bothered him, as it did Satie in this regard, was the discrepancy between the music and the place. The fact that a music that *could* be listened to is *not* simply means that music is reduced to a background—not conceived as one. And insisting on such specificity was one of Satie's main promotional arguments.

Promoting Industrial Sounds

Strictly speaking, of course, there should be no audience for furniture music, since it should fulfill its function without attracting notice. Yet listeners have to change their conduct and must be trained to this end. It is the role of advertising, in modern society, to convince them that they desire such change. Satie's ambition was, in his own words, "to establish a kind of [industrial] music designed to satisfy 'useful' needs."[106] Typically, as already stated, a piece of furniture music consists of a short musical phrase to be repeated at will, but not more. Even though the principle could apply to a form of mechanical repetition, the "at will" indicates clearly that the performance of furniture music is still dependent on human factors: the small orchestra performing the piece and the customer who is using this musical appliance (who may switch it on or off when needed, as indeed one would do with light or heat). "Art"—Satie insisted—"has no part in such needs. 'Furniture Music' creates vibrations; it has no other goal; it plays a role similar to light, heat—& comfort in every possible way."[107] "Art"—"*L'Art*" with a capital A—writes Satie, "does not fit in those needs."[108] Strictly speaking, furniture music is not art and does not pretend to be so. Introducing it through a manifesto would have been nonsensical. It is a commercial product, "advantageously replacing Marches, Polkas, Tangos, Gavottes, etc.," which too often played in a background they were not suited for. In order to market his product, Satie even attempted to formulate a few promotional slogans targeting specific consumers, among which were statements such as: "Do not set foot in a household that does not use Furniture

Music!"[109] A more finalized and wide-ranging publicity leaflet was written by the composer for an aborted premiere of furniture music, scheduled to take place in the fashion showroom Jove in spring 1918.[110]

> First Attempt at Furniture Music
> (Industrial sounds)
> Furnishing divertissement organized by the group of 'Nouveaux Jeunes' for Jove, fashion design and decoration.
>
> ---
>
> Furniture music for evening receptions, gatherings, etc . . . What is Furniture Music?—a pleasure!
> Furniture Music replaces
> "waltzes"
> "operatic fantasies" [*fantaisies sur les opéras*], etc
> Don't be fooled! It's really something!!!
> No more 'counterfeit music' [*fausse musique*]: musical furnishing now!
> Furnishing music completes one's décor [*mobilier*];
> It frees you up; It's worth its weight in gold; It's new; It doesn't upset conventions;
> It won't tire you out; It's French; It won't wear out; It's not boring.
> To take it up will make things better!
> Listen at your ease [*sans vous gêner*]
> Elaborate craftsmanship [*confection*] & Tailor-made to the highest specifications.[111]

Most of the arguments are spoofing the rhetoric of advertising to the point of saying nothing at all, but very loudly ("Don't be mistaken! It is something else!!!"), while keeping, nonetheless, a tongue-in-cheek allure of credibility. Stressing the "Frenchness" of furniture music, in particular, is certainly suitable considering the context of World War I, but it sounds superficial enough when speaking of nonartistic "industrial sounds" that had more to do with matching the exigency of modern life than with the affirmation of a perennial national cultural identity. In a sense, promoting his product as being French in essence is as ridiculous as the recent and fleeting coinage in the United States of the absurd label "freedom fries," in order to save fried potatoes (aka French fries) from becoming politically indigestible.

In such terms, however, Satie surreptitiously debunks Cocteau's nationalistic views, by reducing their value to that of selling arguments: "It is not tiresome; It is French; It won't wear out; It is not boring." By equating propaganda and advertising, Satie walks a thin line. First, he may implicitly satisfy a nationalistic rhetoric that fears the weakening of French culture through the contamination of anything "German" (and music, Cocteau argued, is on the front line). At the same time, the surrounding imagery of advertising explicitly exposes the arbitrariness of the claim: French culture is, in this light, no more and no less a manufactured product of mass consumption than any other. In this regard, furniture music may not be art, but it strives for what the progressive artists of the time were expressly trying to achieve: positioning their art as a productive force shaping a future society, an art integrated with the dynamic of everyday life and ready to affect directly the life of individuals. To this end, Satie's promotional strategy clearly and only logically strives to reconcile a wide range of expectations. If Satie typically conveys his idea with a certain wit, he is not simply joking around. Introducing furniture music in the context of a fashion show, Satie presents his product as a luxury item, tailor-made in a one-man factory. It must thus be properly and efficiently advertised as bearing all the qualities suitable to the high standing of Jove. Founded by Germaine Bongard (the sister of Paul Poiret), the showroom was not only—as Le Corbusier noted—a place where all "the grand courtesans" went.[112] As the purist painter Amédée Ozenfant, who was then running Jove, made clear in his memoir, Jove's conception of haute couture was distinct from the vagaries of fashion. "Painter and poet of class [Germaine Bongard] knew that the true haute couture is not submitting to the seasonal decrees of the *petit* commercial fashions, but to the same permanent laws that have always ruled all the plastic arts. The dresses that she created were never out of fashion because they were not à la mode of the instant: they were simply beautiful."[113]

The point was not, as was already happening in retail stores or fashion showrooms since the late nineteenth and early twentieth centuries, to hire an orchestra to accompany the spring fashion show or promote a sale.[114] This was what Satie would call "counterfeit music," that is, an orchestra playing arrangements of tunes that were not designed to become background music. Furniture music was not an ornament but in itself a product for sale on an equal footing with Jove's haute couture. While the music itself, as is now understood, was not supposed to attract attention, the scores were meant to be displayed on the walls.[115] This wallpaper in the literal sense would make visible the music and its function and would possibly, as a complement to the advertising pamphlet, display the craft involved in its making. Clearly, furniture music was introduced not as a one-liner joke, a mere novelty item (soon boring, and eventually wearing off) but as a profitable and durable investment. Neither Jove nor Satie intended to abuse the patience of their potential consumers. As Satie asserted in conjunction with a sketch for furniture music, "the artist has no right to waste the time of his/her listeners."[116] And furniture music, stresses the advertising pamphlet in this regard, "is not boring." This may sound like a simple preventative strategy, aiming at convincing the audience beforehand that the repetition of a few bars bears a hitherto unknown entertaining quality.

For Satie, however, denying that furniture music is boring does not imply that it is entertaining. To the contrary, furniture music intends to make positive use of boredom, which, as Satie realized, "the audience worships."[117] For the listeners, he noted, "boredom is mysterious and profound," and, curiously, they find themselves "defenseless," and "tamed" (*dompter*). Why, then, would composers and artists consider boredom a failure and avoid at all costs making it an active component of their work? Boredom, at first, is essentially associated with repetition as it appears in some of Satie's scores such as *Vexations* or the less famous *Vieux séquins et vieilles cuirasses* (Old Sequins and Old Armor, 1913). Just as *Vexations* fascinated Cage, the artist Dick Higgins (1938–1998)—who studied with Cage at the New School of Social Research in the late 1950s—became interested in the ending of *Vieux séquins*, which consists of "an eight-beat passage evocative of old marches and patriotic songs, but which is to be repeated 380 times."[118] In reality, the score indicates that the passage, quoting the air of the popular song *Le bon roi Dagobert*, is to be repeated (only!) 267 times.[119] The passage comes under the title "The Defeat of the Cimbri (Nightmare)" (La Défaite des cimbres [Cauchemar]), and before the score begins, one reads the following contextualization:

> A very small child is sleeping in his very small bed. Every day his very aged grandfather gives him a kind of strange very small lesson in universal history, drawn from his vague memories./ He often tells him about the famous king Dagobert, the Duke of Marlborough and the great Roman general Marius. In his dreams the very small child sees these heroes fighting the Cimbri at the battle of Mons-en-Puelle [near Lille] (1304).[120]

The musical reference to the king Dagobert (who, says the song, had put on his trousers inside out) arrives, as a last illustrative bit following notably a "portrait of Marius," and an evocation of "Boirix, King of the Cimbri" under the heading "Le Sacre de Charles X,"[121] followed by the indication (267 bis), when the nightmare, presumably, begins.

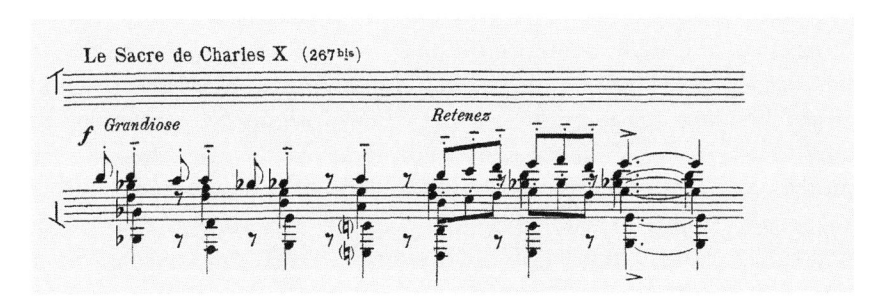

Figure 1.2. Erik Satie, ending of *Vieux séquins et vieilles cuirasses* (1913).

Apparently, Satie's improbable number of repetitions ending *Vieux séquins* waited some fifty years before being performed. The circumstances of this performance are not known, but clearly remembering his experience of a faithful execution of this finale, Higgins relates its strange effect: "In performance the satirical intent of this repetition comes through very clearly, but at the same time other very interesting results begin to appear. The music first becomes so familiar that it seems extremely offensive and objectionable. But after that the mind slowly becomes incapable of taking further offense, and a very strange, euphoric acceptance and enjoyment begin to set in."[122] The full repetition of the fragment, which itself lasts an average of ten seconds, would thus go on for a maximum of forty-five minutes, and it is surely enough to generate a rather hypnotic effect. What is then "enjoyed," suggests Higgins, is not the music anymore but the fact that the repetition has ceased to become offensive, opening up a new "dialectic between boredom and intensity."[123] Similarly, furniture music may guarantee boredom only to overcome its negative connotation. Boredom is boring only when one is supposed to pay attention to something that nonetheless challenges one's attentiveness. Once removed from a conventional artistic framework in which it is dreaded, boredom can become the central instrument of a functional appliance that—to use Brian Eno's words—becomes "as ignorable as it is interesting."[124]

One might wonder, nonetheless, the extent to which some of those pieces could be positively ignored. The titles given by the composer to some sets of furniture music identify them as an improbable and ostentatious decorative fixtures (such as *Tapisserie en fer forgé* (1917)—"Cast-Iron Tapestry"). Even though such a work certainly promises not to wear out too soon, such an item would doubtfully pass unnoticed. However, it should be stressed again, being functional, such a piece is not an object of contemplation. *Tapisserie en fer forgé*, for instance, is thus specifically designed "for the arrival of the guests (grand reception)." It is to be played in the vestibule, a transitional space of the residence, and its interpretation is meant to be "very rich"—fittingly so considering the implied social standing of the occasion.[125]

It is not the setting (a reception, a lounge, an engagement party, a bar . . .) that qualifies furniture music as "industrial" and even less, despite its repetitive quality, the mechanization of the musical content, but the level of engineering that goes into the making of a specialized functional product of aesthetic worth. Satie is thus already in line with the spirit of the Bauhaus, whose 1919 manifesto would call for "a new guild of craftsmen" that ignores "the class-distinctions that raise an arrogant barrier between craftsmen and artists."[126] In such terms, the reconciliation of the industrially skilled craftsman and the exalted, inspired artist constituted the foundational program

Figure 1.3. Erik Satie, *Tapisserie en fer forgé* (1917–18), four bars for flute, B♭ clarinet, trumpet in C, and strings, to be played ad lib—Tempo: Très riche ("very wealthy," or simply: "very rich").

of the Bauhaus school. It promised both to (re)introduce the arts within the very fabric of society and to elevate the industrial product to the level of aesthetic creation. Furniture music clearly appears as an independent effort to achieve such reconciliation. Yet, at the same time, Satie did not necessarily aim for a democratic distribution of his product.

Who, indeed, could afford the need for Satie's creation? When Satie, mimicking an advertising slogan, writes, "Do not enter a house which does not use Furniture Music!"[127] the composer implies that his ambition for such music is, in part, to enhance domestic life—and mostly a bourgeois one. Robert Orledge, notably, remarked that while Satie was in contact with the Dadaists and was moving in "more exalted social circles," taking delight in "shocking society with his Bolshevist sympathy," the composer also seemed to have an "increasing concern in his final years to make his music new, chic, and Parisian."[128] In accordance, wrote the artist Francis Picabia in 1920, Satie might have essentially found, with his furniture music to be rented for special occasions, a means of infiltrating high society ("Erik Satie a trouvé la musique d'ameublement, façon de s'introduire dans le monde [locations pour soirée]").[129] Picabia's comment suggests that the music, and maybe the composer, could be "rented" for the evening, thereby prostituting himself

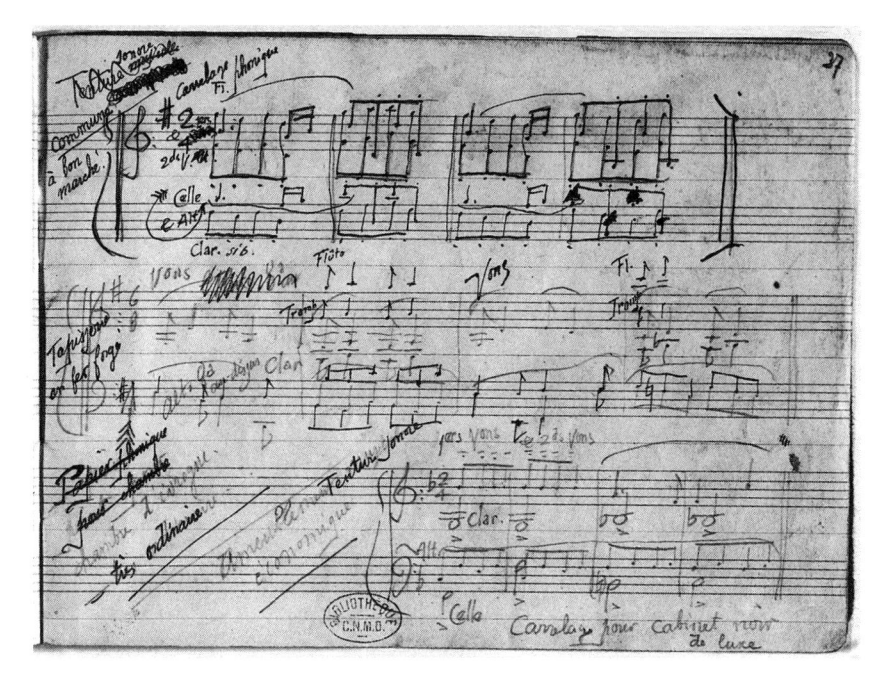

Figure 1.4. Erik Satie, "Notes, brouillons et esquisses c. 1918–1919," Bibliothèque Nationale de France, Paris, Département de la Musique, Ref. Ms 9623 (2), pp. 26–27.

and his art. But it also closely identifies furniture music with a product of consumption, even though only a select audience could afford it. As a final counterpoint, one existing note for an unfinished piece of furniture music titled *Papier phonique* (Sonic [wall]paper) was apparently designed to fit "a very ordinary drunkard's bedroom, with cheap furniture" [*chambre d'ivrogne—très ordinaire / ameublement économique*].[130] To some extent, given Satie's notable inclination for alcohol and his modest living conditions, *Papier phonique* almost sounds like a self-commissioned piece to furnish the "unforgettable rubbish heap" of his own dwelling.[131]

Cinéma

The corpus of furniture music remains ultimately open to question. Should we, for instance, include the score that Satie composed for René Clair's film *Entr'acte*, screened during the interlude of Francis Picabia's ballet *Relâche* in 1924? Such was the conviction of Douglas W. Gallez in his study of this piece, which has been variously referred to as *Cinéma*, *Entr'acte cinématographique*, and *Entr'acte symphonique*.[132] *Cinéma* shares obvious characteristics with furniture music, beyond the context of the intermission, which recalls the failed premiere of the latter. As Shattuck pointed out, *Cinéma* is made of short musical units deprived of "any strong tonal feeling," each repeated eight times but "[lending] themselves to infinite repetition."[133] Gallez, in turn, describes very aptly the music as "ruthlessly mechanical, characterized by endless repetitions without variation."[134] Stressing the absence of any emotional content, Gallez qualifies the piece as "[devoid] of passion, pictorialism, and drama, often cool and detached." The composer, he argues, "denuded" and "nullified" his musical ideas, making them "impotent" to the point that "[the] static quality of [*Cinéma*] deadens many listeners."[135] By comparison, a piece of furniture music like the throbbing *Tenture de cabinet prefectoral*, evoking to some "a pitiful and repetitive march, whose conclusion conjoins the musicians in a descending motif simulating extreme fatigue," gains in expressiveness and also takes on an irony when associated with its pompous bourgeois interior.[136]

Following Gallez's analysis, however, *Cinéma* would only kill anyone attempting to listen to it for its own sake. For the piece is so irreducibly suitable to film scoring that it is only (or especially?) when it is stripped from the filmic support that it sounds "tediously obnoxious."[137] In this regard, one could argue that Satie composed a perfect soundtrack—a music, as Hanns Eisler would later define the soundtrack of mainstream cinema, that "even if it is listened to inattentively, can as a whole be perceived correctly and adequately to its function."[138] But this "function," when attached to a nonnarrative, experimental film is delicate to pinpoint: no plot to elucidate, no dramaturgy to emphasize, no lurking disaster to announce. There is little doubt that, while watching such a film, the excruciating nature of Satie's music only exacerbated the frustration of some viewers, and this might certainly be envisaged as a possible (subversive) function. But, perhaps more importantly, Satie's score does not become insufferable because it is suddenly deprived of a context that the music would attempt to illustrate or mimic, and behind which it would tend to disappear.[139] *Cinéma* cannot exist by itself because, as both Shattuck and Gallez stressed, the music is indeed purely cinematographic. Not only do the "abrupt and arbitrary" transitions of the score respond to the filmic montage (thereby stressing it), but the sheer *mechanical* character of the music also fits the nature of the medium with which it is associated. *Cinéma* is clearly not a negligible experiment in incidental music. But how can we estimate the condition of its appreciation? Clearly, a film starting by shooting a cannonball at the viewers and ending with a man bursting through the screen does not treat the audience as a *remote* entity. Yet two divergent accounts exist of the effect of *Entr'acte* on the audience. First, the filmmaker himself, René Clair, recalls the immediate reaction and ensuing involvement of the audience. As the film started, laughter was heard, followed by a growing rumbling, shouting, and hissing, all "merging with the melodious buffooneries of Satie who, no doubt, appreciated as a connoisseur the sonic backup (*les renforts sonores*) that the protesters brought to his music."[140] In this turmoil, it becomes quite difficult to identify what is the background of what, to the utmost satisfaction of the filmmaker. Hans Richter's recollection of the event, however, contradicts Clair's version. As he remembered it, Picabia had intended to use the murmur of the audience during the intermission as a background noise for this silent film, but the plan did not succeed: "They all fell silent, as though the sight of this extraordinary cortege had taken their breath away. Picabia, enraged, shouted at the audience, 'Talk, can't you, talk!' Nobody did."[141]

Such a failure, of course, strangely recalls the premiere of Satie's furniture music . . . Is it due to Richter's confusion? Both Clair's and Richter's accounts came quite late (in the 1960s), and the point here is not to judge their respective reliability. At any rate, it is clear that one cannot not evaluate the role of Satie's music in *Entr'acte*, according to the standards of film music that developed later, in a different cinematographic tradition and under different conditions of spectatorship (seated in the dark, silent . . .). With *Entr'acte*, it is the entire cinematographic object (i.e., including Satie's music) that one must reconsider . . . As a piece of "furnishing cinema," maybe?

An Absence of Resolution?

Up to and including *Cinéma*, the dilemmas of furniture music are certainly not easier to resolve than the music itself. Reducing it to a "good armchair" may just drain an unusually strange yet paradoxically familiar music of any critical value. Considering it as a mere ironic gesture tends to cover up the aspiration to conceive a form of music in tune with the "roaring twenties." Putting the blame on Muzak for implementing Satie's concept simply offers an easy way to forget how much the artists of the time were eager to turn their art into positive, functional tools of social production. Of course, humor infiltrates some pieces through and through. It is impossible to miss the intoxicated quality of *Chez un bistrot*, the exaggerated pompousness of the *Tenture de cabinet préfectoral*, and once the quotes of *Un Salon* (especially the tacky Thomas song) have been discerned, the underlying mockery of the process becomes audible. Still, beyond sarcasm, one may remember that Satie's endeavor was conceived in reaction to the inappropriateness of existing music as background. Even though it is done with wit—that is, without missing the possibility to mock its own purpose (that of satisfying the "needs" of the wealthy, for instance)—furniture music was nonetheless conceived to reduce an existing gap between music as an independent art form and music used as a functional product in modern life. In this regard, Satie's concept could be first understood as a typical avant-garde gesture. "It has always been one of the primary tasks of art," wrote Walter Benjamin, "to create a demand whose hour of full satisfaction has not yet come."[142] Yet to fulfill this essential task with the prospect of reforming society, artists had to face an increased struggle. Since the futurists, at least, the necessity for artists to compete with the strength of industrial creations and the increasing power of mass-media communication had become a priority. Fernand Léger, for instance, famously remembered visiting the Paris Air Show with Constantin Brancusi and Marcel Duchamp in 1912 when the latter exclaimed: "Painting is finished! Who can do better than this propeller? Tell me, can you do that?"[143] A bit later, Mondrian similarly recognized that "it is not only the fine arts that show the rhythm of basic opposition [neo-plasticism]; the new music and especially American jazz, as well as modern dancing, also tends to express it emphatically."[144] In other words, observed Mondrian, what Adorno defined as the culture industry constituted a vehicle of positive change in society that ran parallel to, and sometimes ahead of, the fine arts. Satie's furniture music is "industrial" to this extent. It is not, like a propeller, designed to be a self-sufficient object of pure aesthetic contemplation—no matter how beautiful one finds it to be.

Ultimately, the insights of the first avant-gardes of the twentieth century regarding increasing competition between the fine arts and the products of industrial society would essentially reflect the critical recognition of their failure to win the contest, and thus to impact society. In Eric Hobsbawm's words, for instance, "the real revolution in the twentieth century arts was achieved . . . outside the range of the area formally recognized as 'art.' It was achieved by the combined logic of technology and the mass market; that is to say the democratization of aesthetic consumption."[145] Hobsbawm's sweeping argument is generalized to the point of caricature—which actually gives it some strength. Furthermore, while he contends that his purpose is not to formulate "aesthetic judgments on twentieth century avant-garde," his remarks are full of superficial judgments betraying a curious and profound hatred of his subject.[146] Yet, beyond its reactionary inflections,[147] or rather because of them, Hobsbawm's analysis touches upon one of the most sensitive points of the history of modern art. Undeniably, as Darius Milhaud suggested, it appeared that the role of the avant-garde artist had been taken over and fulfilled by the culture industry, without necessarily subverting the hypothetical "original" impulse of the former.

Leaving any critical distance aside, Muzak certainly represents the fulfillment of Satie's dream of a music perfectly integrated to and shaping its surroundings. Eventually, the most pessimistic account (or, for that matter, the most lucid one) would argue that, in effect, the "commercialisation of every aspect of Western life has been a perverse realisation of the avant-garde dream that high art would lose its autonomy in the general aesthetisation of life—in this, at least, modernism has been a notable success."[148] Certainly, concludes Julian Stallabrass, "non-utilitarian" art may still be produced, but it can exist only against a world of products that are themselves already "saturated with aesthetics."[149] Muzak provided John Cage with a sense of what such saturation implied for a composer who, influenced by Satie, perceived the need to redefine the function of art in society.

"Environments are invisible. Their groundrules, pervasive

structure, and overall patterns, elude easy perception."[1]

CHAPTER 2

Muzak Incorporated

> I'm not going to reform man because he is not reformable. I'm going to reform the environment.[2]
> —Buckminster Fuller
>
> Of all the arts, music possesses the greatest power for social organization.[3]
> —Arseni Avraamov

Muzak Proper

In the beginning was the word, which the Oxford English Dictionary defines as follows: *Muzak* (also erron. *Musak*): "The proprietary name of a system of piped music for factories, restaurants, supermarkets, etc.; also used loosely, with small initial, to designate recorded light background music generally." Muzak "proper" owes its name to General George Owen Squier (1865–1934), a chief signal officer in the United States Army who, in 1922, founded Wired Inc., a company "employ[ing] electric power lines to transmit news programs, music, lectures, general entertainment and advertising directly into private homes."[4] In 1934, inspired by the catchy, popular brand name of Kodak, Squier himself renamed his company Muzak. Since then, like "Vaseline," the brand name Muzak has eased itself into the vernacular language to become a common name denoting an entire genre of music. True to its Kodak-inspired origin, the name muzak has become a powerful

Figure 2.1. Muzak Logo "The planned music service" in Muzak ad in *Fortune* (February 1957), "How Much is Worker Tension Costing your Company?"

and adaptable cliché. It serves equally well in belittling a composer ("the sound you make is muzak to my ears"[5]) and in expressing contempt for the "mindless art" deriving from Clement Greenberg's formalist canon ("visual Muzak"[6]).

More than anything else, muzak defined itself in the sheer impact of a word bearing powerful resonances, no matter how controversial they may be. From early on, one essential function of Muzak has been to project a strong, convincing image, and the 1934 rebranding of the company already served this purpose. *Image*, in this context, does only not mean "picture"; it refers to the evocative connotations associated with the watchword *muzak*. Simply uttering the word thus triggers the pacifying images of "[feeling] more relaxed, contemplative, distracted from problems."[7] One may be seduced or terrified by the prospect, but Muzak succeeds in subjugating its proponents and detractors alike. Whether they aim to promote it or condemn it, interpretations of Muzak overwhelmingly subscribe to the premises of its efficiency. This clearly indicates that, in order to be effective, Muzak needs more than just to be implemented. It requires, above all, a collective suspension of disbelief. It is in the formulation of a persuasive concept, designed for a society meant to be shaped to its image, that Muzak can be characterized as an artistic endeavor. After all, stressed Barnett Newman, Adolph Gottlieb, and Mark Rothko in the 1940s, wasn't it the primary task of the artists to subjugate their viewers? "It is our function as artists," they famously declared, "to make the spectator see the world our way—not his way."[8] The following study of muzak is primarily an inquiry into the formation of the discourse (the set of beliefs, solidified in a doctrine) out of which Muzak and muzak emerge. For an artist like John Cage, it was Muzak's power to project the powerful image of a reformed society to come that constituted an object of competition, not its music.

In the second half of the twentieth century, Muzak presented itself as the most successful form of "environmental music." Responding acutely to what John Cage defined as his musical ideal, one could say that it has been perfectly integrated into "the rest of our life."[9] Whenever we encounter Muzak, "[it] flows through channels parallel to those providing air, electricity and information."[10] An ideal image of Muzak resembles the double blank page of Marshall McLuhan's and Quentin Fiore's 1967 book *The Medium Is the Massage: An Inventory of Effects*. It is easy to miss its caption, printed in a small typeface and running on the upper edge of the page: "Environments are invisible. Their groundrules [*sic*], pervasive structure, and overall patterns elude easy perception."[11]

Regardless of its sophistication, a critical consensus surrounds Muzak: it is bad. Despite the company's relentless efforts to improve or simply to correct its image, the reputation of Muzak remains frankly disastrous. Even specialists in marketing, who could be expected to be sensitive to the product, feel compelled to condemn it. Most recently, Alan Bradshaw and Morris B. Holbrook reiterated and amplified the common rejection of muzak on conventional grounds.[12] Muzak, they complain, is formulaic and predictable, and overall it dispenses to the masses "incalculably insipid instrumental inanities."[13] As a corruption of music, they observe with indignation, muzak does nothing less than embody the "elevation of commerce over art" that "pervades our culture of consumption"—for there is clearly no other.[14] The question of the function of Muzak remains, as it appears, only incidental. Of course, stress the authors, Muzak intends to "manipulate us by changing our shopping habits," with the sole aim of generating ever-increasing "commercial gain for greedy capitalist pigs."[15] But there is much worse. As a consequence, are we warned in near panic, "contemporary consumers in general and young ones in particular have grown too desensitized to appreciate true aesthetic excellence."[16]

In truth, the claims that Muzak is neither music nor art have only facilitated its expansion, and can only continue to do so. Being the target of violent criticisms and becoming an object of utter contempt are not only expected, but somehow encouraged by the producers of Muzak. Rather than debating the dubious virtues of "true aesthetic excellence," some of the company's executives suggested that Muzak requires, more radically, the overcoming of individual likes and dislikes. "[It] has nothing to do with what I like and what I don't like," claimed the president of Muzak Corporation in the 1970s. His company, he explained, is "not in the culture business," and "[we] are not trying to get [intellectual or emotional involvement], any more than you do with air-conditioning or the color of an office."[17] Muzak Corp. could not agree more with the careful distinctions made between music and muzak upheld by those claiming to be guardians of genuine culture. "'Music by Muzak' is perhaps an unfortunate slogan," admitted the company in the early 1970s. "It is not music, nor even 'background music,' but something called 'functional music,' a wholly different commodity."[18] To this day, the company carefully avoids defining its product in musical terms. Still, its functional and aesthetic qualities are sometimes stressed conjointly: Muzak, they proclaim, is "Audio Architecture," or in other words, "emotion by design."[19] As Jean Baudrillard suggests, one must take into account the full "etymological breadth" of the word design in such context: from the conception of the product (*dessin*) to its embedded purpose (*dessein*), and, finally, the actual process of *Gestaltung* implied in the shaping of our emotion.[20]

Muzak's recent ambition to fulfill a function in environmental design is less innovative than reactualizing of older theories that had fostered the development of industrial, functional music. From this perspective, a coherent image of Muzak can be gathered from the company's promotional material, countless journalistic pieces recording its evolution, a fair number of scholarly articles, and a small number of "comprehensive" studies of disputable value.[21] But it must also, and primarily, be grounded in early studies of functional music and industrial psychology, both of which helped to define Muzak's subsequent ambitions and contributed to its rising, albeit disputed, status. This chapter, however, does not intend to provide a comprehensive overview of the development of Muzak, whether as a trademark or as a genre. This task has already been fulfilled more or less successfully.[22] Taking as a point of reference a seminal study conducted in 1937 by Wyatt and Langdon and observing its ramifications, the following inquiry will offer only a partial overview of the discourses that contributed to outline Muzak's powerful image. This includes a dominantly negative critical stance that, despite itself, only strengthens the basis on which muzak operates.

Navigating through the history of muzak, one must also be prepared to admit its peculiar temporality. On the one hand, any historical perspective moving from past to present cannot miss that the primary function of "audio architecture" is to shape the better society of tomorrow. This ever-coming future of "emotion by design" can be utopian or dystopian. Either way, it will have fulfilled its function in transforming society. As the company put it in 2009, while celebrating its seventy-fifth birthday, "we think the best is yet to come."[23] To accompany this statement on their website, a tongue-in-cheek sound byte praising "man's eternal search for a brighter future" has been extracted from the 1962 Seattle World's Fair commemorative LP[24] (appropriately titled *Man in Space with Sounds*). This anachronistic reference to the golden age of the future is certainly meant to communicate the company's power in mocking its own capacity to improve mankind. But this self-conscious irony cannot conceal that—actually—the temporality of muzak stands strangely still. Of course, the product has evolved and its sphere of influence somehow expanded. But the premises upon which music was implemented in factories during World War II, and which prompted the response of an artist like John Cage, still constitute the underpinning principles of the contemporary achievements of Muzak (and muzak). From early on, Muzak is synonymous not with bad music, but with inevitable progress.

The Menace of Mechanical Music

From the mid-1930s on, Muzak Co. started to build its own transcription library[25] (recordings exclusively made for broadcasting) using a high-fidelity sound-on-disc technology that would not become commercially available until after World War II.[26] Depending on this specially recorded material as "a standing reserve of musical performances," the technology of Muzak was directly involved in what Tim Anderson identifies as the construction, from the late 1920s into the 1940s, of a "new, dominant economy of music production that would be based on recordings rather than the production of musical performances."[27] To some extent, professional musicians were, in this context, faced with a cruel paradox as they witnessed the "constant growth in the popularity and use of music accompanied by a diminishing curve of musician employment."[28] In this context, argued James Petrillo—the most controversial leader of the American Federation of Musicians (AFM)[29]—recording for radio broadcast could be described as a form of economic suicide for professional musicians: "[It] was like the iceman making a mechanical refrigerator which would ruin his route."[30] The response of the AFM to these changes, discussed by Anderson, culminated in two national strikes organized by the union in 1942 and 1948. Using its ultimate weapon for the first time in 1942, the AFM warned all major recording companies in the United States that, as of August 1, 1942, musicians affiliated with the AFM "will not play or contract for any other forms of mechanical reproductions of music."[31]

By that time, however, the AFM had already been engaged in a long and complex struggle. A decisive blow had come, between 1927 and 1929, with the rise of sound films, which swiftly rendered live music in theaters obsolete.[32] The AFM's immediate response, it appears, was to fight technology itself. In one paid advertisement published in *Variety* in 1929, part of a broad campaign meant to raise public awareness, the union dispatched a dystopian vision of a mechanized future: "Can a 'cold' house, devoid of all personality beyond that contributed by doorman and ushers, retain the atmosphere of the theatre? . . . The Robot is a bulging, pushing sort, quite impervious to audience reactions and his disposition to 'hog the whole show' may disgust the movie-going public."[33]

The pamphlet was illustrated by a cartoon showing a mindless robot butchering a harp, to the sole effect of making the angel decorating the instrument cry, while a dog standing by howls at the moon. The argument was not new. In 1906, John Philip Sousa (1854–1932) had tried to persuade his readers that no mechanical device (such as the pianola) could replace "human skill, intelligence, and soul."[34] Even though the technology of the player piano was central to Sousa's discussion of what he called "canned music," phonograph recordings were not the least of his concerns.[35]

Yet by the early 1940s, the "now-old story of men against machines"[36] seemed to have been told and the war fought by the AFM appeared to be a "hopeless" one: "The country's 500,000 juke boxes and the use of 'canned' music by hundreds of radio stations have destroyed employment opportunities for thousands of musicians. Many taverns and hotels, which formerly employed small bands now use the juke box; it costs less and provides music by Benny Goodman instead of Joe Doakes. Of some 800 radio stations in the United States, fewer than 300 employ musicians; the rest use recordings only."[37] For the AFM, such numbers were indeed telling. They showed that radio and the jukebox industries were profiting increasingly from the commercial use of recordings, while Joe Doakes was not properly compensated. The AFM might have lost the fight against technology, but it could still expect to see technology's use being controlled so that the interests of professional musicians would be protected. Observing, for instance, that radio programs were relying more and more on phonograph recordings, the AFM asked the Federal Radio Commission to limit (or even to eliminate) their use in broadcasting.[38] At a loss, it seems, the union subsequently attempted, equally unsuccessfully, to restrict the use of commercial phonograph recordings by printing "for home use only" on the record.[39] It was as a part of this struggle that, in 1938, the New York local chapter of the AFM signed a contract with Muzak, guaranteeing that it would not—in theory—"make its facilities available to any establishment if such action would cause the replacement of live musicians."[40] The agreement was clearly responding to Muzak as a cause of technological unemployment and an attempt to limit its expansion. In practice, however, Muzak was piped into hotels and restaurants that could have used small ensembles. Yet as Muzak programming relied on its own transcription library, not on commercial phonograph recordings, the AFM local refrained from further exercising its right for fear that the company, in return, "might substitute ordinary phonograph records for the special records it now uses."[41]

Still, the actions of AFM's leader Petrillo (as well as his powerful public persona) were undeniably getting in the way of Muzak Co.'s expansion and, at times, effectively silencing it. While Muzak already counted five thousand installations across the United States in the mid-1940s (a thousand of them in New York alone), the company had avoided the Chicago market (Petrillo's turf). In February 1946, Muzak finally licensed its product to a Chicago sound equipment company named Boom Electric and Amplifier in order to move in.[42] Promoting the operation, the presidents of Boom Electric and Amplifier were careful to claim their intention to target industrial plants and department stores, thereby staying clear of cocktail lounges and avoiding competing with live talent. Over the next four years, however, Muzak faced Petrillo's resistance. Ultimately, in July 1949, the union leader ordered AFM musicians to "quit work in hotels which used Boom services"[43] on the grounds that the company should hire AFM members in place of the six disabled war veterans operating their turntables, themselves members of the local 134 Electrical Workers union. Hotels immediately decided to give up the canned music rather than the orchestras.[44] In response, Boom and Muzak charged Petrillo, the Chicago Federation of Musicians, and the AFM with unfair labor practices,[45] dropping the case only after Petrillo finally agreed, in the summer of 1950, to give up his struggle.[46]

Fast-Forward

A brief consideration of the progressive dynamic of Muzak's history is essential to sketch out its image. Not only does the fast pace of Muzak's development appear ineluctable, it also—and from its inception—inscribes the company into a fast-forward-moving time. While it serviced only New York in the early 1940s, the Muzak company had already designed a colorful catalogue of different networks (purple, red, blue, and green) tailored to the needs of their subscribers: banks, restaurants, post offices, medical environments, retail stores, and private residences.[47] Starting in 1945, Muzak launched its product in more cities and expanded its services into the realm of transport: elevators, buses, airplanes, and so on.[48] According to a study published in 1950 by the U.S. Chamber of Commerce, Muzak was a fast-growing business whose network now covered two hundred cities with more than seven thousand subscribers, ten times more than ten years earlier.[49] It would be misleading, however, to attribute this success simply to the largely undisputed power of "music by Muzak" to make us feel more relaxed, contemplative, and so forth. The expansion of Muzak in the postwar era is more, it seems, the consequence of a more complex combination of factors, including—in first rank—the propitious advent of World War II.

As with much of our modern technological surroundings, the momentum of Muzak was—first and foremost—a product of the war industry. According to two acousticians from the Stevens Institute of Technology, writing in 1947, the development of functional music owed much to its "vigorous promotion by persons anxious to be in on a good thing."[50] These promoters included first the British government, followed by the American War Production Board, record and radio companies,[51] and of course, the Muzak Corporation itself. As part of the war effort between the late 1930s and the mid-1940s, acousticians, work scientists, and industrial psychologists collaboratively explored the potential of applying music to industry. These studies defined the criteria that both prompted and informed the subsequent expansion of one major company, Muzak, dedicated to the fabrication and distribution of a specialized product. During World War II, improving morale and productivity were perceived as necessary correlates, and the intense research conducted on the use of music in industry definitely inflected the ambition of Muzak from entertainment to functionality. By the early 1950s, it appears, the integration of Muzak into our surroundings was already fully achieved. *Nation's Business* reported that the latest trend in architecture was "to install loudspeakers and wiring in office and professional buildings during the process of construction" so that they would be "wired for Muzak from basement to roof."[52] The technology of Muzak was thereby orchestrated to function as unobtrusively as its product. Muzak, noted another observer, had definitely found its place "alongside air conditioning, sound-proof ceilings, indirect lightning, contour chairs and the coffee-break as a commodity designed to help us meet the tension of our daily life."[53] By then, the influence of muzak resonated far beyond the limits of the working day. Concurrently, while "Music by Muzak" was never released commercially (it was available only to subscribers and occasionally circulated in the form of promotional LPs), companies like RCA or Capitol distributed easy-listening compilations (muzak) designed to "stimulate people to greater interest in and enjoyment of"[54] reading, dining, relaxing,[55] quitting smoking,[56] socializing,[57] or, occasionally, having sex.[58] From the 1950s on, the warm arrangements of classical or popular numbers by George Melachrino, Mantovani, Paul Mauriat, or the Mystic Moods Orchestra (with a notable contribution entitled *Erogenus*, c. 1972) sought to remedy the "trouble [that] so few records can be used as background music, [for] most recorded products these days demand the listener's attention."[59]

By encouraging its consumption in a state of distraction,[60] the broad genre of muzak presented itself as an essential contribution to the development of our design-intensive society. In the 1960s it was no longer "Complementary music by Muzak" that was promoted alongside a "scientifically planned kitchen" and telephone service.[61] Instead, it was guaranteed that alongside "quiet central air conditioning for all season comfort" and "dishwashers in all bedroom apartments," a truly modern residence would be furnished with "music by Muzak in the lobby, elevators, laundry room—and on your own TV set."[62] Little by little, the company gained enough confidence to consider diversifying its product applications to a near-delirious level. As William Wokoun, one of the company's engineers, trumpeted loudly in the liner notes of a 1969 Muzak promotional LP entitled *Reveille*:

> Today, as specialists in the physiological and psychological applications of music, MUZAK is concerned with developments in vigilance and human factors

Muzak Speakers and Grilles: Specially designed for full-range reproduction of both music and voice under continuous operational conditions.

Muzak Volume Control: Virtually failure proof, these efficiency tapped-transformer-type units are ideal for selective control of volume in specific areas.

Muzak Amplifiers: Specially engineered for continuous, dependable, heavy-duty performance.

Muzak Microphones: A wide range of reliable Muzak-approved units for all types of systems available for quality sound reproduction.

Wired for sound by Muzak®...
The great new First National Bank in Dallas

Tallest building west of the Mississippi, First National Bank in Dallas is now completely *wired for sound*...the sound of Muzak. And the entire sound system was especially designed by Muzak.

Officials of First National recognized how important Music by Muzak is for improving employee morale. That's why they specified it for their new headquarters. Muzak was selected because of its unique ability to mask noise, boost worker efficiency, and create an atmosphere that is pleasant and stimulating to employees and public alike.

But there's another side to the Muzak story: complete communications systems. At First National, all voice paging, public address and signalling are handled exclusively by Muzak equipment.

Complete Muzak sound systems and components are specially engineered and installed for continuous heavy-duty, dependable performance. They meet highest quality standards for both music and voice distribution. Muzak systems now operate efficiently in thousands of commercial, industrial and institutional installations throughout the world.

To save time and expense, specify Muzak in the early planning stages.

music by Muzak

MUZAK A Division of Wrather Corporation, 229 Park Avenue South, New York, N.Y. 10003
Argentina, Australia, Belgium, Brazil, Canada, Colombia, Denmark, Finland, Germany, Great Britain, Israel, Japan, Mexico, Peru, The Philippines, Switzerland, United States, Uruguay

For more data, circle 99 on Inquiry Card

Figure 2.2. Advertisement "Wired for Sound by Muzak," *Architectural Record* (July 1965): 217.

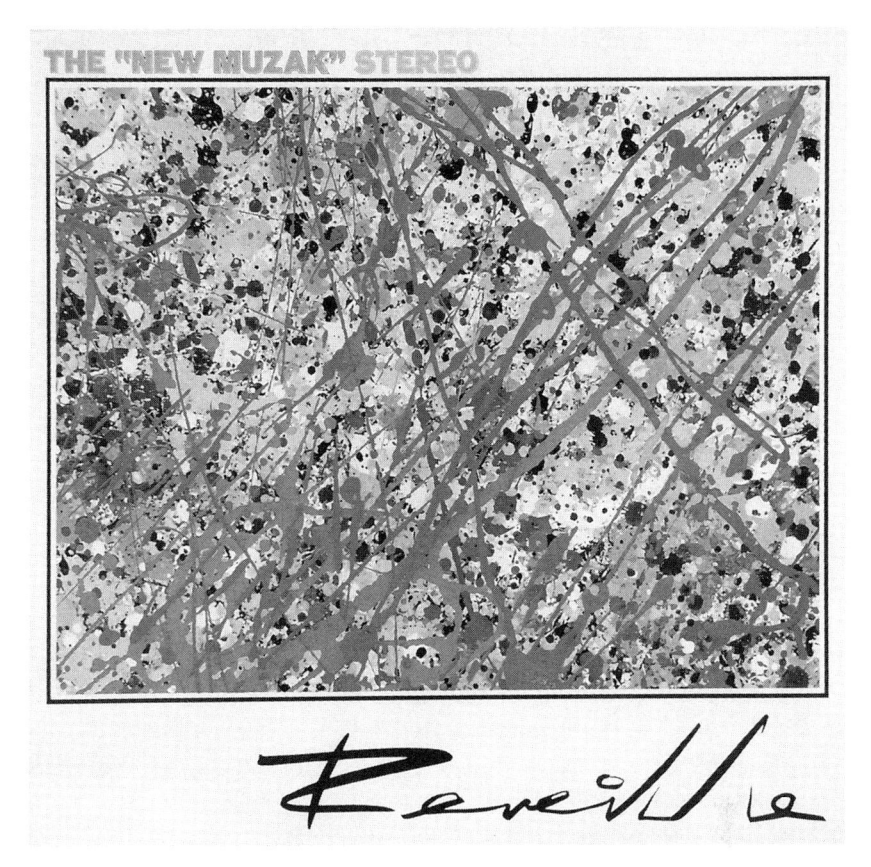

Figure 2.3. LP cover, *Reveille*, 1969, H-1(1) 79 by Muzak. Photograph courtesy of Rob Micallef.

research, automobile driver safety, medical and dental studies, noise control, the influence of color and music on emotions and of course, the effects of scientifically planned music on work productivity and efficiency, among others. Professional guidance is provided by the MUZAK Board of Scientific Advisors which consists of distinguished professionals in the field of education, industrial engineering, medicine, psychology and human factors. Under the guidance of the Board, MUZAK aims to make dramatic contributions to the business community through new discoveries in the scientific applications of music.[63]

Relying on an inflated scientific pretention—backed up by a "Board of Scientific Advisors"—the ambitious prospect of Muzak as a functional device served well, in the postwar era, the definition of an ever-expectant, scientific, and techno-utopian vision of the world. Of course, the futuristic image presented by Muzak is extravagant. But inducing such extraordinary expectations is meant to lead even the most moderate or incredulous observers to actually resolve the gap between anticipation and realization. Hence, reported a journalist a few years later, under Wokoun's direction the company was successfully exploring new applications, "the most prominent of which is medical therapy." Indeed, at "one hospital, Muzak seems to be having a beneficial effect on patients in the intensive care unit; a mental hospital reports it has been able to cut use of tranquilizers and sleeping pills by 50 percent since Muzak was introduced. It has been used to help ex–drug addicts relax, and to help students study. Dr. Wokoun believes it may be applicable to automobile safety, perhaps in specially programmed tape cassettes for the weary driver."[64] Such incredible determination to expand the reach of its product reflects what could be called the quasi-messianic ambition of Muzak. For the company, to borrow Michel Foucault's words, it was "no longer a question of leading people to their salvation in the next world but rather ensuring it in this world. And in this context, the word 'salvation' takes on different meanings: health, well-being (that is, sufficient wealth, standard of living), security, protection against accidents."[65] Despite guaranteeing a collective reveille, Muzak's promise of salvation was not grounded in the longing for any spiritual "awakening." The utopian, messianic nature of Muzak targets a well-defined space and time: the real space, now. To this end, during the late 1940s and 1950s, factories and war plants provided a propitious field of experimentation in order to prepare for the full emancipation of functional music in the civil sector.

Making Work Pleasant

From the postwar era to today, "Making Work Pleasant" has remained one of Muzak's company mottos.[66] As the invaluable research of Anson Rabinbach signals, the beautification of labor as a part of a state social policy might have been unique to National Socialism, but its principles were anticipated much earlier. One finds them, for instance, at the core of the utopian socialism of Charles Fourier, who envisioned "attractive labour," where "the workshops and husbandry offer the labourer the allurements of elegance and cleanliness."[67] At the beginning of the 1930s, Rabinbach points out, the English Industrial Welfare Society relied on the slogan "Beauty and success in work go hand in hand," to which a company like Wallace Scott & Co. responded by "paint[ing] its machines blue, its girders grey, its railings green, and other parts of the plant red and gold so that the colours would reflect light and 'make the plant lively.'"[68] Such a response plainly rewarded the efforts of "psychotechnics" schools of research that had emerged since the early twentieth century. Thanks to the development of industrial psychology, numerous studies contributed to the scientific measurement of the effects of "fatigue, temperature, dampness, body positions" (for example) on worker performance.[69] There is no doubt that these studies, and more specifically the careful examination of fatigue, conjoined to shape what Rabinbach calls a "rational deployment of the body's force in the interest of productivity."[70] It is in this context that the influences of "overeating, flower aromas, coloured lights, dance music" on the emotional life of the workers were envisaged and studied.[71]

The use of a time-based medium like music, in this context, seems to fit well the purpose of disciplinary techniques designed to impose upon the workers an internalization of the mechanical time clock of the factory day. As Simon Jones and Thomas Schumacher summarized it, "Taylor saw that the key to increasing output was to remove knowledge and control over the production process from labor and to place them in the hands of management. That knowledge, in the form of time and motion studies that examined the physical movements of workers with detailed precision, was then returned to the worker through practices that were exercised directly on the human body."[72]

With workers "practically danc[ing] up to their machines,"[73] as the president of Muzak Co. put it in 1946, functional music seemed to have perfected the choreography of factory work. At first, it is certainly tempting, as critics do eagerly with muzak, to interpret functional music in purely repressive terms, supplementing the rational organization of factory time and space in the pursuit for maximum productivity. Yet again, Rabinbach observed that the interest in energetic calculus has never been the privilege of any single political doctrine or ideology: "it could be applied on different sides of the political spectrum by liberal reformers, by socialists, and by Marxists."[74] In this regard, the various schools of industrial psychology shared the common objective of "reintegrating the individual into an industrial work process which, as a result of Taylorization, had been reduced to the carrying out of predesigned detailed tasks."[75] There is thus a distinction between "Taylorist engineers and progressive capitalists . . . whose chief interest was productivity" and "work scientists, who saw the reduction of fatigue as an anti-Taylorist, proworker humanization of labor relations."[76] However, emphasizes Rabinbach, it is true that

> these paths ultimately converged in the shared vision of rationalized society, dominated by "neutral" scientists dedicated to eliminating the atavistic conflict between labor and capital and expanding productive forces. The reduction

of fatigue proposed by the work scientists, labor's call for shorter hours, and the industrialist's ideal of scientifically determined productivism combined to establish the notion of an 'optimum' (as opposed to Taylor's maximum) duration of work.[77]

Managing this transition toward an optimization of the working conditions certainly motivated the seminal study *Fatigue and Boredom in Repetitive Work*, conducted in 1937 on the behalf of the British Industrial Health Research Board.[78] According to the authors, S. Wyatt and J. N. Langdon, studies in this field were justified not only because of the increasing number of repetitive processes, but, most importantly, because of the negative effects of the latter on "personal abilities and desires" that actually could extend beyond work proper.[79] Through the monitoring of the physical and psychological health of the worker (from "abilities" to "desires"), it is not only individuals' bodies that are turned into a stage of power relationships. Repercussions beyond the workplace are considered, and it becomes apparent that the immediate interest in producing and maintaining a vigorous labor force encompasses a larger concern for public health.[80] This concern, as we have seen, later permeated Muzak's ambition. The purpose of functional music was not only to produce better workers, but also to contribute to the shaping of the lives that it (incidentally) regulated. From factory to daily life, researchers in industrial and functional music aimed at "establishing" and "maintaining" "a desired emotional relationship between the man, his work, and his environment."[81]

At first sight, Wyatt and Langdon's inquiry simply provided a means for efficient workforce management. To this end, however, the scientists also intended to "remove sources of misunderstanding" between workers and employers.[82] In other words, this meant some consideration of the workers' standpoint. After six months of inquiry, they were able to inform the (surprised?) management that, actually, "repetitive work contains little that is inherently interesting or satisfying."[83] Who, one wonders, couldn't have formed such "general impression" without scrutinizing the workdays of chocolate packers and makers of paper-crackers? From a scientific point of view, however, it appeared worthy of note that, considering the latter task, "the papers of many colours which were used in the making of different batches" positively introduced a notable "degree of variety" into the work. Furthermore, they noted, the "attractive appearance of the finished article undoubtedly appeals to the creative tendencies in human nature."[84] Why, then, would this "fairly interesting and satisfying" task not be a popular one among workers? No matter how puzzling these considerations may appear today, they illustrate well the scientists' genuine, yet tainted, eagerness to

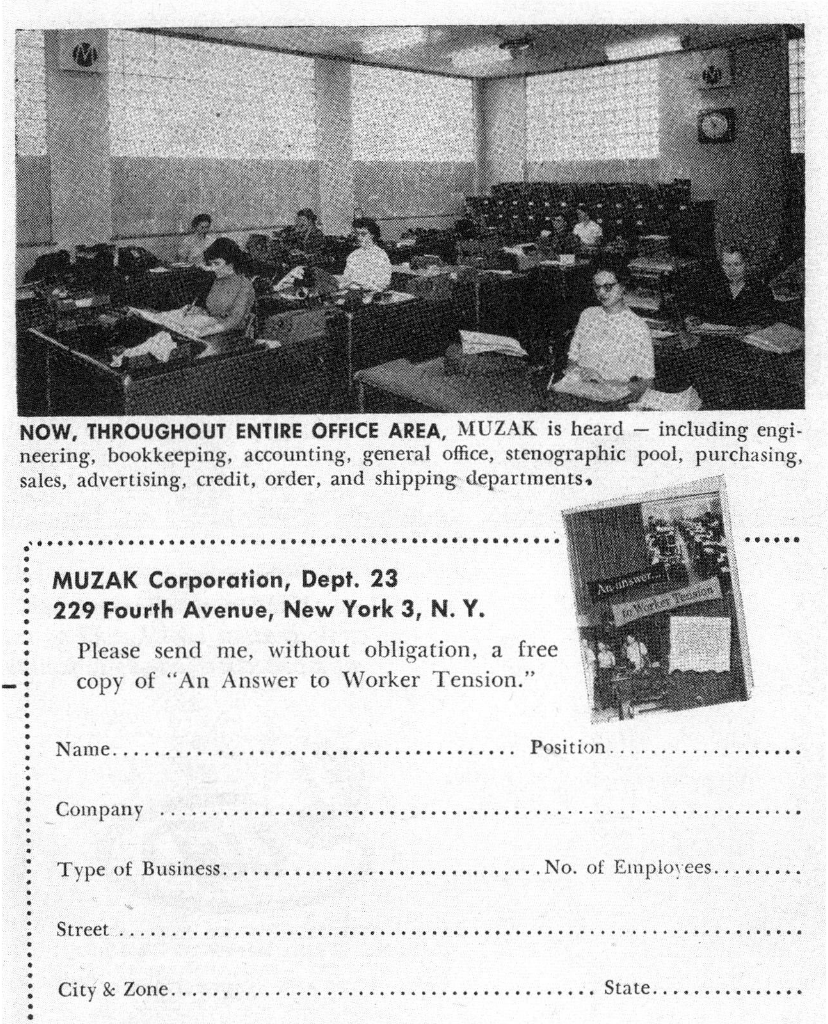

MUZAK INCORPORATED 59

NOW, THROUGHOUT ENTIRE OFFICE AREA, MUZAK is heard — including engineering, bookkeeping, accounting, general office, stenographic pool, purchasing, sales, advertising, credit, order, and shipping departments.

MUZAK Corporation, Dept. 23
229 Fourth Avenue, New York 3, N. Y.

Please send me, without obligation, a free copy of "An Answer to Worker Tension."

Name.................................... Position....................

Company ....

Type of Business............................No. of Employees.........

Street ....

City & Zone.. State..............

Figure 2.4. "More Striking Proof that It Pays to RELIEVE WORKERS' TENSION WITH MUZAK." Employees of The Fischer Lime and Cement Company, Memphis, Tennessee, in a photograph used for Muzak Advertisement, *Fortune* (March 1957): 53.

improve the working conditions of their subjects. From this perspective, their study presented a seminal special experiment on "the effects of gramophone music," using a fairly primitive technical device. Quite simply, the factory "was equipped with a gramophone, amplifier, and loud speakers, and the music was provided by records obtained from a local lending library."[85]

Music While You Work

In itself, the decision to utilize music was not primarily influenced by any belief in its intrinsic power. It was rather motivated by a very pragmatic and logical concern. If one argues that the alleviation of boredom depends "upon the extent to which the mind can be distracted from this condition," it is only common sense in a workplace to pick a form of distraction to "appeal to the ear rather than to the eye."[86] Music is not itself more or less efficient than anything else; it is only—wrote the researchers—"the most suitable medium" in the context of industry. As for its actual (favorable) effect, Wyatt and Langdon could only remain circumspect in their conclusions. First, it appeared that the impact on output was "most marked during the music period," but, they added, it "was not confined to the time the music was played."[87] Second, despite the fact that "the majority of workers responded to the music by an increased output . . . there were isolated cases in which the music seemed to have little or no effect."[88] Does the first observation signal a lingering effect, or rather, does it weaken the immediate correlation between the use of music and increased output? And why would music work on some workers and not on others? Did the presence of a pair of scientists observing them over a period of several months influence, in one way or another, the workers' behavior? Their research certainly contained many gray areas and left behind many wobbly conclusions to be later widely disregarded in further studies and analyses of functional music.

Wyatt and Langdon's study was highly specific, and as a result of their limited framework they could only vaguely speculate ("it is highly probable . . .") that their findings would apply to "most industrial workers."[89] They had started by observing and questioning 355 experienced female workers from fourteen to thirty-five years of age. In order to prevent extraneous factors from corrupting their study, Wyatt and Langdon elected unmarried subjects only, convinced that "they started the day fresh, i.e. without having any housework to do at home before starting for the factory."[90] If anything, this principle shows well that beyond work—even housework—there is no life worth considering. Eventually, certain focused experiments on the effects of music involved only 68 workers, and the statistical results were obtained from recording the output of 12 workers "uniform in type."[91] Wyatt and Langdon experimented with five types of music—marches, waltzes, one-steps, fox-trots, and "light" music—but it appears that their choices were prejudiced: "[a] preponderance of dance music was included in the programme," they admit, "because of its undoubted appeal to the modern female worker."[92] Nevertheless, beyond any doubt, Wyatt and Langdon's results contributed to the passage from the experimental field to systematic application. Already, starting in 1940 and inspired by their findings, the BBC *Music While You Work* program had been launched and was soon heard daily by more than 8 million war workers in Britain. This was supplemented by the use of phonograph records and the hiring of traveling bands and orchestras.[93] In 1943, a survey conducted in American war plants would thus conclude confidently that not only was the music program "universally liked by the workers," but that they demanded it emphatically.[94]

Functional Music

Certainly, the use of music in industry is not entirely a product of the war years. In 1927, as reported in the *American Journal of Public Health*, the president of the Section on Industrial Hygiene of the Royal Institute of Public Health, eager to improve general health in factories, estimated that music, through the introduction of gramophones with amplifiers "in departments where the operations consist of endless repetitions, such as stamping, wrapping and packeting goods, and are therefore monotonous," had "an inspiring effect during the later hours of a working day."[95] Similarly, responding to a growing interest in this field during the war years, a representative of RCA Victor reminded its readers that by the early 1930s, management staff had already recognized the experimental use of music as an "outstanding aid to . . . production efficiency" in their plant in Harrison, New Jersey.[96] This positive effect, however, strictly depended on the presentation of this musical background "as a service to employees for their benefit."[97] Early on, it was understood that, in order to be in a "good thing," the "idea of speeding production should never be mentioned" to the workers.[98] Very swiftly, it seems, this deceitful principle was recognized as a cornerstone for program efficiency:

> The psychological attitude of the workers to the music program is important. For example, in one or two plants the programs were rendered relatively ineffective because the workers suspected that they were "guinea pigs" for a music experiment. On the other hand, very effective programs . . . were carried out under conditions where the workers were reminded daily that "this is your program—tell us what you want and we will try to give it to you." This attitude, provided care, is taken to secure sufficiently large samples of opinion, seems to produce the best results.[99]

Yet, if one believes this study published by the U.S. War Production Drive Headquarters in 1943, functional music was still—despite such refinement—in its infancy. In fact, despite the great expectations surrounding the possibility of using music in American industry during the war, a dearth of informative studies existed in the field. Very little was actually known in this domain, remarked the author, except for "one investigation made under controlled conditions and the report from the British Ministry of Information, 'Music While you Work.'" What mattered most, clearly, was that all this "fragmentary information indicated that its use was growing at mushroom speed."[100]

Cited as an example, the development of functional music in Great Britain was undeniably inspirational to American acousticians and work scientists. In 1941, a year after its installment, the seminal BBC program *Music While You Work* was already reviewed as an incipient "national institution," and its function was summarized as follows: First, it reintroduced music into social life, for "to ease manual work has been one of the functions of music throughout many centuries of past history." Second, "the output of war production is substantially raised, as has been proved," and at last "the twice daily broadcasts . . . welcomed by the workers," and providing "refreshment for their minds and bodies," could also be regarded as "a factor in the musical education of millions of women and men who are listening to it."[101] The efficiency of the program was further noticed by the head of the Broadcasting Section of the British Army who allegedly praised it as "easy to hear" and implying "no necessity to listen."[102] By 1945, a study conducted by the BBC reported that "[over] 9,000 major industrial organisations are now relaying the programmes through their factories—1,000 more than last year."[103] It is in this context that the premises upon which music could be considered functional were defined.

Musical Antidote

How could music be functional? At first, Wyatt and Langdon suggested that it simply intervened to fight boredom and prevent fatigue by affecting workers' sense of time. "Most people," they contend, "will agree that time seems to pass quickly when work is interesting, but slowly when the worker is bored."[104] More precisely, argued Wyatt and Langdon, music could help establish a form of positive "day-dreaming or reverie."[105] Of course, within the walls of a factory, the functional value of daydreaming did not go without saying. Yet again, as work scientists, Wyatt and Langdon opposed the views of "the majority of employers," who regarded "singing as a form of frivolity which would desecrate the atmosphere of serious work." To their detriment, those employers

> overlook the fact that singing is not only a wholesome means of escape from boredom, but is also a stimulant to cheerful feelings and increased activity. /

> Since boredom is due to an awareness of the monotonous conditions of work, its alleviation will depend upon the extent to which the mind can be distracted from these conditions.[106]

Naturally, the point was not to divert the workers from their task but to regulate what would otherwise constitute "undesirable" or even "harmful" "prolonged indulgence in flights of fancy."[107] Ultimately, Wyatt and Langdon's reasoning and experiments did not only seduce factory managements. From the start, their study was received as much as an economic rationale as a medically legitimate answer to boredom and fatigue, which were viewed as a treatable physical and psychological deterioration. The *British Medical Journal* relayed and amplified these findings. From a psychological point of view, the main medical interest was certainly the correlation established between the level of boredom and the level of "intelligence" of the workers, their potential "extrovert temperamental tendencies," and their desire for "creative work" (as opposed to repetitive).[108] Yet the British medical review of Wyatt and Langdon's study was quick to recognize music not simply as the "most suitable medium" but, more definitely, as "the most effective antidote to boredom."[109] As a later study would assert, "on the theory that an ounce of prevention is worth a pound of cure, it is conceivable that fatigue and boredom can in some degree be forestalled with a well-timed program of music."[110] Moreover, even for the medical corps, workers' health was evidently not the final concern. For the *British Medical Journal* reviewer, the efficiency of the cure was primarily gauged economically upon a "6 to 11 per cent" increase in output "during the music, while the total daily output increased 3 to 6 per cent."[111] Already, the demonstration that music constitutes an effective antidote to boredom relies on the sheer, almost magical power of statistics. Without delay, the emergent science of functional music quickly clarified the inextricable interdependence of the medical and economic spheres in their joint capacity to shape a powerful nation.

This correspondence between the therapeutic and the economic spheres never ceased to inform research in functional music. Eventually, as a researcher formulated it, "[to] be functionally effective the music must be used to counteract the natural degeneration and reinforce desirable changes which take place in the individual during his normal working day."[112] Music, in this light, offered an efficient vaccine to a form of physical and mental disorder. Throughout the 1940s, researchers of music in industry continued to find their inspiration in the medical field, and most especially in mental institutions. "With respect to mental illness," remarked one work scientist, "there is a growing disposition to try music as a means of calming the manic, stimulating the depressive, arousing the lethargic and reaching the withdrawn."[113] Conversely, the same researchers relied on a previous study undertaken in an industrial context to encourage hospitals to "exploit the now empirically validated techniques for applying music specifically to the relief of boredom, one small segment of the field for which we have specific data."[114] In other words, medical research could, in turn, benefit from the progress made in industry. In effect, among the implied "empirically validated techniques," the elaboration of careful programming—determining what music should be played and when—had become an object of increasing refinement within factories.

Programming Strategies

Considering when to play music, as Wyatt and Langdon wrote on behalf of the workers, "there was a decided preference for the introduction of music during alternate half-hours throughout the spell of work."[115] Only a "small minority" of workers, they noted, raised the objection that this regular, timed intervention of music (half hour with music / half hour without music) actually "increased awareness of the passage of time," and one subject claimed, "I don't want to be reminded of the amount of time still to be worked."[116] Here again, no matter how much concern is shown for the workers' well being, the study is clearly driven by the scientists' interest in enabling increased productivity. Most often, after this example, studies subordinated music's effect on productive output to its physiological effect. Hence, concluded a 1943 study conducted in more than 100 plants, "the principal value of music in relation to efficiency is not in speeding up the worker to greater effort, but in relaxing unnecessary nervous tensions and creating a pleasant atmosphere for work."[117] Consequently, since the purpose of music is "to relieve boredom and allay fatigue, . . . the right moments to use it are suggested by these factors."[118] Even though differences between plants were taken into account, one basic structure reads as follows:

> Whenever possible, music should be carried over into the actual beginning of the work period. The next installment of music should act as a restorative to the so-called fatigue period, occurring usually toward the end of the first half of the shift; or, if 10-minute rest periods are instituted 2 or 3 minutes of music should precede and follow news and announcements at this time. . . . During the last half of the shift, short intervals of music may be used with great effectiveness to take the worker's mind off the fatigue of work and make the day seem shorter. It also serves to bridge the after-lunch fatigue period. Where music is not carried right up to the closing time, martial airs used to play the old shift out and the new shift in are very effective.[119]

EXAMPLE II

Title	Artist
1. Two Hearts in Three-quarter Time	Harry Horlick Orchestra
2. I Love You (Porter)	Bing Crosby
3. Avalon	Al Goodman Orchestra
4. On the Sunny Side of the Street	Benny Goodman Sextet
5. Brazil	Xavier Cugat Orchestra
6. Surrey with the Fringe on Top	Carmen Cavallaro, Piano
7. Something to Remember You By	Dinah Shore
8. Orchids in the Moonlight	Xavier Cugat Orchestra

Figure 2.5. Playlist (example II): "Programming Music for Industry," Barbara Elna Benson, *Music and Sound Systems in Industry* (New York; McGraw-Hill, 1945), 24.

When to play music appeared to be a rational enough matter, conditioned by data coordinating productivity drops with points of utmost degeneration. What to play and to what effect, however, appeared to be a more delicate issue. While Wyatt and Langdon's choice of music remained dominated by their belief in what would "appeal to the modern female worker,"[120] their followers started to attach more and more importance to the dynamic relationship between the structure (timing) and the content (playlist) of the programs. On the American side, echoing the BBC's rhetoric, the supplemental educational value of music influenced this process, according to the peculiar belief that the workers' appreciation of "good music" would ultimately "assist the war effort more than swing."[121] As a result, the researcher could rejoice in the observation that introducing more "music of good quality" (rather than "popular swing") led one third of the workers to "now favor classical music during lunch period."[122] Still, what exactly constitutes good and bad beyond a rough dichotomy between "classical" and "popular" requires elucidation. Evidently, experiments in industrial broadcasting only relocate within the workplace a broader debate over cultural legitimacy, which, in the 1920s and early 1930s, accompanied the emergence of acoustic media (phonograph, radio, film). In factories, introducing selections of the operatic canon as the antithesis of and the antidote to the deleterious effect of jazz only reiterated a politics well established in radio broadcasting.[123] Following this logic, the question of what to play necessarily led to the issue of what not to play. In relation to the workers' performance, an immediate correlation was drawn between "boogie-woogie, hot swing, jive, vocals and all forms of bizarre music" and their negative effect on the workers.[124] In effect, beyond notable dissension about whether or not workers' likes and dislikes should be taken into consideration, researchers generally agreed that "eccentric" performers—such as Art Tatum, Eddy Duchin, Hazel Scott, Fats Waller, and Earl Hines[125]—should be banned. Similarly, the avoidance of vocals, characteristic of music by Muzak until the early 1980s, stemmed from the industrial context, where

> there are very few vocals listed, and those used are either part of the background or else soft low voices that are very well known. Every orchestra has a definite full-bodied style minus eccentricities to be found in some of the more stylized bands, for example, Glenn Miller, Duke Ellington, or Tommy Dorsey. Each recording has a sustained melody throughout, which means that it is easier to monitor and will be heard with ease in almost every plant area.[126]

Out of such experiments, some general rules ultimately emerged. Functional music, it was concluded, "must not seize and hold [the] conscious attention of the listener, to the detriment of his activity," even during the lunch break. To this end, the music should possess what the researchers called a "high acceptance factor."[127] That is why, after relying on commercially available material, it was eventually considered necessary to control every level of the music: "from the creation or composition ... through its instrumental arrangement, its performance, its interpretation, its preservation, its reproduction, and distribution and finally the manner of its presentation [in order] to achieve the desired psychological effect upon the ultimate listener."[128] From the late 1940s to the late 1970s, Muzak continued to pay special attention to all the factors contributing to the careful crafting of its product: "the melody line; the number of musicians involved ... the instrumentation; the placement of the musicians at the time of the recording; the content of the arrangement; the personality and style of the arranger ... the use of the instruments, the percussiveness; the impulses; the pulse, the accent, the tempo, the rhythm."[129] It appears misleading, in this light, to assume that functional music relies on a general disregard for aesthetic concerns. To the contrary, the very elaborate set of principles that slowly emerged out of research in the industrial use of music defines a specific mode of musical understanding and appreciation, no matter how remote from conventions it may at first appear.

Figure 2.6. "Time Out for Lunch," illustration from Barbara Elna Benson, *Music and Sound Systems in Industry* (New York: McGraw-Hill, 1945).

The Aesthetic of Functional Music

At first, the aesthetic of functional music offers an inverted image of the cultural codes defining the place and space of music in society. The producers of the BBC *Music While You Work* program, recognized very clearly, in 1940, that a programming of functional music was the antithesis of a regular (i.e., entertaining) radio broadcast. If one takes the point of view of the general listener, they wrote, "we are asking for a bad piece of programme building." Consequently, a proper musical selection would include "as little variation of tempo as possible, the ideal being to maintain the same beat through the whole programme." Defining a radical aesthetic later refined by Muzak, this already meant that "[artistic] value must not be considered. The aim is to produce something which is rhythmically monotonous and repetitive; a 'sustaining' background of brisk, cheerful but unobtrusive music. Slow sentimental numbers and selections are ruled out." And last, stressed the producers, "[subtlety] of any kind is out of place. Quiet pieces should be avoided. A more or less steady volume of moderately loud to loud power should be used throughout, and items selected accordingly."[130] Even though it is formulated mostly as a negation of traditional musical values, it is nevertheless clear that from its structure (tempo) to its emotional quality (cheerfulness), functional music necessitates the elaboration of a comprehensive aesthetic system.

The broadcast of music in the industrial workplace notably faced the expectation that listening to music required at least relative silence. This was simply not an option in a factory, and researchers rapidly understood that, without proper monitoring of the levels (volume, dynamic range), "the problem of continuous audibility and enjoyment of music" in this context could not be solved.[131] What was needed, suggested a study, were special recordings created for industrial use wherein the volume would not vary more than "plus or minus two decibels."[132] It was in this domain, notably, that Muzak was able demonstrate its expertise. As a 1943 study in war plants recognized, conclusions pertaining to the technical issue of audibility were based

> on the excellent effect on workers of good music wired over telephone lines from companies furnishing industrial music. These programs are, in general, of a definitely higher value than those supplied by the plant themselves. This reason for this superiority is found in the fact that these companies have already re-recorded thousands of standard compositions in order to make them suitable for use in restaurants where there is considerable noise interference. The changes in intensity of volume between restaurant and plant are small, making them ideal for industrial use also; but unfortunately they are not obtainable in the open market.[133]

The same year, Muzak Corporation contributed to the Symposium on Music and Industry held in New York by the Acoustical Society of America (founded in 1928 by a group of scientists and engineers) with a concise presentation by Ben Selvin (1898–1980), then director of the company's Programming and Recording Department. Following the lengthy account given by the representative of RCA, the expertise of Muzak Corporation on the overall aesthetic of functional music is notable. Ben Selvin, who had been a successful recording artist since the 1910s and a renowned bandleader, entered Muzak at its inception in 1934 and stayed until 1947. First, on the question of what to play, his programming strategy appears to be close to RCA's position. The music, says Selvin, must be "the type of tune the 'man of the street' understands," ranging from popular tunes and old-time favorites to Latin American tunes (about once an hour), and "americanized polkas." An occasional "operatic selection" is acceptable, adds Selvin, but only if it is a familiar melody "such as the Sextet from 'Lucia,' the Quartet from 'Rigoletto' or the Soldier's Chorus from 'Faust.'" However, warns Selvin, proper content is not sufficient to guarantee the functionality of the program. The issue, he insists, is not only what to play, but also how to play it. In other words, says Selvin, good industrial music must be transcribed music: each tune needs to be specially arranged and carefully interpreted. From his days in the recording industry, Selvin knew all the tricks to produce a catchy arrangement. For example: a startling opening, a change of color "every twenty or thirty seconds," a "change of key between choruses," a "vocal refrain," and a "fancy ending" are just some of the features that are required to manufacture a successful tune. Efficient industrial music, concludes Selvin, is just the opposite. It should be "strictly instrumental . . . and never over-arranged or tricky."[134]

Following this crucial observation, the author also signals a coming and important shift in the production of "Music by Muzak," when he reports that the company "recently commissioned several composers to write special industrial music. These writers have been taken through various plants and will compose with a good understanding of the need of the workers and the employer's problem." And finally, beyond the production of custom-built music, Muzak's expertise also led them to analyze the problem of when to play music. Here again, Muzak shows a growing professionalism in its consciousness that music is not an all-purpose panacea: "We recommend, too, that no music be played when the bell rings and the workers start at their jobs. . . . Playing music simultaneously with the start of the shift suggests a speed-up and may be resented by employees." Hence, quite in opposition to the definition of an uninterrupted and saturated musical environment envisioned by RCA, Muzak Corporation suggests, on the contrary, that music as a functional tool must be carefully rationed. Selvin's lesson resurfaced in the survey published in 1947 by Cardinell and Burris-Meyer, the former being then credited as the director of the Research Department at Muzak Corporation. Industrial music, they reiterated, is indeed a "highly complex technique," and it cannot be stated that "any kind of music presented in any manner would result in the desired industrial benefits."[135] In the end, from the early use of commercially available gramophone music to this late-1940s proposal of an inclusive system of production and broadcasting, a product ultimately known as Muzak slowly emerged. As it imposed itself in the civil sector in the postwar-era, significant transformations may have affected the way functional music was implemented in society (from background to foreground music; from labor to consumption). Yet, turning to more recent implementations and critical evaluations of the device, a strong and irremediable sense of continuity dominates.

Earworms

As a broadly distributed genre of music, the muzak of the postwar era can be characterized by its string-oriented and/or melody-centered arrangements, deprived of syncopation and of any strong dynamic change. This stripping "of any distinctive elements" from the music, observed Jonathan Sterne in the late 1990s, still defined most background music in opposition to the majority of "industrially recorded and disseminated music."[136] "Controversial songs" with a "catchy tune" (such as Madonna's "Like a Virgin" or Nirvana's "All Apologies"), noted Sterne, can become background music only after being subjected to "quiet jazz arrangements . . . with a piano or saxophone playing the vocal melody."[137]

Still, opening the understanding of Muzak to a wider musical scope can be beneficial in some regard. In his *Surreal History of Muzak, Easy-Listening, and Other Moodsong*, for instance, Joseph Lanza encouraged his readers to revise their swift value judgments: "This book will have succeeded if I can help efface (or at least make all the more confusing) the distinction between one person's elevator music and another's prized recording."[138] Lanza's purpose is not simply to nurture a kitsch appreciation of muzak. While background music is mostly associated with a specific mellow sound, the author suggested that its sedating quality might pervade a much wider array of musical productions ranging from the string-heavy arrangements of Mantovani to the "parsimony" of Philip Glass.[139] Why not? Muzak Co., however, did not need assistance to blur the distinction between music and muzak. In an advertising supplement published in 1994 celebrating the sixtieth anniversary of the company, the vice president of programming and licensing made it clear: "If you go to a store and you're hearing Muzak, it probably isn't Muzak . . . There are still a couple of companies out there doing that old-style 1,001-string, ruin-your-favorite-song kind of thing but we dropped all that in '87."[140] Only one of the twelve music channels, the article stressed, was still distributing the "old Muzak tradition of remaking popular tunes."[141] As a definite blurring between the objective of Muzak Corporation and the purpose of Lanza's study (whose conclusions, warned the author, "do not necessarily reflect [the company's] present-day official policies"[142]), the same 1994 infomercial brochure singled out and recommended the author's *Surreal History* as the only "easy reading" reference for those who would like "more information" on Muzak and ambient music.[143]

More recently, to the question "Is Muzak still elevator music?" the company's website answered even more vehemently and precisely: "No way! Muzak started working with original artist material in 1984—one of the first songs was Michael Jackson's 'Thriller.' Since then, our business music programs have expanded to include genres such as new indie rock, skate punk, hip-hop, alternative country, contemporary Italian, '80s hits, American roots, classic soul, Latin pop, and New Orleans music, among many others."[144] This shift in marketing strategy is not superficial. It corresponds to an expansion of the functionality of muzak from background ("striving toward anonymity and gradual changes in mood"[145]) to foreground music ("[striving] for an absolutely consistent identity and unchanging mood"). All the listed genres and sophisticated subgenres evoking many shades of culture (alternative country, contemporary Italian, classic soul . . .) give a good sense that the music industry, relayed by radio stations dedicated to specific "subaltern voices," does not need Muzak Co. or any of its competitors to package and channel music as a commodity whose social function in identity production could not be clearer. Hence, diversity only encourages normalization. Musical and artistic valorization of differences against a unifying "mainstream" only fosters the illusion that "all that is required is to break . . . repressive deadlocks," in order to be "reconciled with [oneself]."[146] Actually, as Michael Hardt and Antonio Negri have stressed, "many of the concepts dear to postmodernists and postcolonialists" have found their "perfect correspondence in the current ideology of corporate capital and the world market":

> The ideology of the world market has always been the anti-foundational and anti-essentialist discourse par excellence. Circulation, mobility, diversity and mixture are its very conditions of possibility. Trade brings differences together and the more the merrier! Differences (of commodities, populations, cultures, and so forth) seem to multiply infinitely in the world market, which attacks nothing more violently than fixed boundaries; it overwhelms any binary division with its infinite multiplicities.[147]

As much as it had been a matter of reinstituting individuality in an alienating, homogenizing work process, foreground music puts the process of identity formation at the service of a dominant political and economical force. As soon as differences are asserted and no longer in the making, suspected Michel Foucault, individuals are simply expected to "regain contact with [their] origin" and to reestablish "a full and positive relationship with [themselves]."[148] To a certain extent, the role of foreground music, in concert with the recording industry, is to foster identification with such irreducible lifestyles. In the end, foreground and background music are equally functional, the distinction between them residing essentially in how they are meant to be heard: "Foreground music is the industry name for music programming that consists of songs in their original form, as recorded by the original artist. The music itself is still meant to serve as a background wherever it plays, but it is 'foreground' in that it can draw attention to itself in ways that background music cannot."[149] Of course, as both many critics and the company concur, one may easily conclude that muzak is not music. But when it comes to promoting the functionality of its product, the company itself tends to overlook this distinction. A 2009 promotional brochure, "The Positive Impact of Music in a Business Environment,"[150] does not advertise muzak (whether as a genre or as a brand) but, rather, the Muzak company's skill in implementing the scientifically proven efficiency of music as a functional device. Whether Muzak especially composes music or uses its expertise to craft programs of functional music out of commercial material, the final product is designed to influence the environment—and, more specifically, the environment conceived as workplace. This, however, should not lead us to generalize the "meaning of this functional, highly rationalized music" as simply "maintain[ing] the present social order"[151] without questioning the nature of such "order." Our modern society, as Rabinbach emphasized, has consistently conceptualized labor as the activity that "which produces and constitutes society as such," and thereby defined "all other activities as non-economic, and consequently nonessential."[152]

In this context, the relative question of the musical "quality" of Muzak appears strictly irrelevant. Nonetheless, as reflected in the commentary of the critic Nick Groom, it may be more convenient to confine muzak to the genre of "soft and sweet and sticky; lubricious and lubricating" music. It makes it possible to wonder whether this "proprietary sonic vaseline" (i.e., this distinguishable form of cheesy music) may succeed in its purpose to "ease social intercourse, or facilitate cultural buggery."[153] The answer comes later, as the author reiterates a common refrain equating muzak "with containment, imprisonment, and control, a denial of human emotions—what [Joseph] Lanza* christens 'melodic surveillance.'"[154] In this last catchphrase, it would seem, the two extremes in the critical evaluation of muzak convene.

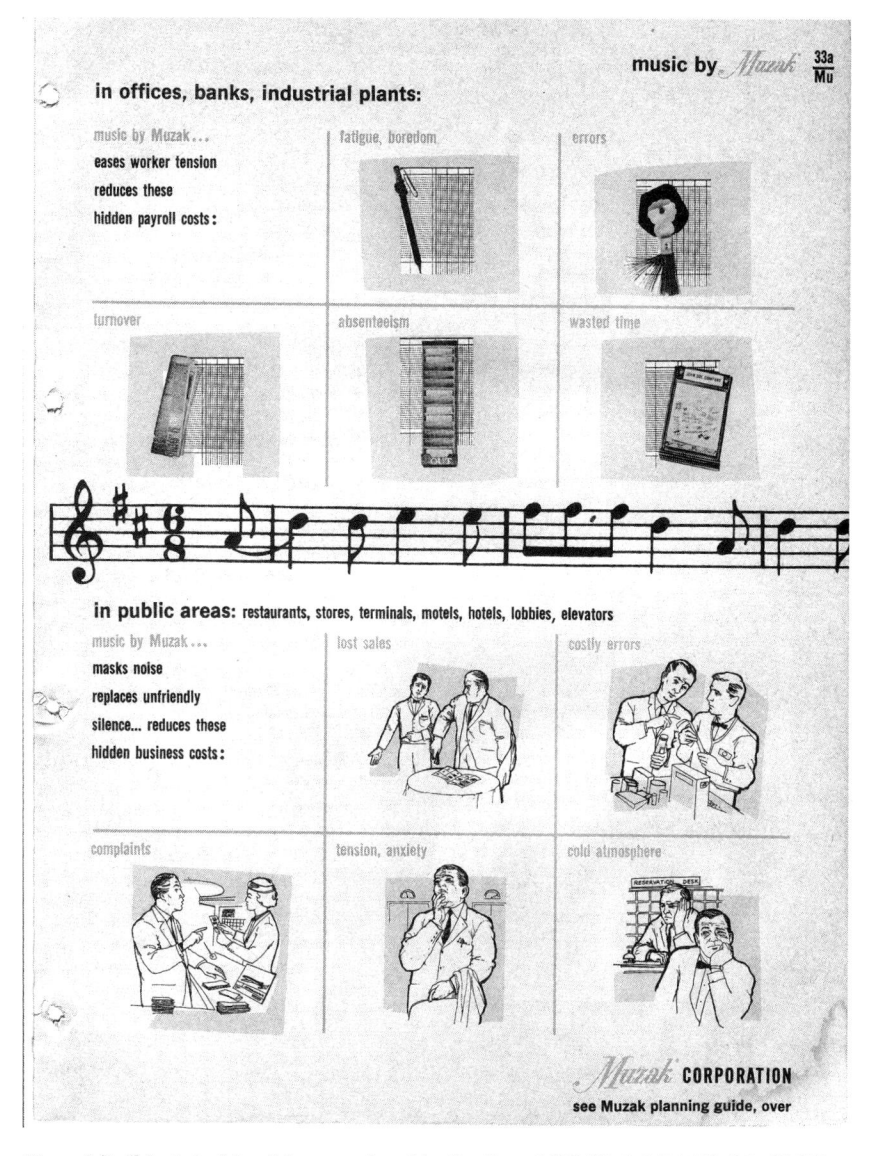

Figure 2.7. "Music by Muzak" promotional leaflet from 1962 [Ref. A.I.A File No 31-I-7].

The qualification of "melodic surveillance" combines, undeniably, the two poles of criticism generally associated with functional music. The aesthetic one, first, judging it to be a degraded form of sugarcoated music, literally reaching to the confines of "nonmusic"; and, on the other side of the same coin, the ideological criticism insisting on the coercive effect that Muzak has on individuals, "perpetuating alienation and false consciousness."[155] Whether right or wrong, the problem with such overdetermined criticism is twofold. First, it takes the effectiveness of Muzak for granted, only occasionally rejecting the hypothesis according to which changes in workers behaviors may be due, at least to a certain extent, to the result of their awareness of being watched (an observation better known as the "Hawthorne effect").[156] Consequently, the very "scientificity" of functional music is never called into doubt, its efficiency never questioned: it is assumed that Muzak positively "disguises stress, controls and directs human activity to generate the maximum productivity and the minimum discontent" and "calms the workers as they are led to the abattoir."[157]

Second, and as a result, such critical pretense tends to present the aesthetic quality of Muzak as the cause of its coercive power. Even without considering the wide range of musical genres qualifying for Muzak programming, the argument barely stands. At first, one may argue, the predictability of a musical tune, beyond Muzak and the so-called field of popular music, may well be part of a listener's pleasure. Thus, even though it remains the "most prestigious of music genres," writes Charles Rosen, "Opera as a whole has a shabby reputation." As the historian and pianist argues:

> The banality of the tunes is the heaviest charge, and this might seem to be a relative, even a subjective, matter—the banal is the overfamiliar, the too often-heard. But that was exactly what was wanted—or, rather, the initial success of an opera demanded at least one original melody that seemed long familiar at first hearing, and could be whistled by the audience on leaving the opera house. Both Donizetti and Verdi needed such tunes, at once original and instantly banal, for their dramatic structures to work: neither the sextet from Lucia di Lammermoor nor "La donna è mobile" from Rigoletto, to take only two examples, would have the right effect if they did not sound immediately as if one had known them all one's life.[158]

Whether or not one considers the potentially tormenting effect of "La donna è mobile" as coercive, it is difficult to understand how a sugarcoated melody or, for that matter, any overfamiliar tune could qualify, then, as a "denial of human emotions." To the contrary, it has been observed that if music impacts the listeners negatively, it is when it affects them excessively.

An example of such tormenting circumstances[159] is the irritation caused by some tune stuck in your head—a "musical itch" of the brain—that has been called "earworms."[160] The most identifiable form of "Music by Muzak" certainly relied on such effect. Phil Bodner's instrumental version of Dusty Springfield's "The Look of Love" opening Muzak's promotional LP *New Dimensions, Volume 2* (1969),[161] for instance, can be heard (while not listened to) as an earworm version of the 1967 original single composed by Burt Bacharach and Hal David. Certainly, one may regret Muzak's exclusion of the sensuous ratchet sound of the güiro, which, in counterpoint to Springfield's low, whispery voice, gave to the original a marked sexual innuendo. Springfield's voice is undeniably central to the sex appeal of the original, but so are the lengthy and smoky saxophone breaks saying, as the lyrics foretell, "much more than words could ever say." Following this lead to the letter, Bodner's full instrumental arrangement took its distance from the original while preserving enough of it to be caught as an earworm. While hearing it in the background, one gets the sensation of recalling Springfield's "soft, sweet and sticky" rendition inside one's head. Muzak, as it turns out, cannot afford to be as bad as Verdi. If too familiar and too recognizable, Muzak would run the risk of holding the "conscious attention of the listener."[162] The design of an "anonymous or 'unobtrusive yet familiar'"[163] music is therefore a fragile balance that ought to achieve the prowess of producing music that is not only not meant to be listened to, but actually not listened to. Still, as we've noted, the undeniable craft of the company in producing background music could please only the amateur of so-called "bad" music. What muzak requires, in order to convince more unanimously, is to situate itself on a more rational, scientific ground.

The Science of Muzak

Muzak Co.'s advertising strategy reveals a strong and longstanding reliance on scientific arguments. Over the years, the company's repeated claims that their products positively affect individuals' bodies physiologically and psychologically varied only slightly:

> 1956: "Not so many years ago people thought of music as a distraction when there was work to be done, especially mental activity. But since the development of MUZAK, progressive business management has awakened to a new concept of music. Alert executives have discovered that the right kind of music—unobtrusive background music by MUZAK, scientifically planned and custom-created—actually aids mental concentration."[164]

76   CHAPTER 2

> 1962: "Scientific studies show what happens when Music by Muzak eases worker tension and fatigue, the monotony of repetitive operations, the boredom of dull routine. Your people become more interested, more efficient, less prone to time-wasting, errors, lateness and absenteeism."[165]
>
> c. 2009: "Studies have shown that music can promote a less stressful and more enjoyable customer experience. People who are exposed to music experience reduced blood pressure, score higher on emotional wellness tests and experience reduced levels of anxiety and lower levels of stress. . . . The benefits of music extend beyond the customers. Increased employee satisfaction and productivity can have a significant financial impact for business locations, as well in result in increased customer satisfaction."[166]

In this promotional context, the notable shift of emphasis from worker to consumer, and from labor to leisure, seems nearly incidental. Inspired by studies in work psychology, Muzak's sustained logic was that time passes quickly when work is interesting, and slowly when the worker is bored. The principle was seamlessly transferred to consumption: in restaurants, for instance, "waiting periods never seem as long . . . with Muzak in the air."[167] This smooth transition was supported by a relentless insistence upon the scientific quality of the product. A typical reference to outside ("objective," "neutral") research, highlighting Muzak's willingness to advertise the efficiency of its product on an independent and objective ground, reads as follows:

> Findings: R. E. Milliman studied the effectiveness of music in a national chain of supermarkets and discovered that the use of slow music increased sales more than the use of fast music. The length of shopper stay expanded, and more items were purchased ranging in increased sales from $12,112.35 per store to $16,740.23 (an increase of 39.2%). In a 1991 study commissioned by Muzak, it was reported that sales to shoppers under age 25 increased 51%, age 26–50 increased 11%, and over age 50 increased by 26% when music was present. The addition of low arousal music in a retail environment results in an 18.9% increase in impulse purchases.[168]

That the company had not commissioned the first study, as opposed to the second, does not imply that Muzak had no influence on the experiment. Actually, Muzak directly influenced the conditions of Milliman's experiment. The use of slow-tempo and fast-tempo music, explained the author, was chosen as experimental criterion "because of a claim made in the sales literature of a nationally known marketer of programmed background music systems that music tempo, among several other factors, could be varied to affect human behavior."[169] Yet, he continued, "[when] contacted, the firm refused to produce research data in support of its claim. Therefore, tempo was selected as the independent variable for this research to find out whether, in fact, a link existed between music tempo and human behavior."[170] Seen through the lens of Muzak, the most significant segment of Milliman's argument, which is meant to turn skeptics around, lies in the succession of and, at times, the level of sheer precision of numbers (the increase in profit reported down to the penny, and reflected in a sales increase of precisely 39.2 percent!). But what do such numbers really amount to, beyond raising a facade of rational, irrefutable, objective truth? As a professor of marketing, Milliman had indeed concluded that, generally speaking, it appeared "possible to influence behavior with music," but this influence, he also noted, "can either contribute to the process of achieving business objectives or interfere with it."[171] What Muzak ultimately disregarded was the overall value that Milliman assigned to his own study. His readers, he insisted, "must be cautioned against generalizing these findings too far beyond the scope of this study. The results may not apply to all supermarkets, nor to any other market situation."[172] Moreover, in contrast to Muzak's advertising strategy, Milliman stressed that "exact figures are not important, as they pertain only to this research situation."[173] If anything, a closer look at some of the scientific studies referenced by Muzak reveals a mutual, yet at times conflicting, dependency between the company's arguments and those of "independent" researchers. Researchers regularly qualified their results in ways that Muzak easily elided for its promotional materials and guiding principles.

Figure 2.8. "How Much is Worker Tension Costing your Company?" The need for Muzak as demonstrated in an advertisement published in *Fortune* (February 1957): 53.

While Muzak always sought to legitimate its product scientifically, the company—understandably—does not readily acknowledge its underlying influence on particular scientific experiments. In the early 1980s, for instance, a study examining music as "an external psychological input that may elicit psychological change" experimented with hyperactive children, using an "ascending music progression cycle." This cycle was essentially a version of Muzak—what the company called a "stimulus progression curve." In the study, the author's hypothesis that "as the cognitive processes focus on the available stimulation of the environment . . . hyperactive children will be significantly less active during the ascending music progression cycle"[174] was openly grounded in at least three major precedents: Wyatt, Langdon, and Stock (1937) found that music was a successful means of combating boredom and increasing productivity. Muzak Co. found a significant increase in employees' work production when intervals of stimulus-ascending music were played. The subjects' alertness in an unstimulating environment was improved and attention span was increased (Wokoun, 1963, 1968).[175] One might be surprised, at first, to discover that studies conducted in the late 1930s in factories still constitute a dependable landmark for a child psychologist and still represent a valid reference for Muzak Co. In 2009, tracing back the history and genesis of Muzak on the occasion of its seventy-fifth birthday, the company presented Wyatt and Langdon's study as a turning point. The team of British industrial psychologists, they report in the "1930s" section of a self-celebratory website, "established that music increased workers' efficiency and concentration as a scientific fact."[176] The reference to William Wokoun's research is even more significant. The latter, actually, had worked at the Human Engineering Laboratory for the U.S. Army in the 1960s, before becoming "Director of Human Engineering" at Muzak Co. in 1968.[177] Muzak had already been central to Wokoun's military research; his 1963 experiment on vigilance with background music used "specially programmed" Muzak tape recordings to test the subject responses.[178]

Expectations regarding the therapeutic value of music inspired, equally durably, researchers and Muzak Co. alike. A 1995 study in consumer behavior, for instance (incidentally referenced by Muzak Co. to promote its product[179]) presents itself in light of two inquiries dating back to the mid-1950s.[180] Results, one could read in 1995, demonstrated that the use of background music in psychiatric hospital settings and in the context of group psychotherapy fostered an increase in verbal interaction: "the presence (compared to the absence) of background music," report contemporary researchers, "increases verbal exchange and affiliated behaviors such as smiles and eye contacts."[181] Forty years later, nothing much had changed:

"The empirical evidence presented here suggests that background music may influence buyer–seller interactions in some systematic way."[182] The most innovative finding, it appears, is that "soothing background music" rather than "stimulating music" is now associated with "more interpersonal interaction."[183] On this basis, marketing strategists expected to establish a strictly balanced emotional state, in effect the maintenance of an "optimal" point of arousal—speculated about in the 1960s—and located at the "intermediate level" between not enough and too much arousal.[184] Such researchers are certainly not attempting to conceal the semantic shift from the medical to the economic sphere. From their point of view, "findings from studying abnormal conditions help our understanding of normal functions," and even though some caution is required, "findings from clinical research" can be quite confidently "generalized to buyer–seller interactions."[185] Hence, one is to believe, from hospitals to retail stores, the adjustment of the subject can be efficiently monitored: "smile," "say hello," and "chat" can be measured on a seven-point scale from very "unlikely" to "very likely."[186] All in all, mentally ill subjects have simply become maladjusted consumers, who are basically expected to open up to the world of retailing. Muzak, from this perspective, is not simply "bad music." It belongs to a complex network of industrial, military, medical, and commercial interests, and it seeks to situate itself (productively) at their intersection.

Audio-Architecture: A Sense of Place

By and large, the function assigned to the programming of music, whether in workplaces, retail spaces, or elevators, is to eliminate inevitable frictions between humans and their environment in order to establish an "ideal" relationship. Logically, then, its efficiency can be measured according to its effect during catastrophic circumstances. If one is to believe the *New York Times*, piped-in music might actually have achieved such a goal when, in July 1945, a bomber hit the seventy-ninth floor of the Empire State Building. At that time, reported a journalist, about fifty people were in the glass-enclosed observatory situated on the eighty-sixth floor, close enough to the crash to see the debris of the plane landing on the open balcony. However, wrote the journalist: "the 'canned' music that is wired into the observatory continued to play and the soothing sound of a waltz helped the spectators there to control themselves. There was no panic, but within a few minutes the heat and choking fumes from the fire below made the observatory uncomfortable."[187] The situation was certainly not ideal, but it nonetheless indicates that functional music somehow systematized the

80 CHAPTER 2

Figure 2.9. Photograph, July 18, 1945, B-25 army bomber crashed into the Empire State Building (photo by Ernie Sisto / *New York Times* / Redux).

legendary lesson of the *Titanic*'s sinking to the sound of a cheerful tune.[188] In a way, Muzak presents itself as the technological, modern equivalent of a permanently available orchestra carefully designed to avoid panic in a society where passengers are constantly being assured that there is no danger.

Responding to its regulating effect, a certain sense of catastrophe defines the concept of background music. In the late 1970s, the composer Brian Eno summarized the musical ethos of "conventional background music" as a stripping away of "all sense of doubt and uncertainty."[189] For him, it was less the relegation of the music in the background that was condemnable than the concurrent attempt of "canned-music companies" at "regularizing environments by blanketing their acoustic and atmospheric idiosyncrasies."[190] In response, Eno famously developed the concept of an ambient music, "as ignorable as it is interesting,"[191] and able to "accommodate many levels of listening attention without enforcing one in particular."[192] The highly immersive, richly textured soundscape he created following these principles are certainly far more subtle (and discreet) than any standard background music. Still, his *Music for Airport* (1978) may not fully contradict the fundamental rhetoric of functional music. Predicated upon the capacity of the music to strengthen rather than to weaken listeners' sense of place, Eno's concept ends up meeting—even critically—the essential requirement of more "conventional" functional music. As the composer emphasized:

> And, most importantly for me, [the music] has to have something to do with where you are and what you're there for—flying, floating and, secretly, flirting with death. I thought, "I want to make a kind of music that prepares you for dying—that doesn't get all bright and cheerful and pretend you're not a little apprehensive, but which makes you say to yourself, 'Actually, it's not that big a deal if I die.'"[193]

Undoubtedly, Brian Eno was interested in the musical structure and texture of background music in an attempt to redefine them entirely, in strict opposition to the cliché of Muzak. His purpose, however, was not unlike that of Muzak in his attempt to generate a sense of place. Moreover, Eno's eagerness to foster a sense of intense awareness—to a point of full resignation—may only clarify what specialists of functional music had defined more vaguely in terms of a "desired" emotional relationship between man and its environment. Both ambient music and more conventional functional music are, to a certain extent, predicated upon the establishment of a positive, harmonious relationship between man and environment, which reveals itself all the more acutely in extreme instances. As an undated Muzak research document reportedly stated, panic could even be avoided "[in] the advent of nuclear war."[194] According to the performer and musician Genesis P. Orridge, for whom muzak represented the ultimate totalitarian evil, the company had designed its own "power generators to ensure no failure of the Basic Programme to those facilities still functioning and able to receive ... transmissions."[195] True or not, such a claim follows the logic of functional music. Whether you have to work, buy, or die, the purpose of ambient music (as reiterated by Muzak's chief programmer in the mid-1990s) "is to make [us] realize that [we've] come to the right place."[196]

Correspondences between music and architecture, as Xenakis reminded the readers of Le Corbusier's *Modulor 2*, are old ones. Quoted by Le Corbusier, the composer stated: "Goethe said that 'architecture was music become stone.' From the composer's point of view—added Xenakis—the proposition could be reversed by saying that 'music is architecture in movement.'"[197] Following this analogy, muzak is not simply added to the architecture as a decorative element. As Jonathan Sterne summarized it considering the semi-public commercial space of the Mall of America, music becomes a form of architecture: "Rather than simply filling up an empty space, the music becomes part of the consistency of that space. The sound becomes a presence, and as that presence it becomes an essential part of the building's infrastructure. Music is a central—an architectural—part of [it]."[198] Thus, pursues Sterne, background music "is not devoid of meaning, but its meaning is entirely located in its presence, rather than in the songs in the soundtrack."[199] And such presence suffices to construct "a continuity among the hallways, bathrooms, and entrances. These spaces are somewhat distinguished by architectural motif, but the background music reinforces their common characteristics through its own non-distinctive and generalized character."[200] Whenever foreground music is at stake, it then serves to define its distinctive uniqueness. It is in this light that one must appreciate the wide range of spaces that muzak, in one form or another, has infiltrated and helped to shape: from restaurant to factory, from retail stores to private residences. The physical assimilation of the device, characterizing it as part of the infrastructure of our environment, is the most blatant clue of Muzak's integrative process. To each location, whether public or private, corresponds a task that must be fulfilled efficiently. From increasing "employee productivity" to guaranteeing "stress reduction," or from the sharpening of "brand perception" to contributing to a required design-intensive production of the self, music as a functional device defines itself as an integral part of the social fabric. Profoundly, it defines its structure as a continuum, overcoming distinctions between the artistic and the useful, music and muzak, economic imperatives and medical concerns, military and civil sectors, educational aims and exploitive purposes, work and leisure, retail points and living rooms.

Confronted with this infrastructure, an artist like John Cage forcefully struggled, in the late 1950s and 1960s, to reinstate art as a means of social reformation. Facing the pervasiveness of background music and, beyond, the overwhelming influence of the mass media on society, artists may simply appear to embody a salutary resistance. Yet their objective (to impact society) was no different than that of the forces they opposed. Only art, stated Gyorgy Kepes in 1965, could beneficially participate in the structuring of "our chaotic physical and social environment" and become a key factor in "human self-regulation of the interacting variables of our man-shaped inner and outer world."[201] John Cage was no stranger to this philosophy. Encouraged by the theories of Marshall McLuhan and Buckminster Fuller, the composer ascribed to his art the function of designing "instances of society suitable for social imitation—suitable because they show ways many centers can interpenetrate without obstructing one another."[202]

In the 1960s, Cage's work clearly articulated the general promises of emancipation that relied on the transformative power of art in society. Such an endeavor, as Janet Kraynak perfectly summarized, gave birth to a powerful rhetoric of participation whose "positive attributes" and "potential for critical transformation" have never since ceased to be emphasized within art-historical interpretations: "Whether the Marxian model of de-alienation (in which the redefinition of object relations leads to a politically emancipated subject); or poststructuralist critiques of authorship (where the activation of the reader dismantles the aura of the individual work and authorial intention); or the ideological model of collectivism (as an antidote to the passive lull of bourgeois leisure and media), participation is seen as an interventionist gesture that furthers the ambitions of a progressive avant-garde."[203] With the hopes of opening such liberating space of creative participation, not only did Cage investigate the concept of "furniture music" developed by Satie, but he, in turn, also formulated the concept of a "Muzak-plus," which came close to being realized in the early 1960s for the Pan Am building in New York City. To the extent that Muzak appeared as a powerful instrument to Cage, the composer did much more than attempt to reject it or to silence it. "Our business in living," argued Cage, "is to become fluent with the life we are living, and art can help this."[204] A strangely similar task, indeed, to that of the Muzak Corporation.

CHAPTER 3

Muzak-Plus and the Art of Participation

> I think one day music will be a lot freer. Then the pattern
> for a tune, for instance, will be forgotten and the tune itself
> will be the pattern.
> —Ornette Coleman, *The Shape of Jazz to Come* (1958)

Constructing the Future

If John Cage remains one of the most controversial composers of the second half of the twentieth century, it may be because he had little interest in music, after all. "For many years," he said in 1974, "I've noticed that music as an activity separated from the rest of life doesn't enter my mind. Strictly musical questions are no longer serious questions."[1] There should be no surprise, then, in discovering Cage's long-lasting interest in muzak. His curiosity about the most despised form of canned music does not imply, however, that he liked Muzak, or that he was sympathetic to its alleged power. On the contrary, Cage often stated his distaste and, to a certain extent, his fear of Muzak.[2] Coincidentally, in the late 1950s, Muzak Co. unintentionally reformulated Satie's argument in favor of furniture music while promoting the use of its product in restaurants: "As far as our dining room is concerned," reported one satisfied subscriber, "Muzak is a must—for it helps to create a warm, friendly, enjoyable atmosphere, while subduing the natural restaurant clatter of dishes, knives, forks, etc."[3] Cage might not have come across this obscure ad, but he clearly established a connection between Satie's furniture music and conventional background music in order to distinguish one from the other. "[In] a very weak way," he estimated, "[Muzak] attempts to distract us from what we are doing . . . whereas Satie's furniture music would like us to pay attention to whatever else we are doing."[4] At first, Cage's distinction may appear to be nothing more than rhetorical. Yet whether or not it is that easy to separate one from the other, Cage succeeds, at least, in marking the thin line that distinguishes an artistic aspiration to emancipate society from an industrial/commercial venture meant to regulate an essentially dysfunctional social body of workers and consumers.

In Cage's words, encouraging distraction or, conversely, triggering a form of awareness is not intrinsic to the music. Both effects partake, more problematically, in the question of the intended purpose assigned to the music, whether an *attempt* to divert our attention or the *eagerness* to redirect it. Simply dismissing muzak on the grounds of this distinction did not appear suitable to the composer. Just as his dislike of the vibraphone would not appear to be a sufficient reason to prohibit its use, Cage perceived his aversion for muzak as something to be somehow overcome: "[If] I liked Muzak, which I also don't," he stressed in 1961, "the world would be more open to me. I intend to work on it."[5] Such conviction could only be reinforced by the realization that, after all, in the face of Muzak, resistance is futile. As Marshall McLuhan pointed out: "We are simply not equipped with earlids."[6] Cage, in tune with this prophet of the global village (or the "most convinced imbecile of the century," according to Guy Debord[7]), understood this better than anyone. Accordingly, he ascribed to the art and music of his time the daunting function to "serve to open people's eyes and ears to the enjoyment of Daily environment."[8] In such terms, the composer's position regarding muzak echoes the philosophy of the new media as it unfolds in McLuhan's theory. As the development of functional music indicated, muzak—in the broadest sense of the term—cannot be considered as a part of, or as a supplement added to our environment, but as an environment in itself.

More specifically, McLuhan pointed out, environments are not just containers, but "processes that change the content totally."[9] Whatever we may discern when we oppose these environmental processes (for example, that muzak is bad music) is only fragmentary and irrelevant compared to their "total and saturating" quality. Conversely, Cage responded to McLuhan's understanding of the artist's function as "taking over the task of programming the environment itself as a work of art, instead of programming the content as a work of art."[10] A condensed and optimistic summary of Cage's appreciation of the artist's role in relation to new technologies appears in a letter he sent to the engineer Billy Klüver in late June 1965:

> [Changes] in technology make other things possible to do than were done before. These scientific ideas are very superficially understood by artists and

artists are only slightly aware of technology. Nevertheless, many artists now feel that due to these changes anything is possible, or that if it isn't, it soon will be.

If I imagine myself then as composer in a situation where anything can be done, I imagine making a music little different from the concerts of ambient sounds we nowadays hear wherever we are when we listen. I imagine this music as technically like my daily experience: wireless. I imagine all distinctions between art and life removed. Art would then have to do with the opening of ourselves to the world in which we live.[11]

By following these principles, as the composer Cornelius Cardew observed, Cage did not try to represent the dynamics of our new environments "as an oppressive chaos."[12] Still, one cannot fully assume that he (or McLuhan) ignored their "underlying tensions and contradictions."[13] Cage's art does not translate changes in the environment into an uncritical celebration of our advanced technological society. Yet, suggested McLuhan, one cannot solve the issue by concluding that "the environment is bad," but by understanding its modes of operation upon us, which are—plainly put— "total and ruthless."[14] To this extent, he argued, the "environment is always the brainwasher, so that the well-adjusted person, by definition, has been brainwashed. He is adjusted."[15] In response, continued McLuhan, the artist increasingly appears as a maker of counter- or anti-environments designed to allow a perception of an otherwise invisible process. And to McLuhan, Cage undeniably fulfilled this function:

> . . . anti-environments, or counter-environments created by the artist, are indispensable means of becoming aware of the environment, in which we live and of the environments we create for ourselves technically. John Cage has a book called *Silence* in which, very early in the book, he explains that silence consists of all of the unintended noises of the environment. All the things that are going on all the time in any environment, but things that were never programmed or intended—that is silence. The unheeded world is silence. That is what James Joyce calls thunder in the "Wake." In the "Wake" all the consequences of social change—all of the disturbances and metamorphoses resulting from technological change create a vast environmental roar or thunder that is yet completely inaudible.[16]

Of course, one cannot argue that Cage's entire musical endeavor was geared toward the conception and realization of a form of muzak, which, as much as its industrial counterpart, would be intended to affect society at large. Still, the concept of "Muzak-plus," as the following inquiry suggests, may have some implications beyond its theoretical formulation. "Our business in living," Cage repeatedly claimed, "is to become fluent with the life we are living, and art can help this."[17]

Figure 3.1. Flyer designed by Andrei Hudiakoff for Léon Théremin's American debut at the Metropolitan Opera House, January 31, 1928. Music Research Collection, New York Public Library for the Performing Arts; Astor, Lenox, and Tilden Foundation.

Cage's mixture of interest in, and dislike for, Muzak is neither paradoxical nor ambiguous. He had a similar reaction to the Theremin, an early electronic instrument (eerie-sounding and touch-free) invented in 1917 by Lev Termen,[18] and commercialized by RCA in 1929. As Cage perceived it, the Theremin was undoubtedly "an instrument with genuinely new possibilities."[19] To a certain extent, Termen himself exploited such possibilities with the Terpsiton, a device allowing dancers "to create music by the movement of [their] bodies."[20] Nevertheless, the problem remained, said Cage, that the "Thereministes [such as Clara Rockmore] did their utmost to make the instrument sound like [an] old instrument . . . performing upon it, with difficulty, masterpieces from the past."[21] In other words, the problem of the Theremin, as it might be for Muzak, is not the instrument itself but its use. In the case of the Theremin, concluded Cage, it amounts to "imitat[ing] the past rather than construct[ing] the future."[22] Similarly, why not grant Muzak the genuinely new possibility of constructing the future? It may be necessary to admit this potential, even reluctantly, in order to understand why, in the early 1970s, Cage was still seriously keeping "muzak in mind as a project."[23] Only in this context can the possible nature of Cage's project, the extent to which it has been realized or not, and its consequences in music and society be discussed. In the end, it seems, the difference between the art of Cage (here, his Muzak-plus) and the commercial music by the Muzak Corporation lies less in what superficially opposes them ("commercial" vs. "experimental"; "bad music" vs. "serious music"; "coercive tool" vs. "emancipative experience") than in their common attempt to affect and shape society by the means of an aesthetic product designed to dissolve into life itself. Muzak could thus be seen as a missing link between the ambition of Happenings to rehearse, in the space of art, new dynamic interactions between individuals and their environment,[24] and the possibility to actually reify such an image of a future society in the present. This potential was not lost to a professor at the University of Wisconsin School of Music, who in the late 1980s speculated boldly that Muzak might have accomplished what John Cage "hoped to achieve with a highly radical musical language": "it places the responsibility for creating a meaningful experience in the realm of the receiver, circumventing the dichotomy of artist and listener."[25] Such a conclusion may be hard to swallow, but it nevertheless indicates how Cage's art had helped that author to become (perhaps a bit too) fluent with the life he was living.

Happenings are, by definition, ill-defined artistic events. There is no need, as did Michael Kirby in the mid-1960s, to reject the "prevalent mythology about happenings" ("widely known and believed" but "entirely false"), according to which "there's no script and 'things just happen' . . . there is little or no planning, control or purpose . . . no rehearsals."[26] Undeniably, happenings varied greatly according to the type of location ("a room or a nation"[27]), their temporality (closed or open), and the type of action (scripted, unscripted, rehearsed or not . . .). Still, while many happenings may have been more rules-dependent—less "improvised"—than one suspected, the diffusion of this mythology was essential to the promotion and perception of such events as being essentially liberating.

The difference between some of Cage's compositional tools (meant to generate indeterminacy) and the performance of the pieces may offer a good example of the issue at stake. From the late 1950s on, Cage often insisted that the indeterminacy governing his music was a means of challenging the primacy of the composer's intentions (his authority) and giving performer(s) "an active hand in giving the piece a form."[28] This, notably, confers to his music the (mythological) characteristic of happening, implying both a participative process and the relative unpredictability of the (simply sonic or interdisciplinary) event. Starting with *Variations I* (1958), Cage elaborated a well-known compositional tool—subsequently used for all *Variations*—consisting of transparent sheets with lines and dots. Randomly throwing them on top of one another, the performer(s)/composers could create an arbitrary visual map, indicating the time of occurrence, duration, loudness, pitch, and timbre to be assigned to the sounds. According to composer Cornelius Cardew, this process, as much as the music potentially ensuing suggested the appealing, liberating vision of the world "as a multiplicity of fragments without cohesion."[29] Yet after executing what he called a "pure performance" of *Variations I* with Kurt Schwertsik ("just reading the lines and dots and notating the results"), Cardew formed a rather different opinion.

> Contrary to his "beautiful idea" [of letting sounds be sounds and people people], Cage, in his performances of this piece with Tudor, never let the sounds be just sounds. Their performances were full of crashes, bangs, juicy chords, radio music and speech. No opportunity for including emotive material was lost. And musically they were right. Without the emotive sounds, the long silences that are a feature of the piece in its later stages would have been deprived of their drama and the work would have disintegrated into the driest dust—as Schwertsik and I found out by painful experience.[30]

Relating his experience in the early 1970s, Cardew clearly meant to debunk the myth surrounding the emancipative quality of Cage's music. What was painful was not only the dryness, or lack of interest of the musical output, but the feeling of having been duped. In actuality the music did not represent the idea—or, rather, it did so too well: leading a fragmentary vision to

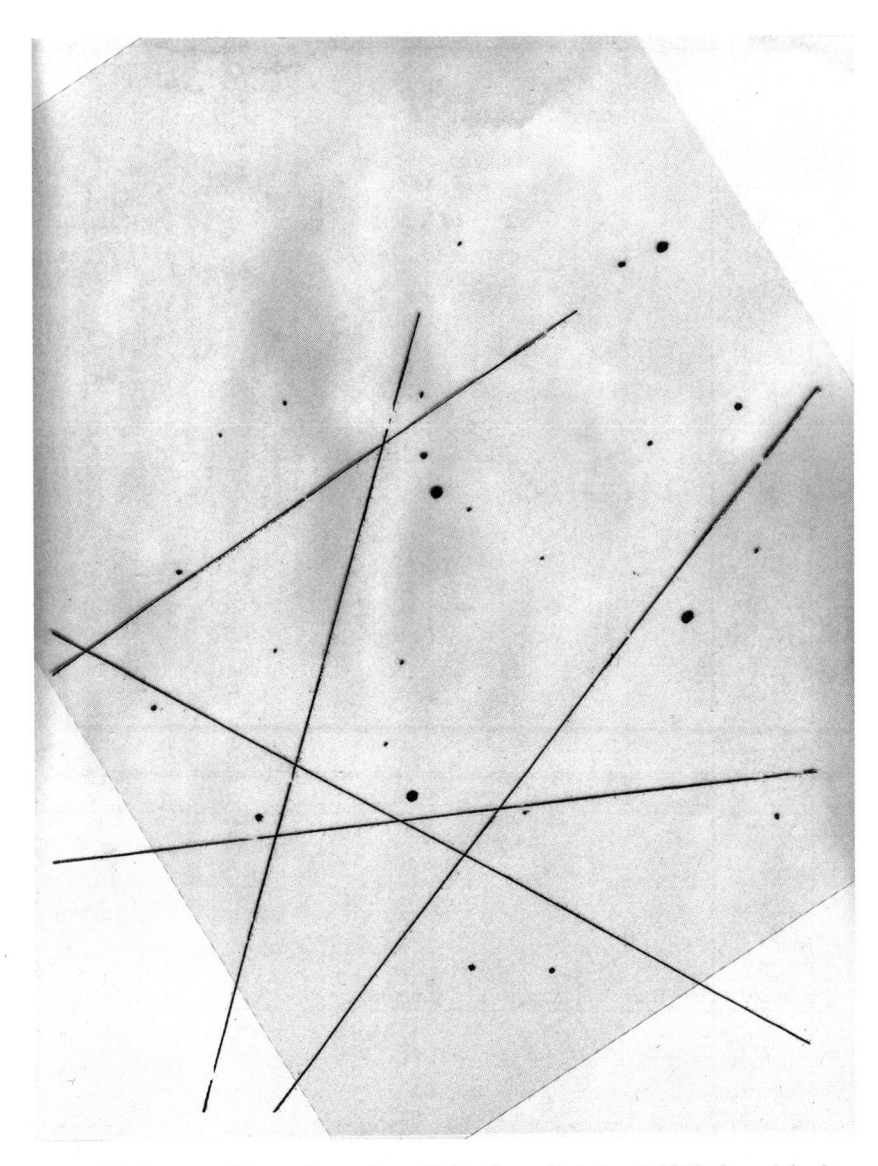

Figure 3.2. One possible configuration of John Cage, *Variations I*, 1958, Copyright © 1960 by Henmar Press, Inc. Used by permission of C. F. Peters Corporation. All rights reserved.

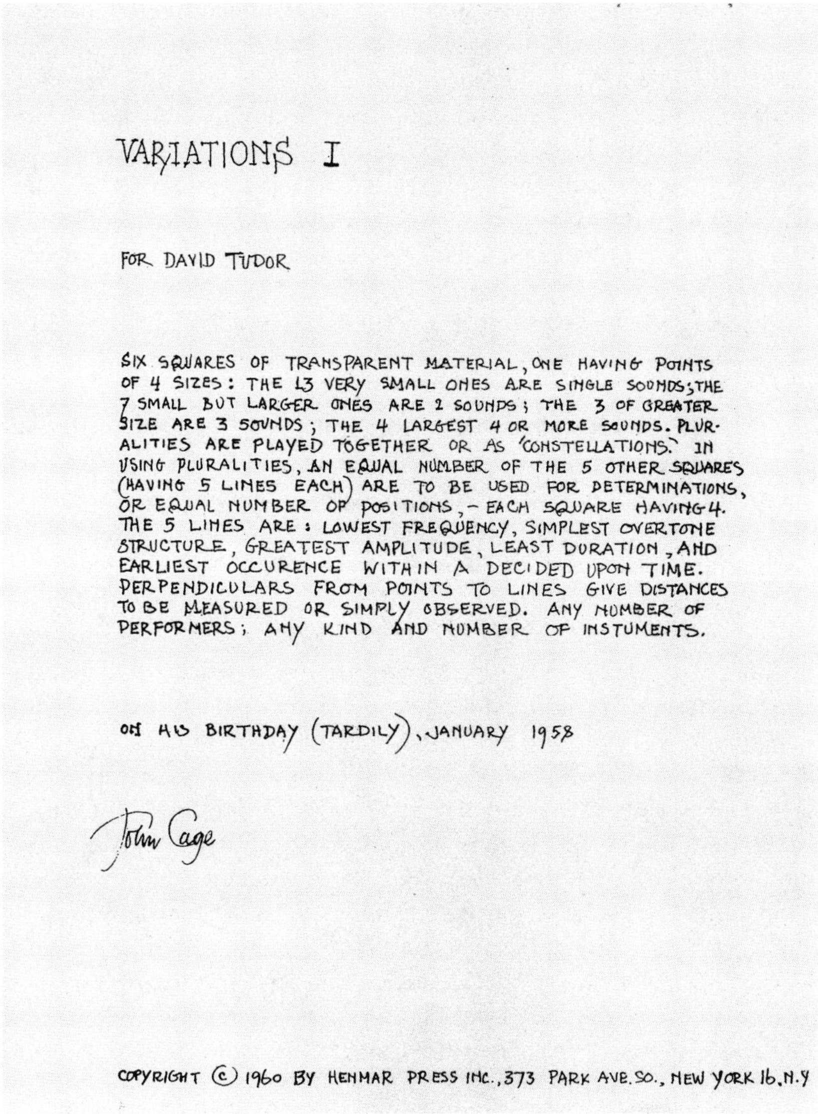

VARIATIONS I

FOR DAVID TUDOR

SIX SQUARES OF TRANSPARENT MATERIAL, ONE HAVING POINTS OF 4 SIZES: THE 13 VERY SMALL ONES ARE SINGLE SOUNDS; THE 7 SMALL BUT LARGER ONES ARE 2 SOUNDS; THE 3 OF GREATER SIZE ARE 3 SOUNDS; THE 4 LARGEST 4 OR MORE SOUNDS. PLURALITIES ARE PLAYED TOGETHER OR AS 'CONSTELLATIONS.' IN USING PLURALITIES, AN EQUAL NUMBER OF THE 5 OTHER SQUARES (HAVING 5 LINES EACH) ARE TO BE USED FOR DETERMINATIONS, OR EQUAL NUMBER OF POSITIONS, — EACH SQUARE HAVING 4. THE 5 LINES ARE: LOWEST FREQUENCY, SIMPLEST OVERTONE STRUCTURE, GREATEST AMPLITUDE, LEAST DURATION, AND EARLIEST OCCURENCE WITHIN A DECIDED UPON TIME. PERPENDICULARS FROM POINTS TO LINES GIVE DISTANCES TO BE MEASURED OR SIMPLY OBSERVED. ANY NUMBER OF PERFORMERS; ANY KIND AND NUMBER OF INSTRUMENTS.

ON HIS BIRTHDAY (TARDILY), JANUARY 1958

John Cage

COPYRIGHT © 1960 BY HENMAR PRESS INC., 373 PARK AVE. SO., NEW YORK 16, N.Y.

Figure 3.3. Introductory note to John Cage, *Variations I*, 1958, Copyright © 1960 by Henmar Press, Inc. Used by permission of C. F. Peters Corporation. All rights reserved.

the point of complete disintegration. Independently of its grief, however, Cardew's account clarifies other noteworthy issues. At first, of course, it emphasizes the function of participation in Cage's music: fulfilling—even poorly—Cage's desire to see the performers becoming composers. More significantly, Cardew stresses the importance of the element of (intellectual) seduction that goes into the appreciation of Cage's music (his "beautiful idea"). Without the capacity of Cage's concept to subjugate Cardew, there is no *raison d'être* to *Variations I*. This, in a sense, pushes the success or the failure of the music into the background. It only becomes relevant when Cardew's experience reveals that, in order to be made audible (or physically appealing), the "beautiful idea" of indetermination may require some additional makeup.

In this light, it is not what happenings really were that matters, but the kind of image they projected for the audience to identify with. To a certain extent, an illusionistic tradition prevailed in happenings: "It is art but seems closer to life."[31] What was plainly at stake, in Allan Kaprow's terms, was "to provide as much liberation . . . as possible,"[32] and achieving this goal began by stressing a rejection of rehearsals, actors, roles, repeats of the happening, etc.[33] A strong collective identification with the emancipatory image of happenings appears to be the first participative step toward the realization of art in life. It is necessary, indeed, to believe that thanks to happenings "[the] time will come when life will no longer be a simple matter of bread and labor, nor a life of idleness either, but a work of art." As RoseLee Goldberg suggested, this "radical art proposition," formulated by Marinetti in the early twentieth century, constituted the subterranean impulse of most subsequent performance-oriented arts.[34] In this regard, Happenings fundamentally evoke a reconciled community of individuals, emancipated from work, liberated from their isolated, alienating condition of passive consumers and, at last, freed to release their hitherto repressed creative nature. Yet in their eagerness to give form to a harmonious community of human beings, artists inevitably faced powerful competition. As the history of functional music suggested, indeed, the idea of muzak resulted in one of the most successful, or at least in one of the most influential happenings of the past sixty years.

Silent Prayer

A first and notable encounter between John Cage and Muzak took place in February 1948, on the occasion of an intercollegiate conference hosted by Vassar College. In a lecture titled "A Composer's Confessions," explaining to students from thirty colleges how he developed as a composer, Cage expressed "new desires," which no matter how *absurd* they may seem, he warned his audience, were fundamentally *serious*. One of them, said Cage, was to compose and have performed "a composition using as instruments nothing but twelve radios. It will be my *Imaginary Landscape No. 4*."[35] Another (and related) desire expressed by Cage was to "compose a piece of uninterrupted silence and sell it to Muzak Co." He described the latter as follows: "It will be 3 or 4½ minutes long—those being the standard length of 'canned music'—and its title will be *Silent Prayer*. It will be open with a single idea, which I will attempt to make as seductive as the color and shape and fragrance of a flower. The ending will approach imperceptibility."[36] Only published long after it was delivered as a speech, Cage's idea has nonetheless received much critical attention. Most notably, *Silent Prayer* has often been discussed as a premise to Cage's famous "silent piece" *4'33"* from 1952. In this regard, Christopher Shultis bypasses entirely Cage's reference to Muzak. For him, Cage's "single idea" opening *Silent Prayer*, "became a process of making music that Cage learned from Ananda Coomeraswamy [*sic*]"[37] whose 1934 book *The Transformation of Nature in Art*, taught the composer that "for the East, as for St. Thomas, *ars imitatur naturam in sua operatione*."[38] More pragmatically, maybe, Kyle Gann suggested that, among the many factors leading to the genesis of *4'33"*, one might regard Cage's reaction to Muzak as one piece (no matter how minor) of a complex puzzle.

> It is intriguing that Cage first mentioned the idea of *Silent Prayer* in early 1948, just at the time some public uproar against Muzak was beginning to take shape, and that he completed *4'33"* in 1952, just as the court were ruling that forced listening to music was not a violation of the first Amendment. Perhaps Cage felt strongly enough about the right to be left alone that he conceived his *Silent Prayer* as something that might be programmed on Muzak stations to provide listeners with a blessed four-and-a-half-minute respite from forced listening. One can imagine many musicians who resented Muzak coming up with such a rueful idea.[39]

The uproar had started, indeed, after the company Capital Transit, based in Washington, implemented in March 1948 the "music as you ride" program, using radio programs amplified through speakers in buses and streetcars.[40] Even though, strictly speaking, *Silent Prayer* predates this controversy over the rights of people not to be subjected to unwanted music, it may appear as an anticipated response to it. Other factors are nonetheless at stake. By 1948, the term "canned music," used by Cage in quotes, was already an old one and a popular one[41] and did not refer to Muzak's product only. Significantly, at the time Cage delivered his lecture, the expression "canned music" was strongly associated with the powerful and controversial figure of James Petrillo,[42] then president of the American Federation of Musicians (AFM). In union speech, "canned music" encompassed a whole spectrum of non-live music, ranging from "phonograph record, the radio transcription (a larger form of records), programs carried across the country on a network, the sound tracks of Hollywood films, television, [to] the juke boxes in bars and restaurants."[43] Undeniably, the most contentious measures taken by Petrillo as president of the AFM remain the two recording strikes he instigated first in 1942 and again in 1947.[44]

Delivered two months after the second recording ban started, Cage's lecture obviously found some inspiration in the action taken by the AFM. Toward the end of his lecture, just before introducing *Silent Prayer*, Cage extrapolated:

> Since Petrillo's . . . recent ban on recordings took effect on the New-Year, I allowed myself to indulge in the fantasy of how normalizing the effect might have been had he had the power, and exerted it, to ban not only recordings, but radio, television, the newspapers, and Hollywood. We might then realize that phonographs and radios are not musical instruments, that what the critics write is not a musical matter but rather a literary matter, that it makes little difference if one of us likes one piece and another another; it is rather the age-old process of making and using music and our becoming more integrated as personalities through this making and using that is of real value.[45]

For Douglas Kahn, both the reference to the AFM's ban and the related concept of *Silent Prayer* can be interpreted as seminal moments in the genesis of the composer's notion of silence and, for that matter, as crucial evidence demonstrating Cage's attempt at the "silencing of the social."[46] Interestingly, Douglas Kahn also situates Cage's idea for *Silent Prayer* in relation to Satie's furniture music: "Satie's performance was a displacement of one of his café haunts (people talking, ignoring the music) into an artistic space, whereas *Silent Prayer* returns to the cafés and other non-art settings to replace Muzak with silence, that is, an unobtrusive music with something even more unobtrusive."[47] Of course, Kahn does not suggest that Cage himself elaborated *Silent Prayer* following such streamlined reasoning. Still, the kind of strategic opposition that Kahn induces between *Silent Prayer* and furniture music seems contrived. Construing furniture music as a sheer transfer of an instance of daily life into the artistic field appears to be rather unfounded. It makes sense, possibly, if one assimilates furniture music (according to Kahn, coming from the cafés) to the score that Satie composed for René Clair's film *Entr'acte* (an "artistic space"), screened during the interlude of Francis Picabia's ballet *Relâche* in 1924. Yet, as one may remember, Satie's furniture music originated (at least partly) from a discontent with background music as the French composer experienced it in his café haunts. Furthermore, Kahn's argument does not make sense, to quote only two examples, in relation to *Tenture de cabinet préfectoral* or *Tapisserie en fer forgé*, the latter serving to welcome the guests at a reception (hardly an artistic space). Of course, one may sense Satie's influence in the descriptive mode adopted by Cage to qualify the "color and shape and fragrance" of his silent piece, whose ending would "approach imperceptibility." Ultimately, however, Kahn's interpretation is meant only to support an argument establishing that "when [Cage] celebrates noise, he also promulgates noise abatement. When he speaks of silence, he also speaks of silencing."[48]

Here, Kahn understands Cage's fantasy as a wish "to extend Petrillo's *silencing* further still, to all of radio and other forms of mass media, whether they were audible or not."[49] In this instance, as well as in the project for *Silent Prayer*, Kahn finds evidence that Cage's "emblematic *silence* was founded on a silencing of communications technologies."[50] Furthermore, the author understands Cage's proposal as pitting *recorded music* against *live music* ("arguing for *liveness*," writes Kahn). But such a response, says Kahn, only promotes the false impression that the composer was supporting the AFM struggle against record companies who were purveying "dehumanized entertainment."[51] In reality, suggests the author, such defense of live music only confirms that Cage's vision of the "real social project of music" was overlooking actual social conditions[52]—namely, massive unemployment—against which the ban was supposed to act. All in all, Cage's fantasy is only, in Kahn's view, characteristic of the composer's larger and suspicious "fantasy of a grand silencing of society [which] had long been within his personal repertoire."[53] Yet if Cage attempted (rhetorically) to silence modern means of communication, it was certainly with the corollary understanding that any sudden deprivation of technologies only raises awareness of their existence: Technology remains invisible or, in the case of Muzak, inconspicuous until it fails.[54] In this regard, raising the awareness of Muzak by silencing it—generating a feeling of withdrawal—would act against its fundamental inconspicuousness.

Still, is this what Cage meant by extending Petrillo's ban? Speaking shortly after the second ban took effect, Cage certainly expected his audience to have some knowledge of his referent. Nevertheless, starting with the first ban, the AFM's measures were easily misunderstood. As a 1949 study of the union suggests, the confusion might have started in 1942, when the director of the Office of War Information declared in reaction to the ban that "the elimination of records . . . for use in restaurants, canteens and soda parlors where members of the armed forces go for recreation" would jeopardize the morale of the nation.[55] Of course, pursues the same study, "the AFM's recording ban did not have the effect of 'eliminating,' or even diminishing, the production of phonograph records, but operated only to prevent the recording of new musical compositions after August 1 [1942]."[56] Thus, even during the first ban, recording companies continued to rely on their existing stock of matrices to press and sell records, and after the ban ended it was found that "the number of pressings has been limited only by the supply of material and mechanical labor."[57] When the second ban took effect in December 1947, record companies had clearly anticipated it, notably by building heavy backlogs.[58] The AFM ban had, nonetheless, some negative effect on the musical scene. Miles Davis, for example, remembered that the new music that he was creating at the time with Charlie Parker and Dizzy Gillespie suffered from a lack of exposure. "The music scene was hurt by . . . the continuing recording ban. The music wasn't being documented. If you didn't hear the bebop in the clubs then you forgot it."[59] Ultimately, to interpret Cage's fantasy of extending the ban as a "silencing of communications technologies"[60] is possible only if one admits that he misinterpreted (fully or in part) the nature of the ban. Petrillo was not, as it was sometimes thought, "forbidding record companies to manufacture copies" of recordings; he was only "forbidding members of his union to accept employment by the companies to make new recordings."[61]

Cage's remark on Petrillo's ban might not have been very clear to start with, but it appears to be a clear follow-up to a point he had made earlier in his lecture, after evoking his study of oriental philosophies and early Christian mystics: "If one makes music, as the Orient would say, *disinterestedly*, that is, without concern for money or fame but simply for the love of making it, it is an integrating activity and one will find moments in his life that are complete and fulfilled."[62] Such a generalizing statement about the Orient is characteristic of Cage's idealization of Eastern philosophies. It could certainly be argued, following Kahn's logic, that in this instance Cage fails to contemplate "the political realities of working musicians outside Western art music who act in an interested manner regarding their occupations."[63] Nonetheless, while looking East, Cage's issue is not to do justice to the life of non-Western musicians. He simply wishes to point out the existence of a value system that contradicts the "corrupting influence of commodification."[64] In his 1946 article titled "The East in the West," Cage had analyzed the beneficial, yet insufficient, infiltration of Eastern influence in the work of Schoenberg, Varèse, and Messiaen. He concluded, "The composers who today wish to imbue their music with the ineffable, seem to find it necessary to make use of musical characteristics not purely Western; they go for inspiration to those places, or return to those times, where or when harmony is not of the essence."[65] Ultimately, it may be strange to notice, following David Patterson's observation, that there is "little if anything in Cage's music that suggests any kind of compelling interest in the musics of Asia, and even less that might constitute direct stylistic borrowing."[66] In fact, concludes Patterson after reviewing and analyzing the numerous sources studied and absorbed by Cage through the 1940s and 1950s, it appears that he extracted from them "with a single-minded discrimination only those malleable ideas that could be used metaphorically to illuminate . . . and reinforce the tenets of his own modernist agenda."[67] Cage's interpretation and rejection of the Western harmonic system in his "Composer's Confessions" was a clear example of this process: "I now saw harmony, for which I had never had any natural feeling, as a device to make music impressive, loud and big, in order to enlarge audiences and increase box-office returns. It had been avoided by the Orient, and our earlier Christian society, since they were interested in music not as an aid in the acquisition of money and fame, but rather as a handmaiden to pleasure and religion."[68]

In this light, Cage's fantasy of extending the ban simply asked his audience to imagine all professional musicians suddenly refusing employment not only from record companies, but also from radio networks, Hollywood, and television. In other words, the suggestion is that musicians would give up entirely performing music *professionally*, that is, in exchange for wages. Cage included newspapers in his extensive ban to imagine that not only the production of music, but also its evaluation (by musicians among other critics) could be cleansed of its exchange value. Musicians and listeners would thus potentially recover the *value* of music as a self-fulfilling activity, implying what Cage describes as return to *normal*, in effect making and using music as a form of self-discovery ("becoming more integrated as personalities"). As such, Cage's point does not ignore the labor issue that motivated the ban. In his own way, he may seek (or dream) a way to overcome the labor issue, but it is not because he ignores it or bypasses it. Yet, quite paradoxically, his extension of Petrillo's ban is antithetical to the union's efforts, which was struggling, after all, to guarantee the economic survival of professional musicians. Cage's fantasy is not, of course, a sensible one: it is a rhetorical device. While the union used the strike as a practical bargaining tool, the composer pushed its logic to his own utopian ends.

Cage's idea for *Silent Prayer* is in the line of his paradoxical response to the AFM struggle. If Cage intended to be simply rational and consistent, rather than speculative, he would not have followed his previous argument about *disinterestedness* by proposing to *sell* a piece of music (most likely a recorded one!), and even less to sell it to a company like Muzak. There is no doubt that, in Cage's view, phonograph recordings falsified our relationship to music by both substituting themselves for live music and reifying music as a commodity fetish.[69] Thus, as a piece of "canned music," *Silent Prayer* basically answers the question of how to make a record that would nonetheless, as James Pritchett puts it, "make a statement about the unimportance of music as a material thing."[70] Of course, *Silent Prayer* remained unrealized, and one can only imagine, following Cage's description, what the piece would have sounded like. Would it, as Kahn suggests, only make use of "conventional silence" and thus result in "the absence of the sound of Muzak"?[71] In this way, Cage would have simply attempted to *silence* Muzak by brutally interrupting its flow.[72] As a sheer gesture of protest against a pervasive musical commodity, the idea may not lack appeal. But it would be naive to think that, as such, could have been implemented (i.e., actually sold to Muzak). If Cage was "serious" about it—as he claimed to be—the project may have been conceived in a slightly more subtle way. From this point of view, Pritchett and Kyle Gann, notably, doubt that *Silent Prayer* was actually thought of as an entirely silent piece.[73] In Pritchett's view, the poetic description of the beginning and ending of the piece clearly suggests a structure that would actually frame a "central silence" in between quiet sounds.[74]

Not long after delivering his "Composer's Confessions," Cage famously clarified, in "Lecture on Nothing" (1950), how his fondness for quiet sounds had developed. "Half intellectual and half sentimentally, when the war came along, I decided to use only quiet sounds. There seemed to me to be no truth, no good, in anything big in society. But quiet sounds were like loneliness, or love or friendship. Permanent, I thought, values, independent at least from Life, Time and Coca-Cola."[75] Formulated in 1948, *Silent Prayer* cannot be thought of as a *reaction* to the war, but following Cage's perspective, it was an unambiguous attempt to supply a corporation like Muzak with a piece of anticapitalist music. In the end, the use of silence in *Silent Prayer* seems to expand upon the conventional (yet problematic) definition of silence in the tradition of Western music. As Elizabeth Hellmuth Margulis explains it, "[silence] is unidimensional acoustically (defined only by its length) but multidimensional perceptually (describable as tense, relaxed, too short, arresting, or disturbing, e.g.)." Yet, she pursues, "it constitutes the ultimate seat of active listening; since literally nothing happens for the extent of its duration."[76] In this regard, *Silent Prayer* may be less of a precursor to *4′33″* than it appeared to be.[77] Following Pritchett's suggestion, Cage's idea for *Silent Prayer* may have relied on the simple principle that "*perceived silences* depend inextricably on musical context."[78] And if he was indeed serious about selling the piece to Muzak, Cage may have planned to introduce, following his charming and colorful beginning (as seductive as the color and shape and fragrance of a flower), a rest that (no matter how long or short) would have thus been contextualized to be perceived as an uninterrupted, dramatically *palpable* silence. Responding to Muzak's attempt to remain inconspicuous, Cage may have imagined a deafening silence as the ultimate weapon. Thus "silencing" Muzak and making it dramatically noticeable at the same time are not incompatible strategies to respond to it critically.

Ultimately, considering the progress made at the time by the programming department of Muzak Corporation, *Silent Prayer* was somehow already integrated into the program and potentially neutralized. Relentlessly studying programming strategies, they themselves had discovered the virtue of silence after realizing that many subscribers of Muzak, saturated by the flow, were actually turning the music off.[79] In restaurants and retail shops, the complaints did not come from the customers, but from individuals permanently exposed to Muzak during their workday: the cashiers and the waiters, for instance. Consequently, to preserve the efficiency of the program, explained Jerri Husch in her study of Muzak, "the programming department introduced a silent interval of 1 ½ to 2 minutes at the end of each quarter hour."[80] Actually, the timing of the interval remains quite unclear. According to the same study, the concept of "quarter-hour programming—15 minutes of music alternating with 15 minutes of silence . . . started in 1948."[81] If the date is correct, Cage's prayer had thus already been answered: interruption had become part of the program, but only to maintain the strength of its continuity. His project nonetheless indicates well how Cage intended to deal with muzak: to infiltrate and to use the medium rather than voicing a circumstantial indignation and advocating its ban. By intention if not in effect, *Silent Prayer* qualifies as a more subtle criticism of a functional program of music than the dominant concert of objections to Muzak and background music.

Pop Sensibility

Cage demonstrated, at least, that one does not resist Muzak by the simple virtue of calling it "bad." Conversely, while he openly disliked it, Cage seemed to have developed what could be called an early "pop" sensibility to Muzak, that is—as Roy Lichtenstein would define it—"an involvement with . . . things we hate, but which are also powerful in their impingement on us."[82] This involvement had, for many artists—including Robert Rauschenberg, James Rosenquist and Andy Warhol, for example—been informed by their work as commercial artists. Hence, responding to a criticism of his 1956 *Radio Music*, Cage explained:

> With the help . . . of some American paintings, Bob Rauschenberg's particularly, I can pass through Times Square without disgust. And similarly, having written radio music has enabled me to accept, not only the sounds I there encounter, but the television, radio, and Muzak ones, which nearly and constantly everywhere offer themselves. Formerly, for me, they were a source of irritation. Now they are just as lively as ever, but I have changed. I am more and more realizing, that is to say, that I have ears and can hear.[83]

Contrary to most critics of background music, Cage did not restrict his definition of muzak to "[music] for factory workers, or for chickens to force them to lay eggs" but extended it to "the miscellaneous music played throughout the day by most radio."[84] Cage's opinion about radio, however, is not really motivated by the "quality" of the music broadcasted, but more

Figure 3.4. James Rosenquist and billboard painters from Artkraft Strauss Company working on BIG Country billboard, exterior of Astor Theater, Times Square, New York City, 1958.

by the mode of broadcasting: both continuous and yet shrugging off listeners' participation. Already, in the 1930s, Brecht had offered a utopian view of radio as a medium of communication, if only "it knew how to receive as well as to transmit, how to let the listener speak as well as hear, how to bring him into a relationship instead of isolating him."[85] On this basis, he pursued: "[Radio] must follow the prime objective of turning the audience not only into pupils but into teachers. It is the radio's formal task to give these educational operations an interesting turn, i.e. to ensure that these interests interest people. Such an attempt by the radio to put its instruction into an artistic form would link up with the efforts of modern artists to give art an instructive character."[86] Cage, from that point of view, fulfilled his duty. Based on chance operations, and composed for one to eight performers using the radio as an instrument, *Radio Music* can actually be heard as a continuation of the criticism of a programming network he inaugurated with his *Silent Prayer*. Cage's piece turns the technology of the programmed radio broadcast, designed for isolated listeners, into an instrument capable of generating a collective experience of a resolutely unpredictable soundscape recalling, in effect, the quality of Times Square. Fundamentally, of course, Cage targets an entire Western musical tradition, not just Muzak or radio programming. But more importantly for our concern, the unpredictability of *Radio Music* can be sustained only if it resists—as did Cage[87]—the technology of recording, which induces repetition and fosters a familiarization capable of turning the most random organization of sound into something perfectly predictable by the listener.[88]

A partial recording of *Variations IV* (1963), for instance—a piece designed for any number of performers, using indeterminate sound sources produced inside or outside of the performance space, for an indeterminate duration—makes no coherent, rational sense at first hearing.[89] Various sound sources follow each other for one hour, overlapping (radio broadcast, electronic buzz, screams, fragments of conversation, toilet flushing), and this concatenation defeats any attentive, focused listening. Rather, it appears a more fitting option to drift in and out of this rich yet confusing soundscape, creating one's own purposeless listening path. Still, after a few listenings, any motivated listener can easily anticipate and enjoy (in a traditional expectative mode) the unfolding of John Cage and David Tudor's 1965 performance. Maybe helped, as Cardew suggested in relation to *Variations I*, by the manipulation of the emotional dynamic of the piece by Cage and Tudor, the reproduction of the performance on record, enabling repeated listenings, can turn *Variations IV* into a programmatic piece.

Recordings of most of Cage's music, in effect, have "no more value than a postcard," providing only "a knowledge of something that happened."[90] In itself, it eradicates the value of whatever happened and cannot happen again. Ideally, Cage's music presents itself as the antithesis of what the recording technology allows.

> The first thing about recording is that it makes repeatable what was otherwise transient and ephemeral. Music, until about 1900, was an event that was perceived in a particular situation, and that disappeared when it was finished. There was no way of actually hearing that piece again, identically, and there was no way of knowing whether your perception was telling you it was different or whether it was different the second time you heard it. The piece disappeared when it was finished, so it was something that only existed in time.[91]

For a musician like Brian Eno, summarizing this shift, recording technologies enabled composers to create elaborated and "artificial acoustic space"[92] shifting the emphasis from the temporal element of music to the crafting of very specific spatial atmospheres characteristic of his *Ambient* works.[93] To the contrary, Cage dreaded recording, seeing it as both a temporal and a spatial ambush. Insisting on the indeterminacy of his compositions, Cage conceived of their performance as "necessarily unique."[94] As he argued logically, any action whose outcome is designed to be unforeseeable (his definition of "experimental") cannot be repeated: "When performed for a second time, the outcome is other than it was. Nothing therefore is accomplished by such a performance, since that performance cannot be grasped as an object in time."[95] On the other hand, following Satie's experiment in furniture music, Cage assigned extraordinary importance to the physical space of the performance. When performing an indeterminate composition, he insisted, "the action of the players is productive of a process" (rather than reproductive) and "*no harmonious fusion of sound is essential.*" Therefore, fearing "the possibility [that] when people are crowded together . . . they will act like sheep," Cage suggested it would be necessary "to separate the performers one from the other, as much as is convenient and in accord with the action and the architectural situation. This separation allows the sounds to issue from their own centers and to interpenetrate in a way which is not obstructed by the conventions of European harmony and theory [in which a fusion of sound was of the essence]."[96]

In this context, naturally, "conventional architecture is often not suitable" (the concert hall, or any compartmentalized spaces), and Cage suggested that, perhaps, an architecture like that of Mies van der Rohe's Crown Hall at the Illinois Institute of Technology, with its open floor plan and transparency, might be more appropriate. Cage's spatial concern focuses not on the unifying of sounds and space, but on their interaction. He highlights well their independence, hoping to generate conflicts rather than produce a synthesis. By no means could any recording (either phonographical or photographical) have registered and conveyed, *a posteriori*, the elements of conflict, inconsistency, and discord that permeate such performances.

Vexations

Striving to disrupt any form of repetition of the same, and eager to foster awareness of an environment as a constant work-in-progress, Cage certainly faced Satie's *Vexations* as a challenge. No other piece of written music, it seems, could promise more stagnation than this one, based as it is on the repetition, 840 times, of the same few repetitive measures. Furthermore, while its performance seems to defy human physical resistance, mechanical reproduction could easily remedy the issue. In 1983, for instance, Reinbert De Leeuw released 35 repetitions of *Vexations*. To hear the entire composition, one simply needs to play the record 24 times.[97] Dismissing this possibility, Cage turned the performance of *Vexations* into an exercise in collective awakening, enlisting twelve pianists to take turns in the unfolding of an ephemeral event of durable influence.

"Ordinarily," admitted Cage regarding the performance of *Vexations*, "one would assume there was no need to have such an experience, since if you hear something said ten times, why should you hear it any more?"[98] However, the event revealed to him the secret nature of repetition: "the funny thing was that it was never the same twice." The musicians were always slightly different with their versions—their strengths fluctuated. I was surprised that something was put into motion that changed me. I wasn't the same after that performance as I was before. The world seemed to have changed.[99] There is no need to pretend that Cage's perception of the "slightest deviation"[100] contained in each repetition was unanimously shared. Conversely, Christian Wolff, one of the twelve pianists, offers a seemingly opposite impression:

> As the first cycle of pianists went round the playing was quite diverse, a variety—quite extreme, from the most sober and cautious to the willful and effusive—of personalities was revealed. Musically the effect seemed disturbing. But after another round the more expansive players began to subside, the more restrained to relax, and by the third round or so the personalities and

Figure 3.5. "Music: A Long, Long, Long Night (and Day) at the Piano," from the *New York Times*, September 11, 1963.

playing techniques of the pianists had been almost completely subsumed by the music. The music simply took over.[101]

The performance, in other words, gradually lifted away the intentions of each performer, resulting in a gradual surrender of their individuality to what Wolff called a collective "state of suspension of self."[102] This outcome may sound rather coercive, but it was essential to the emergence of a sense of community. At first, the ensemble of individuals gathered by Cage formed only a contrived collective. They may have been united by a commonality of goal (Satie's piece), but they were still, consciously or not, competing to affirm a superficial difference (their interpretation of the piece). However, as the night progressed and exhaustion set in, the dynamic reversed: the music, "at first a kind of passive object" subjected to personal inflections, slowly became the "guiding force" requiring each pianist to relinquish individuality in favor of solidarity.

The two points of view are less contradictory than it may appear. Without this beneficial "suspension of self," Cage could not have grasped the most subtle variations within an apparent sameness. Ultimately, even if one admits that the repetitions of *Vexations* changed "nothing in the object repeated," they actually did change something, as Hume famously suggested, "in the mind" that contemplated them.[103] In this light, Cage further clarified the dramatic transformative effect of the performance. His own *reveille* was indeed akin to a form of spiritual enlightenment:

> [After the performance] I slept an unusually long period of time; and when I woke up, I felt different than I had ever felt before. And, furthermore, the environment that I looked out upon looked unfamiliar even though I had been living there. In other words, I had changed and the world had changed, and that's what I meant by that statement. It wasn't an experience that I alone had, but other people who had been in it wrote to me or called me up and said that they had had the same experience.[104]

In this light, Satie's music—stressing the dialectic relationship between boredom and intensity[105]—actively led Cage to "pay attention to whatever else we are doing." As he woke up, his realization that "repetition was in fact a form of difference"[106] went beyond the music and affected his perception of the surroundings. It was as if the "sharpening of the faculty of listening" and the increased awareness that occurred during *Vexations* subsequently permeated all of his senses.[107] The point was not to artificially stress differences: quite the contrary, they needed to be subdued. Only at that point could whatever had seemed to be permanent, stable, and disregarded for its sameness suddenly appear in all its diversity and richness. In addition, consistent with his musical ideal, the solidarity fostered by the performance efficiently demonstrated how "many centers can interpenetrate without obstructing one another."[108] It even succeeded in reconciling Cage's conception of indetermination with the repetitive character of a perfectly written score. In many ways, the performance of Satie's *Vexations* represents a confirmation that music, considered as a productive force rather than a reproductive one, offers "instances of society suitable for social imitation."[109]

On that topic, Cage had many reasons to dislike Muzak. First, the reliance of conventional background music on recordings and playback systems ensures the possibility of elaborating repeatable and standardized programs (no matter how varied in content). As a consequence, Cage may have perceived that the alleged power of background music to subdue tensions resided more in such programming strategies than in the music. Yet, without a doubt, Muzak succeeded in two important areas relative to Cage's artistic concerns. First, it relied on a technological network capable of massively distributing and literally integrating music into our surroundings. Second, Muzak effectively lowered the level of attention devoted to music to a point approximating zero, shifting the focus from the music to the situation. Both the dissemination of sounds in space and the questioning of listening as something that requires a focused and exclusive attention were concerns central to Cage's concept of music. Occasionally, Satie's furniture music appeared as a prologue to new listening experiences concocted by Cage.

Quite literally, Cage placed one of his experiments in the continuity of Satie's concept when he introduced his own work—titled *33⅓*—with pieces of furniture music. The performance was part of a daylong event that Cage called "Mewantemooseicday" and took place on the campus of the University of California, Davis, on November 21, 1969. Undeniably, as a firsthand account of the event and as John Cage remembered it, the presence of furniture music and the work conceived by Cage for the occasion were inextricably linked.

> From 7:30 until midnight, Satie's *Furniture Music* for orchestra was played continuously by members of the University Symphony Orchestra in the lobby of the Freeborn Hall [[110]]. One had to walk through this orchestra in order to reach the performing area where Cage's new piece for the occasion, *33⅓*, was being played for the major portion of the evening. For this piece, Cage had personally purchased three hundred long-play record albums from a dealer in Sacramento.... Cage made no overt choices in his three hundred records, to include a wide range of musics chosen at the manager's discretion. (The records seemed to be those which a music store might find difficult to sell.)[111]

Clearly, *33⅓* does not rely on the assumed "quality" of the individual music played. Rather, in the line of the *Musicircuses* organized by Cage in the late 1960s, it is the simultaneous, collective participation of the audience that determines the quality of the piece. To foster such participation, Cage had not given any instruction, therefore leaving open the possibility for the situation (happening) to fail, and only waiting for the members of the audience to realize that they were in charge of activating the environment by playing or stopping the LPs on the twelve available record players. At first, the connection between Satie's furniture music (which filled the adjacent lobby) and the cacophony of *33⅓* may not be obvious. Yet it is not surprising that Cage, corroborating the above-mentioned account, systematically included Satie's music when he remembered the event.[112] For the experimental composer, indeed, it was less a matter of improving the "quality" of any form of furniture music than, as in *33⅓*, a question of establishing an otherwise nonexistent relationship between the listeners' input and a musical output that required no attention or, at least, scattered it to a point of disintegration. When several people play different records at the same time in the same space, the focus is necessarily less centered on what each one plays than driven toward how the sounds conflict, or maybe on how the sounds merge with one another. The occurring tensions between moments of discord and instances of accord challenge the record.

In December 1977, Cage was given the opportunity to organize a similar debate at the occasion of a four-day conference, titled *The Phonograph and Our Musical Life*, held at Brooklyn College and commemorating the centenary of the phonograph. Wiley Hitchcock, the organizer of this event, had given John Cage the privilege of delivering the opening address. Knowing that he would be (conveniently) unable to attend the conference, the composer offered to prepare a recorded address, "if that would not be too appropriate," of course.[113] The result, called *Address*, offered to an (expert) audience a nonetheless disconcerting combination of different pieces. According to Hitchcock's description, the event lasted an "academic" standard time of forty-five minutes, the end of which was signaled by the sound of a school bell. Members of the audience first entered the auditorium through a dark hall, passing by three clearly separated, spotlighted chamber ensembles, each playing a different piece of furniture music by Satie: *Tapisserie en fer forgé, Carrelage phonique, Tenture de cabinet préfectoral*. Reaching the large backstage, they found hundreds of recordings selected at random from the Brooklyn College music library, piled on phonograph tables. An attendant was ready to assist them in becoming the performers of *33⅓*. On one side of the backstage, five panelists performed a segment entitled

Cassette, which required them to play *ad libitum* tapes of lectures, readings, or addresses prerecorded by Buckminster Fuller, Norman O. Brown, and John Cage. Meanwhile, Satie's furniture music continued to be played throughout *Address*. Apparently, the inclusion of Satie's furniture music was received with perplexity. To the question about whether or not the pieces by Satie were actually parts of the piece, Hitchcock responded quite flatly: "Cage is Cage; Satie is Satie. Their relationship is something else again."[114] For another witness, however, it appeared that Cage had successfully implemented Satie's invention: "Satie would have been delighted with the most recent reaction to his piece. The people did ignore the music. They kept moving as arrows on the floor instructed them to move—literally through the musical groups—in an otherwise empty and cavernous hall. The student performers seemed distracted at being treated like furniture."[115] Following this tour de force, the conference opened the next morning with a panel including the vice president of Muzak Co., who introduced the firm's history (without reference to Satie) and clarified its strategy and ambition in producing an "environmental music" that would successfully regulate our psychological and physiological condition. Cage's response to muzak and, more generally, to the technology and industry of recorded music, anticipated an attitude developed later by an artist like Christian Marclay. Marclay's art, indeed, appears to be rooted in a similar frustration: "Music, one of our most elusive arts, is now available in endless reproduction. Mass production and distribution have engulfed our live-music culture almost completely, leaving us in a solitary relationship to a material object. The distance between live and recorded music is a separation of time and space, an alienation from the original participatory experience of music."[116]

Incidentally, as an instance of resistance, Marclay cited Boyd Rice's 1978 *Pagan Muzak*, a record that "is playable at any speed, centred or off-centred, and for any length of time, since each 'song' is an endless groove. The listener cannot stay passive with such a record and becomes involved in the composition's process."[117] By inducing a counterintuitive use of the technology, *33⅓* was similarly meant to disrupt (or even to derail) the established relationship between the (passive) listeners and the "material object" of recorded music.

Furniture Music and Muzak-Plus

For Muzak, the issue was thus less that of its effectiveness than a question of what model it offered to society. Conventional muzak music relies on the normative definition of the collective, and it projects the future of the community as the product of the unconscious reproduction of such norms. In these terms, Muzak seeks to foster a collective unawareness of the environment (and any of its potential violence), whereas Cage, in accordance with his understanding of furniture music, strives to foster a new awareness of our relationship with a complex, open, and somehow violent environment (or at least an irritating one, as he had said of Times Square).

Undeniably, Cage's desire to promote music as agent of social formation fashioned the image of a community aware of itself and as a constant work in progress (necessarily a happening). As was also the case with *Vexations*, there is no possibility to experience it before it has taken place. Cage's model is actually adequately reflected in the dynamic of the events of May 1968, as Maurice Blanchot depicted them, rather idealistically but nonetheless powerfully:

> "Without a project": such was the essential feature—as much a disquieting one than a happy one—of an incomparable form of society which did not allow itself being fixed, which was not intended to last or to settle, not even thanks to the numerous "committees" devoted to imprecise expertise and through which a disorganized order was simulated. . . . It was rather, beyond any utilitarian interests, [letting] a possibility of being together manifest itself.[118]

Blanchot's use (in French) of the verb *manifester* clearly brings together the dual nature of the event: it means both a *demonstration*, as the collective expression of a revolt against an established order, and a manifestation in the sense of the happening itself, which exists only *without project* as a pure celebration of its own occurrence. For Cage, as well, it seems, a community is, before anything else, a constant manifestation of itself: the permanent demonstration of its ongoing production. If muzak was ever to become an incentive for such a manifestation, it needed a corrective that Cage called Muzak-plus.

The concept of Muzak-plus appeared allusively in a piece of writing titled "Rhythm Etc." that had been commissioned from Cage, in 1961, by Gyorgy Kepes as a contribution to the collective publication *Module, Proportion, Symmetry, Rhythm*. Initially perplexed by the invitation to discuss such notions, Cage quickly came to suspect that "the words might have come from Le Corbusier's book, *The Modulor*."[119] In response to the architect's dogma,[120] Cage made sure to emphasize in his text (completed in 1962) that the ideal promoted by Le Corbusier was meant to be executed through a "grid of proportion . . . *proclaimed by law*."[121] Le Corbusier's model, concluded Cage swiftly, has the "shape of tyranny" because "[the] social inflexibility follows from the initial conception of proportion. . . . Unless we find some way to

Figure 3.6. Asger Jorn, "Vive la revolution pasioné" poster, 1968, © 2012 Donation Jorn, Silkeborg / Artists Rights Society (ARS), NY / COPY-DAN, Copenhagen.

get out, we're lost."[122] In the midst of such polemic, Cage's formulation of Muzak-plus appears, without much warning, simply reading: "There'll be centrally located pulverized Muzak-plus ('You cling to composition') performed by listeners who do nothing more than go through the room."[123]

At first, the prophecy appears fairly enigmatic.[124] No work by Cage bears such a title, and it would seem reasonable to assume that it has actually never been given any other form than this written dream of a music that would rely only on the constant flux of a crowd of listeners whose interaction with the space would actually generate the musical execution. In the early 1960s, this reliance of the concept of Muzak-plus on the existence of listeners-performers-composers clearly relates to what Paul Griffiths identified as a shift in Cage's musical approach. "Where in the 1950s [Cage] had addressed his music to soloists and to individual listeners," wrote Griffith, "he was now working very consciously in society."[125] And this was a society, estimated Cage, whose foundations and structures needed to be changed. How to operate such a revolution, without dictating (or *composing*) a new order, or without simply relocating the center, certainly remained one of his main artistic challenges.

In this regard, Cage strongly relied on the power of music to inflect our relationship to the environment in a powerful and comprehensive way. To this end, he argued, it was necessary to create certain specific "musical situations." It is only by "making musical situations which are analogies to desirable social circumstances which we do not yet have"—wrote Cage in the mid-1970s—that "we make music suggestive and relevant to the serious questions which face Mankind."[126] As he had formulated it in 1962, Muzak-plus qualifies as a situation where being creative never seemed so natural and unnoticeable an act (fulfilled simply while going through the room). In itself, the principle of listeners-performers-composers activating the space by simply traversing it recalls Cage's remark (incidentally inspired by Satie's concept of furniture music) that actually "no one means to circulate his blood."[127] With Muzak-plus, one could barely dream of a more integrated form of art *as* life.

Cage almost realized this dream when, in 1962, the sculptor Richard Lippold asked him to create a sound environment that would complement the sculpture he was designing for the lobby of the Pan Am building in New York City. The two artists had met in 1948 at Black Mountain College, where Lippold was an artist in residence. From 1933 to 1937, Richard Lippold trained at the School of the Art Institute of Chicago and the University of Chicago, where he majored in industrial design and studied music and dance (modern and folk) for six years. In the mid-1940s, he was still pondering whether to pursue music or sculpture as a career. His wife Louise Greusel, whom he had married in 1940, studied with Martha Graham and Merce Cunningham.[128] Quite strikingly, and despite Cage's praise of his art, Lippold's sculptures can easily be qualified as "visual Muzak." In the 1960s, his constructivist-inspired wire sculptures were characteristic of a form of soft modernism that perfectly suited the desire of an airline company like Pan Am to project a modern image without being too threatening.

Two of the main qualities of Lippold's work in this regard are its predictability and its adaptability. This allowed Walter Gropius, at the earliest stage of the commission for the Pan Am building, to envision Lippold's decorative contribution for the Vanderbilt lobby as consisting of "a large metal screen as a prominent feature" and "in front of this screen a large globe designed as an abstract."[129] He could not have described more precisely the equivalence between what he envisioned and what the sculptor delivered. Ultimately, wrote Lippold describing the philosophical substrate of his project, the sculpture would "provide a means for tranquil contemplation in a center of unordered movement, thus being party to the concurrence of law and chance."[130] But that is not all. Following this obvious allusion to Cage's mode of composition, the sculptor finally indicated that

> To further this possibility I have commissioned John Cage to compose a continuous program of music which will provide different sounds for each of ten loud speakers in the ceiling, under the bridges, and in the base of the sculpture—as an alternative to a piped-in program of Musak [*sic*], originally planned for all the public areas of the building. The sounds will be produced by special tapes constructed by Mr. Cage, as well as by noise generators, electronic devices, and the regular Musak [*sic*] programs, altered electronically. The activation of the sounds from each speaker will be photo-electrically accompanied by movement of the public through the lobby. The result will be a constantly changing, continuous concert of music in three-dimensional space, becoming, in effect, part of the sculpture.[131]

This ambitious project did not leave behind much written or visual documentation, beyond a prospective budget listing the necessary materials, which included tape recorders, photocells, oscillators, noise generators, a mysterious TV monitor scope, and of course "Muzac" [*sic*] as an essential part of the technological apparatus.[132] Given that a budget existed, one can reasonably assume that the system was designed, and in his correspondence with Grand Central Building Corp., Lippold insisted that he and Cage had "spent a great deal of time and effort designing [it]" in collaboration with Max Mathews, the director of Human Communication Research at Bell

Figure 3.7. Richard Lippold, "The Globe (or Flight)," 1963, main lobby of the Pan American (now MetLife) building, New York. © 2012 Estate of Richard Lippold / Artists Rights Society (ARS), New York.

Telephone laboratory.[133] Ultimately, while Lippold presented the device as a "part of the sculpture," it appears to have been more of a rescue operation than anything else. In reality, Lippold had not been notified that the Pan Am building, like many other buildings of the time, had been conceived with an already-integrated system of piped-in music. Consequently, the sculptor solicited the musician only after he "became concerned when he learned that Muzak was going to be piped into the lobbies and elevators of the building."[134] Indeed, reported the *New York Times* in August 1962, Lippold "was unhappy with the idea of the conventional Muzak product seeping sweetly out of the surrounding walls and flowing around his sculpture. To him the music and sculpture were incompatible."[135] In the end, the journalist argued, that was the reason why

> Mr. Cage devised a system whereby the people going through the lobby would activate the photo-electric cells. These in turn would release the Muzak music, which would become *pulverized* [italics mine] and filtered in the process. Even people getting in and out of the elevators would have a part in producing the sound. Since the cells would never be activated the same way, the results would be constantly in variation.[136]

In retrospect, this description of the Pan Am project appears like a disguised reminder of the concept of Muzak-plus ("There'll be centrally located *pulverized* Muzak-Plus . . ."), formulated a year before by Cage himself. When Cage surreptitiously mentioned the project years later in his diary, it was less the context of the corporate environment that motivated him than the point of access to Grand Central provided by the lobby.[137] In any case, following Lippold's suggestion, the journalist clearly insisted on the main outcome of the device (its state of constant *variation*) and thereby highlighted its main difference with Muzak. Rather than being a preprogrammed, cyclic broadcast, the Muzak-plus would be indeterminate and in constant flux. Therefore, the space itself would constantly change depending on its unpredictable activation by its users-composers-performers-listeners. However, the journalist could evoke the project only in the conditional tense, knowing that the board of ownership of Pan Am had already rejected a plan that appeared to compromise the integrity of Muzak as a means of regulating the environment. Muzak-plus, by encouraging individuals to pay attention to whatever else they were collectively doing (i.e., becoming artists-composers), might have engendered a disruption potentially affecting the security of the entire building. In the end, in a compromise curiously evoking the *Silent Prayer* that Cage had written fourteen years earlier, it was decided that Muzak would be silenced in the lobby until further notice.

From Life to Art

Rejected from this instance of daily life, the concept of Muzak-plus nevertheless infiltrates Cage's art, more or less evidently. While reviewing Cage's performance of *Variations V* in 1965 for the *Village Voice*, Jill Johnston remarked that the mixer designed by Max Mathews for the Pan Am lobby was actually "similar to the one [Billy] Klüver (also an engineer at Bell Telephone) masterminded for '*Variations V.*'"[138] Thus the continuity among Muzak-plus, the Pan Am project, and *Variations V* is not mere speculation. Johnston's account indicates, at least, that the unfulfilled Cage–Lippold collaboration did not go unnoticed and that the concept apparently informed part of the audience of *Variations V*, who, like the reviewer, witnessed onstage a version of what they had not been allowed to perform in the lobby of the Pan Am

Figure 3.8. Merce Cunningham Dance Company performance of *Variations V*, 1965; television studio Nordeuscherrunfun, Hamburg, Germany, c. 1966. From left to right: John Cage, composer; David Tudor, composer; in the back, dancer Barbara Lloyd; to the right Gordon Mumma, composer. Film by Stan VanDerBeek, TV images by Nam June Paik. (Photo by Hervé Gloaguen [Gamma-Rapho via Getty Images]), courtesy of the Jerome Robbins Dance Division, the New York Public Library for the Performing Arts Dorothy and Lewis B. Cullman Center and courtesy of the Merce Cunningham Trust.

building, that is, what Cage defined in a series of notes for *Variations V*: a "non-focused . . . performance without score or parts" that would ultimately "escape stagnation."[139]

In this regard, Merce Cunningham's recollection of *Variations V* is crucial. As the dancer remembered it, only two of the many ways Cage and Tudor designed for the sound to be affected by movement were ultimately used during the performance. The first, remembered Cunningham, "was a series of poles, twelve in all, like antennae, placed over the stage," each having a sound radius of four feet and different "sound possibilities."[140] Then, "[when] a dancer came into this radius, sound could be triggered." To some extent, this first device is an indication of how Cage himself exploited the "genuinely new possibilities" suggested by the Theremin or, again, Lev Termen's Terpsiton. In addition, recalling the Pan Am project and the concept of Muzak-plus, Cage and Tudor used "a series of photoelectric cells which were to be positioned on the floor along the sides of the stage." Hence, indicated Cunningham, "when a dancer passed between the cell and the light, more sound possibilities were triggered." And at last, completing the environment, "Stan VanDerBeek and Nam June Paik both showed visual elements [film and television images] on screens behind and to the side of the performing area."[141] Though the audience generally failed to perceive the correspondence between the sounds and the movements, the feedback effect was clear enough to Merce Cunningham as a performer/composer. To him, in fact, the general principle of the piece was not unlike certain specific instances of daily life: "[As] far as I was concerned," he concluded, it "was like the doors automatically opening when you enter a supermarket."[142] The comparison is trivial but sensible, surreptitiously conveying the sense of an essential feedback effect between art and life that had informed the Pan Am project. Ultimately, while the possibility of making a work of art out of life had remained unfulfilled in the context of the Pan Am building, Cage continued to promote the transformative power of art in regard to life. Yet, as he clarified in 1967, the dynamic of experimental art forms was, first and foremost, one of anticipation—not one of immediate implementation:

> Changes in music precede equivalent ones in theater, and changes in theater precede general changes in the lives of people. Theater is obligatory eventually because it resembles life more than other arts do. . . . Thus, more and more, we encounter works of art, visual or audible, which are not strictly speaking either painting or music. In New York City they are called "happenings."[143]

That art will eventually affect and transform life is thus an unavoidable outcome. Still, the temporality of the process maintains this ultimate resolution in an indeterminate future. Hence, suggests Cage, beyond the blurring of these ultimate boundaries between the senses and between art and life, the primary strength of happenings as an art form is to lessen a nonetheless necessary gap between *anticipation* and *realization*. Theater, in this regard, only *resembles* life closely to the extent that it is, after all, separated from it. Cage, it seems, perceived acutely that "the identity of art and life is an ideal, not a reality" and, as Richard Shiff put it, that "neither an art possessing the immediacy of life's experience nor a life having the fixed formal structure of art would seem to belong to the world as we know it. Art seems to depend upon its distinction from life, and vice versa."[144] Moreover, the necessity of maintaining the gap between art and life does not only appear as a consequence of the failure of the Pan Am project (a failure that, after all, only heralds its practical impossibility at a given time and in a given place). In reality, as Cage will suggest, any attempt to resolve the gap between art and life runs the risk of generating just another "police situation."

Police Situation

Far beyond Muzak, Cage was especially prompt to point out any attempt at programming or at imposing any kind of grid upon a given environment. Even the genre of the happening, apparently one of the most unrestrained and liberating forms of art to come out of the 1950s (and partly due to the influence of Cage himself[145]), could fail to satisfy his sense of anarchy. Simply being asked "not to sit down" (as in Claes Oldenburg's *Moviehouse*, 1965), or being invited by one of his former students to "move from one room to the other" (as in Allan Kaprow, *18 Happenings in 6 Parts*, in 1959), elicited a sharp response from Cage: "I refuse to be told what to do."[146] So, as did Marcel Duchamp during *Moviehouse*, he sat down—without a word—to express his discontent of being trapped in what he perceived as a "police situation."[147] It was thus crucial for Cage to distance himself from what he might have inspired, at least in part, in Kaprow's art.[148]

> I think what we're doing is something else and not that. So when I go to a Happening that seems to me to have intention in it I go away saying that I'm not interested. . . . Though I don't actively engage in politics I do as an artist have some awareness of art's political content, and it doesn't include policemen. . . . It is not during organized or policed moments that these things [awareness, curiosity . . .] happen.[149]

As a former student of John Cage, Kaprow had nonetheless acquired one fundamental certitude. He was convinced, indeed, that "experimental music, or any other experimental art of our time, can be an introduction to right living; and after that introduction art can be bypassed for the main course."[150] In other words, happenings constituted an experimental platform, a stage upon which collective interactions could be rehearsed before being integrated into life. Once again, one doubts that the product of Muzak fully responded to Kaprow's own sense of "right living," but the pervasiveness of background music had nonetheless opened a path toward what the artist identified as a significant form of *communication programming*.

> TV "snow" and Muzak in restaurants are accompaniments to conscious activity which if suddenly withdrawn, produce a feeling of void in the human situation. Contemporary art, which tends to "think" in multi-media, intermedia, overlays, fusions and hybridizations, is a closer parallel to modern mental life than we have realized. Its judgments, therefore, may be acute. "Art" may soon become a meaningless word. In its place, "communication programming" would be a more imaginative label.[151]

In Kaprow's terms, the reference to Muzak bears no value judgment. Discussing whether it is a coercive tool of the corporate industry, and evaluating its quality, seems to matter less to the artist than asserting its achievement as an addictive product (involving withdrawal symptoms) and as an inconspicuous aesthetic presence in our everyday surroundings. As such, Muzak's ability to become indispensable while being unobtrusive undeniably constitutes a model of sorts for the highest of artistic ambitions: programming instances of communication in society, even though, unlike Muzak, they might disrupt the mechanisms of the society of consumption. While the notion of "communication programming" as formulated by Kaprow remains relatively allusive, it nonetheless implies that, very much like muzak, the art form for which Kaprow coined the term *happening* should neither function as an object of contemplation nor manifest its artiness too strongly. Rather, through the induced participation of a performing audience and with the art component ideally "approximating imperceptibility," the creation of such "rearrangeable environments"[152] (as *Words*, 1962, for instance) ought merely to facilitate all forms of exchange between the people involved in the making or the "production" of the piece and, eventually, between the community of participants and the environment itself. In other words, the primary purpose of "programming" communication is to restore or to reconstitute experimentally an ideal and harmonious community of human beings, thereby sketching out and projecting the forms and conditions of a future emancipated society. As the remark of the critic Udo Kultermann indicated in the early 1970s, the requirement of an all-inclusive and general participation in happenings and performances might have appeared to be a necessity in order to bring about changes in society, but its outcome remained potentially hazardous:

> The participation of actors and audience, artist and society, in an all-encompassing event is analogous to political reality. To reform society—and this is necessary—requires participation. The prerequisites for individual participation, however, are many: a sense of responsibility, the ability to think independently, and the will not to let oneself be manipulated, driven, or coerced.[153]

Kulterman's observation, it seems, is representative of a rhetoric pervading the 1960s discourse on happenings and performances. His urge for "participation" ends up oscillating between the utopian ideal of a lost community and the phantasm of a free and sovereign individual subject.[154] Trapped in the middle, the *required participation* finally appears as the very strength and, at the same time, the ultimate weakness of happenings as a form of artistic "communication programming." And indeed, as Cage's memories of Kaprow's *18 Happenings in 6 Parts* and Oldenburg's *Moviehouse* have suggested, the composer found himself confronted with the likelihood that, as wrote Italo Calvino, "an antirepressive theory taken to its ultimate consequences . . . [would] leave precious little margin to spontaneity, or chance, to the vagueness of psychological impulses."[155]

Following the line of Cage's criticism of the "police situation," regardless of whether it properly reflects Kaprow's ambition, one might conclude that a more or less scripted happening could altogether eliminate frictions, smooth out tensions and contradictions in a given situation, bringing forth a harmonious collective experience. However, as Claire Bishop argued in her criticism of the recent infatuation for "relational aesthetics" in contemporary arts, the problem remains that "without antagonism there is only the imposed consensus of authoritarian order—a total suppression of debate and discussion, which is inimical to democracy."[156] Similarly, suggested Cage, it is possible that beyond any potential emancipative effect, the mode of liberation defined in the loose genre of happening might sometimes simply displace and reproduce existing relationships of power. In those terms, the role of the artist as a *communication programmer* would not be unlike that of the engineers of functional music who, during the war, worked hard to promote the medium as a tool of work management, firmly advocating functional or industrial music for its capacity to establish and to maintain a "desired emotional relationship between the man, his work, and his environment,"[157] reducing or ideally eliminating inevitable frictions and conflicts.

Participation

As with many artists during the 1960s, John Cage's ideal was to turn the community of men into an artistic collective and to make life its constant work in progress. Places like Black Mountain College, a progressive art school where Cage, among others, organized the "first" happening in 1952, or the Gatehill Cooperative Community in Stony Point, New York, where he established himself in 1954, presented themselves as models of this coming collective engendering of life by art. And to reach such a goal, as a former faculty member of Black Mountain remembered, individuals' interests had to be subordinated to collective ones:

> The individual, to be complete, must be aware of his relation to the others. Here the whole community becomes his teacher. Wood-chopping, road-mending, rolling the tennis court, serving tea in the afternoon, and other tasks around the place done by groups composed of students and members of the faculty, help to rub off individualistic corners and give people training in assuming responsibility. They tend to involve the person into participation in the life and issues of the community as a whole.[158]

Hence, in its rough state, still separated from the community, any individual remains incomplete and a captive of his or her unhappy consciousness. It is only thanks to the collective dynamic of the community—conceived as a tool as much as the goal itself of the artistic process—that he or she would take a smoother shape, finally fitting and completing the social puzzle. At the core of this cooperative dynamic lies the same principle of a *feedback* that distinguishes Muzak-plus from standard Muzak. Pretty much like any electronic feedback, the Muzak-plus type of feedback as produced by the listeners-performers might be intentional or unintentional, mastered or uncontrolled without the boundary between one and the other being strictly marked. Such a function, in itself, justifies Cage's interest in the technology of Muzak, which far from simply being a distasteful genre of music, appeared to offer from its inception a new and powerful way of "ordering reality and of structuring social relations."[159]

Yet as much as it characterized his appreciation of Muzak, a mix of approval and resistance tainted Cage's reception of happenings as a possible framework for the implementation of his ideal. The positive appeal of happenings, generally speaking, can be understood clearly in words that criticized their devastating consequences. In this regard, the profound distaste of Clement Greenberg for the sight he was contemplating, in 1968, only made his account of the general state of the arts more perceptive:

> The prevalent notion is that latter-day art is in a state of confusion. . . . Everything conspires, it would seem, in the interests of confusion. The different mediums are exploding: painting turns into sculpture, sculpture into architecture, engineering, theatre, environment, "participation." Not only the boundaries between the different arts, but the boundaries between art and everything that is not art, are being obliterated. At the same time scientific technology is invading the visual arts and transforming them even as they transform one another. And to add to the confusion, high art is on the way to becoming popular art, and vice versa.[160]

Strangely, such a statement may actually be more puzzling than what it describes. How, indeed, can "confusion" be expressed with such clarity? Shouldn't it, by essence, defy any attempt to be sorted out so neatly? Undeniably, the whole picture contradicts Greenberg's understanding of the modernist impulse as a necessary and ongoing struggle to lead each artistic medium toward its proper and irreducible essence. Yet the critic's capacity to encapsulate the diversity and mechanisms of such "confusion" in a nutshell also indicates that it might have already given way, at the time, to an established and perfectly ordered set of conventions against which he could reassert the value of his own "Official History gestalt."[161]

In 1966, for instance, Brian O'Doherty had already referred to the "classic era" of happenings ("say 1955 to '63") and observed how much "the anti-conventions then established" ("randomness, chance, simultaneity, lack of climax and resolution") were now "old-fashioned modes," "conventions themselves, with all the easy traps of avant-garde conformity."[162] Among such conventions, that of "participation"—which Greenberg actually distinguished with quotation marks, suggesting either slight puzzlement or sheer disdain (or both)—was certainly granted a high status. In this context, the disastrous reception of *Nine Evenings: Theatre and Engineering* is certainly telling. Organized in the fall of 1966 by Billy Klüver and Robert Rauschenberg, the evenings consisted of a series of events merging art and technology, to which Cage contributed *Variations VII*, relying on and expanding upon the principles of *Variations V*. The event was clearly expected to provide more participative opportunities than a conventional spectacle. And still today, the capacity to generate an "*easy exchange* between spectator and work" appears to be the preeminent standard of perfection upon which the success of the *Nine Evenings* performances must be historically measured.[163] As Brian O'Doherty observed at the time, the transient medium of happenings and performances possessed a strange capacity—only increased by the subsequent diffusion of photographs—to foster an instant nostalgia for what it was not but could or should have been.[164]

However, when it became evident to members of the audience attending *Nine Evenings* that (for the most part) the "audience was strictly separated from performers"[165] during the events, this structural choice was clearly perceived as a major flaw. It forced the viewers back into their condition of passive observers, which any art form aspiring to the status of "total theatre" should question.[166] That the *Evenings* could contradict such an expectation, intentionally or by omission, actually generated confusion, while not of the kind that Greenberg had in mind. Essentially, the confusion arose from the essential yet capricious technological components of the pieces, frustrating an anticipated reconciliation between the audience as a collective on the one hand, and the arts and technology on the other hand. However, well prepared by his 1960 collaboration with Jean Tinguely on the artist's *Homage to New York* (a self-constructing / self-destroying machine), Billy Klüver never promoted the collaboration between artist and engineer in such a light. "In a purely technocratic society the machine must always be a functional object. Failures of the machine can therefore never be allowed because the control is the necessary element in society. It is when the machine must function *à tout prix* that there can be no *Homage to New York*."[167] Following this logic, during the *Nine Evenings* of theater and engineering, artists and engineers "decided not to interfere with the machine once it was put into operation." But the decision, remembered Klüver, was badly received. As a result, even though the audience was "almost completely unaware of the technical elements" (what triggers what and how?) it vehemently "found failures where there were none and technical successes where no technology was involved."[168] But if only the event had not been marred by "flawed artistry and the faulty technology," wrote the *Village Voice* reviewer, "several hundred people would have become members of the space-age wedding."[169] As such, the "participative" ethos, especially when coupled with technology, undeniably generated its own unattainable vanishing point in the form of "a mechanism without errors, without failures, where nothing jeopardizes the interconnection of the elements and the transparency of the process."[170]

Ultimately, as Cage noted, the artistic ideal of participation was only meant to "precede general changes in the lives of people," and one may regret that they did not take place. Their implementation, nevertheless, has been sharply depicted by the Situationist architect Constant in relation to the all-inclusive, ever-expanding, and cybernetically regulated city-space of his *New Babylon*. There, at last—he declared in 1966—"one's entire life will have become a happening, and the happening itself redundant."[171] In this *New Babylon*, the conditions of an expanded theater, which dominated the

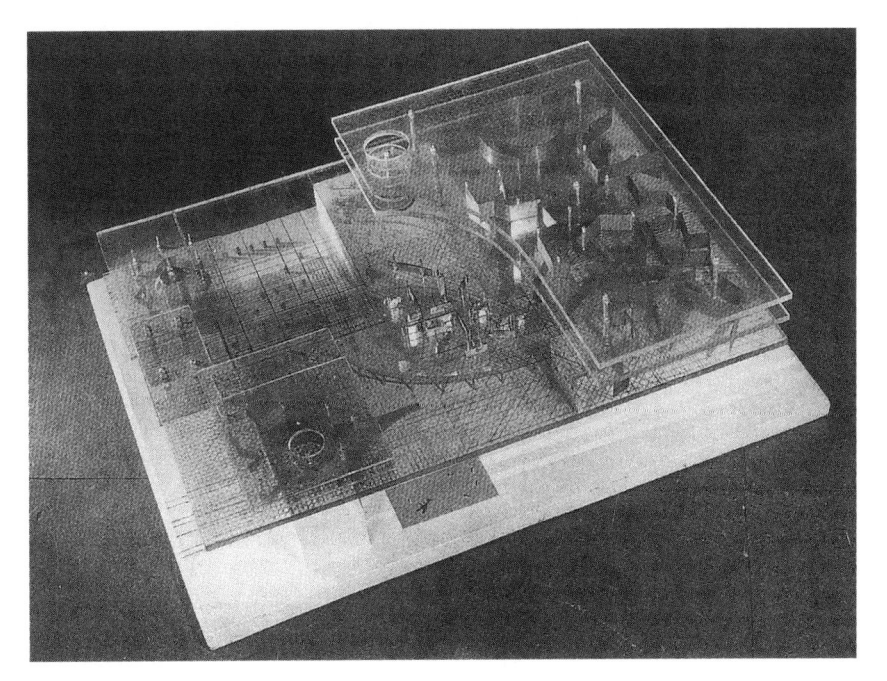

Figure 3.9. Constant Nieuwenhuys, "New Babylon, Orient Sectors," 1959, © 2012 Artists Rights Society (ARS), New York / c/o Pictoright Amsterdam.

early critical appraisal of performance arts, have expanded into the design of a pervasive urban space. This design presented itself simultaneously as a social utopia, an artistic vision, a cultural revolution, a technological conquest, and a solution to the problems of the industrial age.[172] In this space, the community of men would finally live a life of unrestrained creativity, fulfilling an existence determined by the "spontaneous interaction among different individuals, in which the actions of one person trigger the reaction of the other."[173]

One recognizes here the traces of the feedback theory emanating from the science of cybernetics, where moves and countermoves define the relationship between elements of a system geared toward its self-regulation.[174] On the one hand, of course, such a utopian vision can be praised for its strict impossibility: its main value does not reside in its realization, but in providing a standard against which we can measure the conditions of our present. On the other hand, the fundamental unreality of utopian systems seems to mask their ultimate consequence. Pushed to its extreme, indeed, the utopia of art as life is no less dogmatic than its formalist counterpart. In the end, the primary condition of such an emancipated space of permanent collective creativity—as Constant made perfectly clear—is that there will be absolutely "no outsiders."[175] The latter are simply inconceivable and in the end the space of participation can define itself as a Pascalian universe: a sphere whose center is everywhere and circumference nowhere.

That is why, it seems, the genre of happenings only appeared to Cage as a privileged vehicle of change, with the difficult stipulation that it would not enforce or induce any collective conduct. Ideally, the concept of Muzak-plus reversed the dynamic of change: it is not the environment that modifies the conduct of individuals, but the unpredictable conduct of individuals that modifies the environment. Later in the 1960s, Cage named such environments "Musicircuses," or simply "reunions,"[176] and conceived of them as free and non-profit artistic environments where musicians were not paid and tickets were not sold.[177] None of his work could have come closer to artistically defining a desirable social circumstance than the Musicircus, celebrating collectively the suicide of the artist as a "lunatic authoritarian."[178] As a utopian fantasy, noted Daniel Charles, the Musicircus could easily be discarded as inoffensive and naive. Yet, he suggested, it remains more difficult to escape the *fact* that such a utopia had taken shape.[179] "Nowhere," observed Charles Junkerman, had Cage contrived "a more compelling musical model of an amiable anarchic community than in the genre he invented called the Musicircus"[180]—a genre that was mostly an atmosphere, suggested Cage, and in which as "in the case of the weather, though we notice changes in it, we have no clear knowledge of its beginning or ending."[181]

The Musicircus, indeed, had "no score, but consisted of simply inviting all those who would perform in the same time and space to do so," hoping, clarified Cage, "to involve the public in this. I want the performers to be the public. My job is to facilitate their performance."[182] The performance in question, nonetheless, did not follow any script. Combining the experiment of *Variations V* with the premise of Muzak-plus as something to be performed by the listeners, the simultaneity and the spatial explosion of the ephemeral Musicircus were thus intended, argued Cage, to give the audience the possibility of literally "[changing] its experience by where it moves,"[183] therefore leaving to the audience the task of composing its own individual and/or collective experience of the environment. In this regard, added Cage, "if you don't like what you're doing here, you can go there."[184] And in the end, as evidence that one was facing the ultimate participative experience, he also added: "you can leave altogether."[185] These last words are possibly more important than they sound. They do not promote the ideal of a pacified reconciliation between humans and their environment, supported by Muzak or induced in any type of artistic police situation. To be truly all-inclusive, Cage's final view of an artistic community needed to embrace the possibility of voluntary exclusion (rather than fostering the opportunity of becoming voluntary prisoners of a situation). Feeling that one has not come to the right place is an option that Muzak-plus offers, but the question remains of who is going to perform it.

Conclusion
The Community to Come

Ultimately, Cage's Muzak-plus addresses his idealistic belief that art could foster a revolution in society, one that would lead not to a transfer of power but, in an anarchist fashion, to its pulverization in the hands of the individual members of a collective. Still, in the aftermath of World War II, any suggestion that art could be at the service of society was met with increased suspicion. Whether directly or indirectly, suggested Cage himself, any willingness to improve the world may only end up making the matter worse.[1] One could read this warning as a summary of Muzak's self-styled ambition. As Herbert Marcuse emphasized in this regard, "[any] attempt to explain aesthetic categories in terms of their application to society, to the construction of social environment, suggests almost inevitably the swindle of beautification campaigns or the horror of Soviet Realism."[2] Conversely, he concluded: "We have to remember that the realization of art as principle of reconstruction 'presupposes' fundamental social change. At stake is not the beautification of that which is, but the total reorientation of life in a new society. Not political art, not politics as art, but art as the architecture of free society."[3] It remains nonetheless difficult to disentangle politics and art whenever social change appears to be the driving force of the latter. For a composer like Frederic Rzewski, founder of the collective MEV (Musica Elettronica Viva), improvisational practices can be influenced by society as much as they are intended to change it. First, improvisations resemble "Great social movements," in that they "do not have clearly definable causes. Although not totally free of causality, they nevertheless happen spontaneously. No individual can foresee them completely (which is precisely what improvisation is all about)."[4] Music could thus play a role in fostering "some kind of peaceful transition to more generous forms of social organization."[5]

CONCLUSION 127

Ultimately, improvisation tells us: Anything is possible—anything can be changed—now. The world can be changed without having to change human nature. Humans are perfectly all right the way they are. . . . Most of their transactions happen easily, quickly, unconsciously, efficiently, and without money.[6]

Ornette Coleman's *Free Jazz* (1960), to take a famous example, made the message clear. Though making freedom audible required more than one take, the collective dynamic of the piece implied, for the musicians, a mutual awareness of each other's space and time.

> The most important thing was for us to play together, all at the same time, without getting in each other's way, and also to have enough room to ad lib—alone and to follow this idea for the duration of the album. When the soloist played something that suggested a musical idea or direction to me, I played that behind him in my style. He continued his own way in his solo of course.[7]

From the listeners' point of view, the technology of stereo recording fostered the establishment of this sonic community. Each of the two quartets was allocated a channel, and the listener was then confronted with a new order where a fusional totality and the independence of the voices did not contradict each other. As a symbol of this intricate relationship, the dense web of Jackson Pollock's *White Light* was placed on the album cover.

For Cage, as well, there was little purpose to music if it did not provide an abstract model for social organization, and this implied defining a relationship between the individual and the collective. Cage, it seems, believed that "the individual and the collective must be in perfect harmony."[8] What he opposed, however, was that such harmony could be obtained only "if reason can dominate the passions, if there are harsh laws to punish profiteers, and if schools teach children to curb their instincts and vices, and to train themselves thanks to strict disciplines and a familiarity with the great works of the human mind."[9] For Cage, such a society guaranteed, at best, that people would live together like a school of fish, a social figure, as Roland Barthes observed, that appears to be "realizing the perfectly smooth symbiosis of individuals who are nonetheless separated."[10] Can one then expect to see the individual and the collective reconciled? Or should one rather reduce Cage's utopia, following Alain Touraine's very cautious definition, to "the representation of a necessary *yet impossible* society"?[11] The formula may be catchy, but it mostly suggests discarding utopian modes of organizing society collectively as long as it leads to the repression of the "individual." For example, following Touraine's logic, current antiliberal movements may be necessary to the democratic debate, but in reality they mostly promote a *monstrous quest* for social and cultural homogeneity taking the form of *aggressive* and *authoritarian* neo-communitarianism.[12] They should therefore be deemed "impossible."

In this context, Touraine's distrust for utopian thinking reflects and strangely supports the high degree of self-reliance that is expected from contemporary citizens. In the current economy, indeed, individuals are required to assume an entrepreneurial existence, managing and marketing their professional and private lives as a little capitalist venture geared toward ever-increasing performances.[13] In parallel, industrial functional music seeks to *personalize* businesses: "If your business could talk, how would it sound?"[14] And the answer is obvious: as no other. The criticism of Muzak's homogenizing effect is, in this regard, only a lure. The universal value of yesterday's Muzak is now furthering irreducible singularities: "We'll partner with you to discuss your goals and objectives and identify the best solution . . . and we'll deliver a system that meets your specific needs."[15] These are only slogans, but they express well the interchangeability, in contemporary society, between the figure of the free and sovereign individuals and the status of profit-driven corporations. And in such a society, one simply cannot tolerate anymore the idea—so profoundly imbedded in utopias, stresses Touraine—"that the human being is entirely social."[16]

Can we still speak of utopia, logically asks Touraine, when we turn toward one of Cage's models, Henry David Thoreau, who sought to "unite the individual directly with nature, *beyond and against society*"?[17] Thoreau's "extreme individualism" and "voluntary solitude," suggests the author, do not embody a counter-society but rather represent "mystical and ascetic experience *outside of society*."[18] In this light, Cage's reference to Thoreau's adage "Government is best which governs not at all"[19] could very well serve as a criticism of utopian models that, according to Touraine, necessarily "[push] away any nonsocial principle of the legitimacy of the social order."[20] In complete opposition to Touraine's view, however, the composer not only found in Thoreau "a complete absence of interest in self expression,"[21] but also a definition of what he believed to be an "experimental" situation: "one in which nothing is selected in advance, in which there are no obligations or prohibitions, in which nothing is even predictable."

DANIEL CHARLES: A situation of anarchy?
JOHN CAGE: Certainly! Thoreau described it quite clearly [when he replaced Jefferson's maxim "That government is best which governs least" with "That government is best which does not govern at all!"][22]

Cage's "highly eclectic thought," it is true, may appear frustrating in its capacity to reconcile "seemingly irreconcilable differences"[23]: extreme individualism and complete absence of interest in self-expression, the emergence of collective dynamics and independent initiatives. But it is also these tensions that make his reflection still relevant today. Cage certainly believed in the "political economy" of music, but this cannot imply, as Jacques Attali asserted, that "[all] music, any organization of sounds is . . . a tool for the creation or consolidation of a community, of a totality."[24] Cage's view, it seems, is slightly more nuanced, and maybe closer to an ideal formulated by Barthes. Facing the tension between the individual and the collective, Roland Barthes crystallized his personal fantasy of an acceptable, harmonious form of living-together in the musically oriented notion of idiorrhythmy (*idiorrythmie*), which he found to be central to the communal life developed in oriental monasteries. Relying on the association of *Idio* (one's own) and *Ruthmos*, Barthes carefully distinguished his understanding of "rhythm" from the conventional repressive connotations of cadence, metronymic tempo, and measure.[25] Contrastingly, the author ventures to define *Ruthmos* as an equivalent of "swing," a sort of syncopated or offbeat rhythm that, to him, signaled a possible dynamic relationship between the individual and the collective.[26]

Yet no matter how Cage encouraged a form of idiorrhythmic community, any belief that art can assist the elaboration of a harmonious collective life (becoming *fluent* with the life *we* are living) has been met with reservation. The engineer Billy Klüver, who collaborated closely with Cage during the 1960s, maintained strong reservations about the capacity of art—no matter how technologically fluent—to impact society. Clearly, he concluded sensibly, experimental art "will not give people food and housing, and it will not stop the war in Vietnam."[27] And if it fails to do so, does it mean that we have to become fluent with famine, homelessness, and war? To some of his contemporaries already, Cage severely failed to grapple more directly with such real issues. By the late 1960s, this lack of immediate commitment to the reality of a dysfunctional society was regarded as a betrayal of the revolutionary cause. "Nowadays," observed Cornelieus Cardew, "a Cage concert can be quite a Society event."

> The audience has grown enormously, and its class character has become clearer. What happens is that revolutionary students boycott Cage's concerts at American universities, informing those entering the concert hall of the irrelevance of the music to the people's liberation struggles raging in the world. And if his music does not support those struggles, then it is opposing them and serving the cause of exploitation and oppression.[28]

From this point of view, indeed, Cage's music was far too remote from actual struggles to have any immediate consequence. Following Cardew's criticism, one can compare the trajectory of Cage's revolutionary impulse to the history of the saraband: "originally a lively Spanish dance used by prostitutes to attract customers, [it] ended up in the French court as a slow, stately piece of music allowing for the most intricate and refined elaboration of the melodic line."[29] Definitely, Cage's music is not music *of* and *for* the people. "[Despite] the supposed personal freedom it allows," noted Michael Nyman, Cage's work remains "confined to a small elite of players. It takes a musically sophisticated mind to follow the concepts behind his indeterminate pieces, just as it does to unravel and apply his notations."[30] Thirty years after Nyman's criticism, the same argument can be used to cultivate the sense that contemporary art is by essence defiant, for it exists "in a zone of freedom, set apart from mundane, everyday life, and from its rules and restrictions."[31] Hence, remarks Julian Stallabrass, the illusion can be maintained that "the economy and its complementary mass culture function according to strict conventions; contemporary art does the opposite. The idea that capitalism allows space for such free expression could be taken as rather reassuring. The message is that art is a law unto itself, unaffected by the demands of private patrons, religion, business and the state."[32] According to such a view, the "autonomy of art," independent of its subject matter, is not a question but a requirement: it is, in itself, the "decorative" element sustaining the dominant instances of power as their supplementary counterpoint. There is, of course, nothing "reassuring" in this situation. Cage's sociopolitical stance has oftentimes been criticized for its limitations or, worse, scorned for its naiveté.[33] In the end, while it is undeniable that the composer "concentrated on sounds of the world and the interaction of art and life," one might as well conclude, as Douglas Kahn suggested, that the artist failed—despite himself—to deliver his promise.[34]

Such criticism is not new. Modern artists, including Cage, often encouraged their audiences to dream the impossible. Once, said Barnett Newman, "[the critic Harold Rosenberg] challenged me to explain what one of my paintings could possibly mean to the world. My answer was that if he and others could read it properly it would mean the end of all state capitalism and totalitarianism. The answer still goes."[35] Thus the answer—always in becoming—stands at the advent of a "society entirely composed of artists," which, as Newman had already made clear in the 1930s, would be the only one "really worth living in."[36] Newman's perspective not only indicates that, through art, a change might happen on a large scale, but that the responsibility to effect such a change lies within each individual.

Closely attuned to Newman's philosophy in this regard, the primary task that John Cage assigned to his art was not (unlike Joseph Beuys's program for a social sculpture, for example[37]) to lull society into the expectation "of some one artist who will satisfy all our aesthetic needs."[38] His goal was to actively transform himself as an artist in the first place, before anyone else.[39] For as modern artists, suggested Richard Shiff, Newman (or Cage in this regard) served as a model for all members of society[40]—models of "individual[s] who channeled the product of [their] isolated thought back into the flow of society . . . [constituting] a strike force of one dedicated to anarchist principles."[41] In the artistic community of his time and beyond, John Cage embodies such a "strike force," and his art, very much like Newman's, remains in his own terms "a political art which is not about politics but political itself."[42] "I am interested in social ends," admitted Cage, "but not in political ends, because politics deals with power, and society deals with numbers of individuals; and I'm interested both in single individuals and large numbers or medium numbers or any kinds of numbers of individuals. In other words, I'm interested in society, not for purposes of power, but for purposes of cooperation and enjoyment."[43]

Hence Cage's concept of Muzak-plus may be anarchist in spirit and actively threatening to the order of things, but only to the extent that it avoids, as he would say, any "*impracticable* anarchy which provokes the intervention of the police."[44] Cage, quite clearly, never foresaw the outcome of the revolution as an organized, premeditated overthrowing of any governing authority—no matter how artistically done. Suggesting or inducing changes through art does not necessarily imply that art, as such, is politically *productive* in society. In this regard, it is true that Cage's revolutionary edifice remained specifically musical, struggling to preserve an essential and constant flexibility. So that, suggested Cage:

> [Instead] of planning [the revolution], or stopping what we're doing in order to do it, it may be that we are at all times in it. I quote from M. C. Richards' book, *The Crossing Point*: "Instead of revolution being considered exclusively as an attack from outside upon an established form, it is being considered as a potential resource—an art of transformation voluntarily undertaken from within. Revolution arm in arm with evolution, creating a balance which is neither rigid nor explosive."[45]

To a certain extent, one might agree with Richard Taruskin's opinion that it is misleading to think that Cage wanted to liberate people. For the critic, it is clear that "[he] wanted nothing of the kind. He wanted to liberate sounds. People, with their 'memory, tastes, likes and dislikes,' were in the way. Getting rid of them was serious business—not something you could leave to chance"[46] and even less to one single artist, suggested Cage. But no matter how sensible Taruskin's argument may sound, such a conclusion altogether dismisses Cage's political sensibility. For Cage, there is no ambiguity: "[less] anarchic kinds of music give examples of less anarchic states of society. The masterpieces of Western music exemplify monarchies and dictatorships. Composer and conductor: king and prime minister."[47] Fundamentally nurturing a paradox inscribed in the twentieth-century avant-garde, Cage professes both an apolitical stance that privileges the aesthetic and a political stance that stresses the relationship between art and society.[48] Thus, encouraging and noticing the "blurring of the distinctions between composers, performers, and listeners" in contemporary music, Cage would interpret it as "*evidence* of an ongoing change in society, not only in the structure of society, but in the feelings that people have for one another."[49] Of course, beyond musically questioning hierarchical relationships, Cage is not inclined to foster the image of an impossible "better world" in which we would like to live, and against which the (restricted) possibilities imposed by the "real world" only become more prevailing.

Ultimately, it is true that liberating sound and liberating people are not identical, but eventually they are inseparable in Cage's view. Beyond all skepticism—including his own—Cage always maintained that he had written music first "in order to produce a revolution in the mind," and with the hope that, ultimately, "it could further the revolution in society."[50] To be sure, this remains a simple yet ambitious objective, and while it is not beyond criticism, it can still be valued. Whether or not his art and his intellectual positions *effectively* changed society is beside the point. It actually did, to the extent that Cage practiced his responsibility as an artist and "[all] responsibility," as Jacques Derrida reminded us, "is revolutionary, since it seeks to do the impossible, to interrupt the order of things on the basis of nonprogrammable events."[51] For it is true, added the philosopher, that "[a] revolution cannot be programmed. In a certain way, as the only event worthy of the name, it exceeds every possible horizon, every *horizon of possible*—and therefore of potency and power."[52] This interruption is the plus in Muzak-plus and what makes it essentially revolutionary and, therefore, impossible: it belongs only to its unforeseeable future performers, and, to this extent, Cage's answer still holds true. Things might be done that haven't yet...

Figure 4.1. Martha Rosler, *Untitled (O'Hare)*, 1986, from "In the Place of the Public: Airport Series 1981—" Original in color.

Notes

Preface

1. Haskins, "Composition (Not Philosophy)" (1996), 216.
2. Herwitz, "The Security of the Obvious" (1988), 785.
3. See the References section for full bibliographical citations.
4. See in this regard Sundstrom, *Work Places: The Psychology of the Physical Environment in Offices and Factories* (1986).
5. See the References section for full bibliographical citations.
6. Armengaud, *Erik Satie* (2009), 620. ". . . une réflexion sur l'utilisation de la musique pour améliorer l'environnement de l'homme et sur la fonctionnalité de la musique."
7. Ibid., 622. "Satie était évidemment prophétique de toutes les musiques de marketing, capables de stimuler la force de travail de l'ouvrier comme le porte-monnaie du consommateur."
8. Ibid., 625. ("À bas la musique, vive les sons qui repeignent le monde!")
9. Kahn, "John Cage: Silence and Silencing" (1997), 556–98. The argument was subsequently integrated to the author's *Noise, Water, Meat: A History of Sound in the Arts* (1999).
10. Kahn, "John Cage: Silence and Silencing" (1997), 579.
11. Silverman, *Begin Again* (2010), 100.
12. Haskins, "Composition (Not Philosophy)" (1996), 217.
13. Bruce Nauman, "Bruce Nauman: The Center of Yourself," (1975), interview with Jan Butterfield, in *Please Pay Attention Please: Bruce Nauman's Words, Writings and Interviews*, edited by Janet Kraynak (Cambridge, Mass.: MIT Press), 174.
14. Pritchett, "What Silence Taught John Cage," in Julia Robinson (curator), *The Anarchy of Silence: John Cage and Experimental Art* (2009), 176.

Introduction

1. Edgard Varèse's answer to John Cage's question about what the music of the future may be in "Possibilities: Edgard Varèse and Alexei Haeiff Questioned by 8 Composers," *Possibilities* 1 (Winter 1947/48): 97.

2. Cage, introduction to "Rhythm Etc," *A Year from Monday* (1967), 120. "Rhythm Etc," written in 1961–62, was first published in Gyorgy Kepes, ed., *Module, Proportion, Symmetry, Rhythm* (New York: George Braziller, 1966) and reprinted with an introduction by Cage, *A Year from Monday* (1967). Subsequent references to this article are from *A Year from Monday*.

3. For Cage's memory of the commission, see Cage, his introduction to "Rhythm Etc," ibid.

4. On this matter see Revill, *The Roaring Silence—John Cage: A Life* (1992), 199.

5. Ibid.

6. Cage, "Rhythm Etc," in Cage, *A Year from Monday*, 125.

7. Cage, "Diary: How to Improve the World (You Will Only Make Matters Worse) Continued 1973–1982," in Cage, *X: Writings '79–'82* (1983), 165.

8. Ross Davies, "Muzak's Stephen Gottlieb," *The New York Times*, December 15, 1980, p. 19.

9. Jane Jarvis, "Notes on Muzak," in Hitchcock, ed., *The Phonograph and Our Musical Life* (1977), 13.

10. Roger Reynolds, in response to Jane Jarvis, "Notes on Muzak," in Hitchcock, ed., *The Phonograph and Our Musical Life* (1977), 16.

11. Satie, *Correspondance Presque complète*, 396.

12. Mellers, "Erik Satie and the 'Problem' of Contemporary Music" (1942), 223.

13. Klein, "Twentieth Century Analysis" (1966), 26.

14. Ibid.

15. Joan Peyser, "Commentary: 'The Phonograph and Our Musical Life,'" *The Musical Quarterly* 64, no. 2 (April 1978): 253.

16. See Shlomowitz, "Cage's Place in the Reception of Satie," online publication.

17. In 1965, Cage mentioned that "some years ago I gave my collection of Satie to [the pianist] Maro Ajemian, who shares it with other musicians." Letter to Arthur Hill, May 21, 1965, Collection Northwestern University Library.

18. Of course, Cage's piece *Furniture music etcetera* (1980) is a direct reference to Satie's concept and quotes the latter's piece of furniture music *Tenture de Cabinet Prefectoral* (1923).

19. See Kostelanetz, ed., *Conversing with Cage*, 48. A letter from John Cage to the French composer Robert Caby (1905–1992), sent on September 28, 1949, testifies of Cage's interest in Satie's unpublished works ["œuvres inédites"] and notably *musique d'ameublement*. See Imec, Fonds Satie, "Correspondances autour de Satie," SAT 5.12.

20. As Cage writes to Virgil Thompson in 1949, "Three important works of Satie still remain utterly hidden: Le Medecin Malgré Lui (the dialogue you often mentioned); La Musique d'Ameublement (which several say never existed, but yesterday at the Conservatoire I saw a Notebook for it with all the measure[s] marked out and the instrumentation but no notes), and Paul et Virginie." Letter to Virgil Thomson [July or August 1949] from Paris, France. Collection Yale University Library.

21. See Kostelanetz, ed., *Conversing with Cage*, 49.

22. Ibid. See also Cage, "The First Meeting of the Satie Society," New York City, February–March 1985, 2. Typescript consulted in Ornella Volta's collection, Paris.

23. Varèse, "Possibilities: Edgard Varèse and Alexei Haeiff Questioned by 8 Composers," 97.

24. Shattuck's 1958 study *The Banquet Years* includes a chapter on Satie, discussing briefly his furniture music.

25. Cage, Shattuck, and Gillmor, "Erik Satie: A Conversation" (1973), 22.

26. Ibid. As mentioned in the foreword, Douglas Kahn takes Cage's remark quite literally, it seems, and offers in conclusion: "In essence, therefore, he was proposing another version of *Silent Prayer*, this time supplanting Muzak with *musique d'ameublement*."

27. Cage, Shattuck, and Gillmor, "Erik Satie: A Conversation" (1973), 22 (italics mine).

28. Ibid.

29. Ibid.

30. Charles, *For the Birds* (1981), 137. "D.C.: What do you consider Muzak! J.C.: Music for factory workers, or for chickens to force them to lay eggs. The miscellaneous music played throughout the day by most radio stations."

31. Jane Jarvis, "Notes on Muzak," in Hitchcock, ed., *The Phonograph and Our Musical Life* (1977), 16.

32. Ibid., 16–17.

33. See "An Interview with Klaus Maeck," in Jack Sargeant, *Naked Lens: Beat Cinema* (London: Creation Books, 1997; New York: Soft Skull Press, 2009), 202. The interesting soundtrack of the movie, by Psychic TV and Genesis P-Orridge, is available in the box set *Splinter Test*, Caroline Records, 1994, SYARD004. On *Decoder*, see also Steve Goodman, *Sonic Warfare: Sound, Affect, and the Ecology of Fear* (Cambridge, Mass.: MIT Press, 2009), 142.

34. Karen R. Scheel and John S. Westeveld, "Heavy Metal Music and Adolescent Suicidality: An Empirical Observation," *Adolescence* 34, no. 134 (1999): 253–73.

35. See Huron, "Review of Stephen H. Barnes, *The Hidden Messages in Music*," (1990): 183–84.

36. Kaprow, "The Right Living," (1987) in Kaprow, *Essays on the Blurring of Art and Life*, 225.

37. Ibid.

38. Susan Buck-Morss, "Art in the Age of Its Electronic Production," in Susan Buck-Morss, Julian Stallabrass, and Leonidas Donskis, *Ground Control / Technology and Utopia*, (London: Black Dog Publishing, 1997), p.14.

39. Stallabrass, "Money, Disembodied Art, and the Turing Test for Aesthetics," in *Ground Control / Technology and Utopia*, 88.

40. Jane Jarvis, "Notes on Muzak," in Hitchcock, ed., *The Phonograph and Our Musical Life* (1977), 16. "The Muzak that [people] are exposed to is a part of the environment. It's like a pretty painting, or the room decoration."

41. *Reveille*, noncommercial LP by MUZAK, 1969, Ref. MUZAK H-1(1)35B AB284V1H9 (SYB-488/489), liner notes by William Wokoun, PhD.

138 NOTES TO INTRODUCTION AND CHAPTER 1

42. Wassily Kandinsky, "The Psychological Working of Colors," *Spiritual in Art* (1910/1912) (New York: Dover, revised edition, 1977), 24–25.

43. Muzak website, "Why Muzak," http://www.muzak.com/products/music, last accessed July 2011.

44. Jean-Luc Nancy, *La communauté désœuvrée*, (Paris: Christian Bourgois, 1983), translated by Peter Connor, Lisa Garbus, Michael Holland, and Simona Sawhney as *The Inoperative Community* (Minneapolis: University of Minnesota Press, 1991), 1–2.

45. On the revival of communitarian bounds, see the sharp remarks made by Bruce Bégout in *Pensée Privées: Journal Philosophique (1998–2006)* (Grenoble, France: Millon, Collection Krisis, 2007), 315.

46. William Brooks, "Music and Society," in David Nicholls, ed., *The Cambridge Companion to John Cage* (2002), 219.

47. Robert Adlington, "Avant-Garde Music and the Sixties," in Robert Adlington, ed., *Sound Commitments: Avant-Garde Music and the Sixties* (2009), 5.

48. Rainer, "Looking Myself in the Mouth" (1981), 68.

49. Heimbecker, "HPSCHD, Gesamtkunstwerk, and Utopia," 477. This criticism finds its ground in Cage's own words: "As an anarchist, I aim to get rid of politics," he said, "I would prefer to drop the question of power, whether black power, flower power or student power." Kostelanetz, "Environmental Abundance," (1969) in Kostelanetz, ed., *John Cage: An Anthology*, 175.

50. Heimbecker, "HPSCHD, Gesamtkunstwerk, and Utopia" (2008), 492.

51. Paul Virilio, *Art and Fear* (first published in French, 2000), translated by Julie Rose (London: Continuum, 2003), 74.

52. Meyer Schapiro, "The Patrons of Revolutionary Art," *Marxist Quarterly* 1, no. 3 (October–December 1937): 462–66.

53. On these issues, see Jacques Rancière, *Le spectateur émancipé* (Paris: La Fabrique editions, 2008), notably the chapter "Les paradoxes de l'art politique," 56–93.

54. William Brooks, "Music and Society," in David Nicholls, ed., *The Cambridge Companion to John Cage* (2002), 214.

55. Ibid., 225.

56. Ibid., 226.

57. Ibid., 225.

58. Joseph, "The Tower and the Line" (2007), 63–64.

59. Ibid., 62.

60. Cage, "McLuhan's Influence," (1967) in Kostelanetz, ed., *John Cage: An Anthology*, 170–71.

61. Cage, "The Future of Music" (1974), in Cage, *Empty Words: Writings '73–'78* (1980), 183.

Chapter 1. Furniture Music

1. To be fair, Satie was actually considered to be "an accomplished musical analphabet." Indeed, the composer and critique Jean Barraqué (a friend of Michel

Foucault) had qualified Satie, in the 1970s, as being : "[un] analphabète musical accompli, ayant trouvé dans ses relations avec Debussy une occasion inespérée de se faufiler dans les coulisses de l'histoire." Quoted by Ornella Volta in Satie, *Écrits*, 239.

2. Satie, "Mémoires d'un amnésique" (1912), in *Écrits*, 19.

3. Nyman, "Cage and Satie" (1973), 1229.

4. Austin, "Satie before and after Cocteau" (1962), 224.

5. Cage's entire remark reads: "True, one could not endure a performance of *Vexations* (lasting [my estimate] twenty-four hours; 840 repetitions of a fifty-two beat piece itself involving a repetitive structure: A, A1, A, A2, each A thirteen measures long), but why give it a thought?" Cage, "Erik Satie" (1958), in Cage, *Silence* (1961), 78.

6. Andy Warhol, in Paul Taylor, "The Last Interview," *Flash Art* (April 1987), reprinted in Kenneth Goldsmith, ed., *I'll Be Your Mirror: The Selected Andy Warhol Interviews, 1962–1987* (New York: Carroll and Craf, 2004), 389.

7. As Gavin Bryars noted: "A curious feature of several American performances during the 1960s was that newspaper reviews gave the date of composition of Vexations as 'c1920.' This date, which seems to stem from a common (mistaken) source, could have arisen from descriptions of the piece as having an effect akin to musique d'ameublement, the first example of which was written in 1920; but there can be little doubt that the music is located firmly in the early 1890s." Bryars, "Vexations and Its Performers" (1979), 12–20. In his biography of Cage, Kenneth Silverman still assimilates *Vexations* to furniture music. See Silverman, *Begin Again* (2010), 98–99.

8. Orledge, *Satie the Composer* (1990), 143.

9. Adorno, "The Radio Symphony" (1941), in *Essays on Music*, 258.

10. Ibid.

11. See Wilfrid Mellers, "Satie et le musique 'fonctionnelle,'" in Rollo H. Myers, ed., *La Revue musicale, Erik Satie, son temps et ses amis* (1952), 35: "Dans la banalité voulue de la Musique d'ameublement, et, de façon moins tranchée, dans les *Cinq grimaces pour le songe d'une nuit d'été*, Satie a composé de la musique proprement de circonstance, qui se refuse à illustrer ou exprimer quoi que ce soit, et sert tout simplement de musique de fond. Une musique de ce genre n'a évidemment aucune valeur intrinsèque; mais à une époque où la vie émotive et intellectuelle de la 'masse' ne cesse d'être abaissée par l'infériorité de l'art qui lui est offert, il importait de poser de façon clairvoyante la question du matériel de l'émotion musicale' et de la qualité de ce matériel."

12. Hinton, *The Idea of Gebrauchsmusik* (1989), 2.

13. Hence, argued Julian Stallabrass, today's dominant critical discourse assumes that art "exists in a zone of freedom, set apart from mundane, everyday life, and from its rules and restrictions. The economy and its complementary mass culture function according to strict conventions; contemporary art does the opposite. The idea that capitalism allows space for such free expression could be taken as rather reassuring. The message is that art is a law unto itself, unaffected by the demands

of private patrons, religion, business and the state." Julian Stallabrass, "Off Their Trolleys?" *New Statesman* (November 15, 2004): 38.

14. Hinton, *The Idea of Gebrauchsmusik* (1989), 26.

15. Quoted in Nyman, "Cage and Satie" (1973), 1227.

16. In a letter to André Breton from 1922. See Orledge, ed., *Satie Remembered*, 196. Upon Satie's visit, Louise Varèse remembered that, warned by her husband, she "provided a bottle of cognac" (*Satie Remembered*, 184).

17. "He classes himself among the 'fantaisistes' who are, in his opinion, 'highly respectable people.'" Myers, *Erik Satie* (1948), 110.

18. Satie, *Écrits* (no. 9), 21.

19. According to Georges Ribemont-Dessaignes's memory: "I remember him thanking me one day for some words that had been written about him in the magazine *391*. He didn't understand that these words were ambiguous, and that the real meaning was far from flattering." In Orledge, ed., *Satie Remembered* (1995), 199.

20. In 1892 Debussy dedicated "Cinq poèmes de Baudelaire" to Satie: "A gentle medieval musician lost in this century" (*Un musicien médiéval et doux, égaré dans ce siècle*).

21. See Darius Milhaud. "The Death of Erik Satie," in Milhaud's *Notes sans musique* (1949), translated as *Notes without Music* (1967), 148–51. Subsequent references to Milhaud's memoires are from the English translation. See also Orledge, ed., *Satie Remembered*, 215.

22. Cocteau, "Le Coq et l'Arlequin: notes autour de la musique" (1918), in *Le Rappel à l'ordre* (1948), 26.

23. Volta, "Erik Satie," in Laurent Le Bon, ed., *Dada* (2005), 863.

24. Satie, *Écrits*, 31. On the relationship between the composer and the writer, see Volta, *Satie/Cocteau: les malentendus d'une entente* (1993).

25. Satie, *Écrits*, no. 264.

26. I am grateful to Ornella Volta for giving me a copy of the program. It indicates, for the first part of the soirée: 1. *Pièces Brèves* pour piano (A. Honegger); 2. *Sonate* pour deux Clarinettes (Francis Poulenc); 3. *Le Printemps*, suite pour piano (Darius Milhaud); 4. *Hommage à Satie* sur un poème de René Chalupt (Germaine Tailleferre); 5. *Pastorale* and *Fox-Trot* (Georges Auric); 6. *Berceuse du Chat*, suite de chant avec accompagnement de 3 clarinettes (Igor Stravinsky). The details about the exhibition are given by Ornella Volta, in her introduction to the scores published in Satie, *Musique d'ameublement pour petit ensemble* (1999), vii.

27. Ibid. The program reads: "Pendant les entr'actes / Musique d'Ameublement, de M. Erik Satie, composée pour la Pièce."

28. The manuscripts of both scores are at the Institut Mémoires de L'Edition Contemporaine [IMEC], Caen, Fonds Erik Satie, ref. SAT 7 .2.

29. Milhaud's collaboration in the conception of *musique d'ameublement* is acknowledged by Satie in two letters to Milhaud from March 1 and March 5, 1920 (beyond this collaboration, whose exact nature remains unknown, no piece of furniture music is to be found in Milhaud's work). In the first letter, Satie asks Milhaud to

request a written contribution from Cocteau. Actually, Satie himself will send to Cocteau (probably on March 1, 1920) a draft for a prospectus advertising furniture music, soliciting his help to polish the slogans. See Satie, *Correspondance presque complète*, 396–98.

30. The words have been written hastily by Pierre Bertin on the back of a program for a concert (Bach / Debussy) of Marcelle Meyer at the Salle Gaveau on February 20, 1920. Bertin's original manuscript reads: "Nous vous présenterons aussi pour la 1ère fois, par les soins de mmrr Erik Satie et Darius Milhaud et sous la direction de Mr Delgrange la musique d'ameublement, pendant les entr'actes de la pièce. Nous vous prions instamment de ne pas lui attacher d'importance et d'agir pendant l'entracte comme si elle n'existait pas. Cette musique, spécialement écrite pour la pièce de Max Jacob, prétend à contribuer à la vie au même titre qu'une conversation particulière, qu'un tableau de la galerie, ou que le siège sur lequel on est, ou non, assis—vous en ferez l'essai—mmrr Erik Satie et Darius Milhaud se tiennent à votre disposition pour tous renseignements et commandes." Unsigned manuscript, "Présentation de Musique d'ameublement," IMEC, ref. Satie 15.8. An English translation (here modified) is to be found in Pierre-Daniel Templier, *Erik Satie* (1932), trans. Elena L. French and David S. French (Cambridge Mass.: MIT Press, 1969).

31. Milhaud, *Notes without Music* (1967), 37–39.

32. Pierre Bertin, manuscript: "Présentation de Musique d'ameublement," IMEC, Fonds Satie, ref. SAT 15. (Original in French, quoted in note 30).

33. Milhaud, *Notes without Music* (1967), 116–24.

34. Sterne, "Sounds Like the Mall of America: Programmed Music and the Architectonics of Commercial Space" (1997), 25.

35. See Tyler, "Commerce and Poetry Hand in Hand" (1992), 82. "The retailers often preferred to have the musicians hidden from sight, presumably to render the shopping environment more pleasant without distracting shoppers from possible purchases. A reporter in 1912 noted in his description of an elegant New York store that 'musicians are hidden behind vine-hung lattices.' One paradigmatic architectural plan for department stores, published in 1916, featured an ornamental screen on the second floor, behind which an orchestra or organ could play."

36. See Arceneaux, "A Sales Floor in the Sky" (2009), 76–89.

37. On this question, see Sterne, "Sounds Like the Mall of America" (1997), 24.

38. Milhaud, *Notes without Music* (1967), 116–24. In 1923, Ms. Eugène Meyers, the wife of the owner of the *Washington Post*, acquired an autographed score of *Tenture de Cabinet Préfectoral*, a piece of furniture music by Satie. As Milhaud suggests, "[to] have its full meaning, she should have had it recorded and played over and over again, thus forming part of the furniture of her beautiful library in Crescent Place."

39. About *Entrac'te* music, see Orledge, ed., *Satie Remembered*, 117.

40. The first (known) mention of the concept of *musique d'ameublement* was found by Pierre-Daniel Templier in Satie's (now lost) notes for *Socrate* dating 1917. They read: "Le Banquet—Musique d'ameublement—Pour une salle: Encadrement (danse);

Tapisserie (Le Banquet, sujet); Encadrement (danse, reprise) // Phèdre—Musique d'ameublement—Pour un vestibule: Colonnade (danse) Bas-relief (marbre, sujet) Colonnade (danse, reprise) // Phédon—Musique d'ameublement—Pour une vitrine: Ecrin (duvet de porc, danse); Camée (agate d'Asie—Phédon, sujet); Ecrin (danse, reprise). See Volta, in introduction to Satie, *Musiques d'ameublement* (1999), v.

41. All the scores of *Musique d'ameublement* have been published under Ornella Volta's direction in Satie, *Musiques d'ameublement pour petit ensemble* (1999). This edition contains reproduction of the manuscripts of *Carrelage Phonique* (1918), *Tapisserie en fer forgé* (1918), *Un Salon* (1920), *Tenture de Cabinet Préfectoral* (1923).

42. *Un Salon* contains extracts from *Mignon*'s Act 1 Romance ("Connais-tu le pays où fleurit l'oranger?"—Ambroise Thomas's *Mignon*, 1866) and a version of the second theme of Camille Saint-Saëns's *Danse macabre* (1874, bars 50–57). See Orledge, *Satie the Composer* (1990), 319–20. Incidentally, the quotes come from composers that Satie abhorred. Of Thomas he wrote: "La place qu'il occupa dans la musique officielle s'offrit considérable, mais ne l'augmenta pas dans l'esprit des artistes: quelque chose comme les superbes fonctions d'un général commandant de Corps d'Armée, très en vue et très honoraire. Ce n'est pas mal, direz-vous. Je veux bien." See "Observation d'un Imbécile (moi) / Ambroise Thomas" (1912), in Satie, *Les Cahiers d'un Mammifère*, 1.

43. See Satie, *Musiques d'ameublement* (1999). In her introduction, Ornella Volta mentions that Satie obtained the commission thanks to Darius Milhaud's connections in the United States. While Ms. Meyer had funded the gallery 291, Ornella Volta (in conversation with the author) believes that Satie saw her solely as a rich aristocrat (she was the wife of the *Washington Post*'s director), which could explain the irony of the furniture music that the composer delivered to her. Announcing to Milhaud on March 26, 1923, that he had just finished the thing for the American lady, Satie writes about the music—as if to stress its ostentatious character—*Its features are decorative and sumptuous—made to be eye-catching. I'm proud of it*. In Satie, *Correspondance Presque complète*, 529: "je viens de terminer le '*truc*' pour la Dame americaine. Oui. / C'est de la musique d'Ameublement (*Tenture de Cabinet Préfectorale*). . . . / L'aspect en est décorative & somptueux—fait pour la vue. J'en suis fier."

44. Hinton, *The Idea of Gebrauchsmusik* (1989), 27.

45. Matisse's words were published in 1908: "Ce que je rêve, c'est un art d'équilibre, de pureté, de tranquillité, sans sujet inquiétant ou préoccupant, qui soit, pour tout travailleur cérébral, pour l'homme d'affaires aussi bien que pour l'artiste des lettres, par exemple, un lénifiant, un calmant cérébral, quelque chose d'analogue à un bon fauteuil qui le délasse de ses fatigues physiques." In Matisse, *Écrits et propos sur l'art* (Paris: Hermann, 1972, 1992), 50. In Shattuck's words: "Henri Matisse associated himself with the furniture tradition in a remark very similar to Bertin's presentation: 'What I dream of is an art without any disquieting or preoccupying subject, which would be . . . something analogous to a good armchair.'" Roger Shattuck, *The Banquet Years* (1958), 169. In 1945, Rollo Myers had claimed: "The term 'musique

d'ameublement' . . . owes its origin to a statement made by the painter Matisse, who declared that he dreamed of an art without any distracting subject-matter, and which might be compared to an easy chair ('quelque chose d'analogue à un bon fauteuil')." Myers, "The Strange Case of Erik Satie" (1945), 201–3; see also Myers, *Erik Satie* (1948), 60.

46. Matisse's statement, from 1908, has often been used in order to soften the strangeness of his art. Even the *Piano Lesson* (1916), which Kenneth Silver interprets as "[embodying] the new rooted 'sense of limit and of the relative'" in Matisse's art, is not as easily stabilized as it seems. It is also often quoted in relation to the rise of a *rappel à l'ordre* (call to order) as promoted by Cocteau. While Satie's music certainly played a role in the formulation of a form of neoclassicism after World War I, what exactly his *musique d'ameublement* owes to the art of Matisse remains disputable. See Kenneth Silver, *Esprit de Corps*, 45. On the interpretation of Matisse's pictorial space, see Jean-Claude Lebensztejn, "Matisse et l'espace," in *Matisse Aujourd'hui*, Cahiers Henri Matisse, no. 5 (Nice, France: Musée Matisse, 1987), 21–26. The author writes: "Après l'avoir vomi, la France officielle le récupéra [Matisse] dès 1919 en le piégeant à ses propres mots, le ligotant à ce bon vieux fauteuil qui délasse."

47. Orledge, *Satie the Composer*, 222.

48. Ibid.

49. Ibid., 4. According to this classification, the first period (1885–95) was dominated by mysticism and medieval influence, the second (1897–1915) by the composer's work in cabaret. The association between Satie's furniture music and Matisse's statement has since been accepted as a valid premise (see Blickhan, *Erik Satie: Musique d'ameublement* (unpublished, 1976), 6; and more recently Davis, *Erik Satie* (2007), 127: "The inspiration for such an artistic work seems to have come from artist Henri Matisse."

50. Klein, "Twentieth Century Analysis: Essays in Miniature" (1966), 26.

51. Ibid.

52. Umberto V. Muscio (president of the Muzak Division of Wrather Corp.), quoted in Woodley, "Music by Muzak" (1971), 6. About Muscio's experience in the air-conditioning business, see also Haden-Guest, *The Paradise Program* (1973), 15: "What of Muscio himself before his connection with Muzak? He was, he says, with an air-conditioning firm . . . Muscio grins, understandingly. 'There is some sort of correlation . . . I mean, both Muzak and air-conditioning are part of the Environment.'"

53. Lanza, *Elevator Music* (1994), 17.

54. Ibid., 19.

55. Ibid., 2.

56. Ibid., 3.

57. Milhaud, *Notes without Music* (1967), 116—24.

58. See Glazer, "Satie's Entr'acte: A Model of Film Music" (1976), 37, and also Gillmor, *Erik Satie* (1988), 232. Few scholars of Satie's music, beside Ornella Volta, have resisted presenting his furniture music as an anticipation of muzak.

59. Shattuck, *The Banquet Years*, 169. As Roger Shattuck put it, "[all] music, of course, can be traced back to forms or furniture music: rhythmic dance patterns, devotional and inspirational atmosphere for worship, background sounds for courtly gatherings, carnival tunes . . ."

60. David Toop, "Environmental Music (background music)," *The New Grove Dictionary of Music and Musicians*, second edition (New York: Grove, 2001).

61. Orledge, *Satie the Composer* (1990), 1.

62. A term first used by Apollinaire in 1917, in reference to Cocteau's ballet *Parade*, for which Satie wrote the score. "Pour moi, . . . l'Esprit Nouveau est surtout un retour vers la forme classique—avec une sensibilité moderne." In Satie, *Écrits*, 89.

63. A 1918 manuscript from Cocteau's hand, planning an unrealized music-hall evening with music by "Les nouveaux jeunes," includes furniture music during the intermission. Document preserved at the Bibliothèque Nationale de France, département de la musique, Rés Vma 174 (22). I am grateful to Ornella Volta for giving me the missing information about the circumstances surrounding this document.

64. "Assez de nuages, de vagues, d'aquariums, d'ondines et de parfums la nuit; il nous faut une musique sur la terre, UNE MUSIQUE DE TOUS LES JOURS." Cocteau, "Le Coq et l'Arlequin: notes autour de la musique" (1918), reprinted in Cocteau, *Le Rappel à l'ordre*, 28.

65. Ibid., 30.

66. "La partition de Satie est conçue pour servir de fond musical à un premier plan de batterie et de bruits scéniques. / Ainsi elle se soumet très humblement à la réalité qui étouffe le chant du rossignol sous le roulement des tramways." Georges Auric, preface to Erik Satie, *Parade / Ballet réaliste*, réduction pour piano à quatre mains (Paris: Editions Rouart, Lerolle et Cie, 1917). On the rather difficult circumstances surrounding the conception of Satie's music for *Parade*, see Ornella Volta, *Satie/Cocteau: les malentendus d'une entente*.

67. "La partition de parade devait servir de fond musical à des bruits suggestifs, tel que sirènes, machines à écrire, dynamos." Cocteau, *Le Rappel à l'ordre*, 32.

68. Luigi Russolo, "L'arte dei Rumori" (1913), from the translation "The Art of Noise," published in Michael Kirby, *Futurist Performance*, with manifestos and playscripts translated from the Italian by Victoria Nes Kirby (New York: Dutton, 1971).

69. The list goes on: "Rumbles, Roars, Explosions, Crashes, Splashes, Booms, Whistles, Hisses, Snorts, Whispers, Murmurs, Mumbles, Grumbles, Gurgles, Screeches, Creaks, Rumbles, Buzzes, Crackles, Scrapes [rubs], noises obtained by percussion on metal, wood, skin, rock, terracotta, etc. Shouts, Screams, Groans, Shrieks, Howls, Laughs, Groans, Sobs."

70. Joel A. Rogers, "Jazz at Home" (1925), as quoted in Thompson, *The Soundscape of Modernity* (2002), 131.

71. Cocteau, "Notebook on Art, Music, and Poetry," 269, manuscript in the Valentine Hugo Collection, Harry Ransom Humanities Research Center, University of Texas at Austin, quoted in Pasler, "New Music as Confrontation: The Musical Sources of Jean Cocteau's Identity" (1991), 269, and note 56.

72. See Thompson, *The Soundscape of Modernity*, 134. Satie's appreciation of other musicians' efforts to integrate the spirit and the rhythm of industrial modernity in their music translated, as often, in a humorous remark. Hence, remembered George Antheil, while the public (including Man Ray and Duchamp) were arguing loudly at the 1923 Parisian premiere of his new piece *Mécanismes* and *Airplane Sonata*, Satie stood up and, applauding the roaring finale, shouted "Quel precisions!" [*sic*]. In a sense, only humor could capture such essential element of the relation between music and the machine, by praising precisely the quality that the critics of the work would have found missing. See Orledge, *Satie the Composer*, 221.

73. "J'ai composé ... un fond à certains bruits que Cocteau juge indispensable pour préciser l'atmosphère de ses personnages" (Jean Cocteau, *Le Rappel à l'ordre*, 58.) Again, wrote Cocteau on the final copy of Satie's manuscript of *Parade*: "the four-hand piano music of *Parade* is not a work in itself but is intended as a background designed to put the primary subject of sounds and scenic noises into relief." Quoted in Davis, *Erik Satie*, 113.

74. In the end, as Ornella Volta observed, *Parade* went through multiple sketches and "the 'foreground of drums and scenic noises,' for which Cocteau wanted Satie's music to be a mere 'musical background,' against which the sound would stand out, was reduced to the clicking of four typewriters, the squeaks of a lottery wheel and the screams of two sirens (factory and ship). These were to be heard during stretches of silence, which the composer importunately included so the noise would not disturb his composition." See Volta, "The 'French French' Music of Jean Cocteau," in Cat. *Jean Cocteau, sur le fil du siècle*, 107.

75. Yutaka Sado and Ensemble Lamoureux, *L'orchestre de Satie*, CD Erato # 85827, 2002 (recorded in September 2000, Salle Wagram, Paris, France).

76. Fernand Léger, "Le spectacle. Lumière, couleur, image mobile, objet-spectacle" (1924) in *Fonctions de la peinture* (Paris: Gonthier, 1965), 142; English translation slightly modified from Fernand Léger, *Functions of Painting*, trans. Alexandra Anderson, ed. Edward F. Fry, preface by George L. K. Morris (New York: Viking, 1973), 46.

77. "NE FAITES PAS DE L'ART D'APRES L'ART." In Cocteau, *Le Rappel à l'ordre*, 40; line and melody, 27.

78. See Dahlhaus, *The Idea of Absolute Music* (1978).

79. E. T. A. Hoffmann, "Beethoven's Instrumental Music" (1813), translated in Jost Hermand and Michael Gilbert, eds., *German Essays on Music* (New York: Continuum, 1994), p. 59.

80. Dahlhaus, *The Idea of Absolute Music* (1978), 7–8.

81. Hinton, *The Idea of Gebrauchsmusik* (1989), 31.

82. Ibid., 30.

83. Ibid., 26.

84. Ibid., 5.

85. Heinrich Besseler (1926) quoted in Hinton, *The Idea of Gebrauchsmusik*, 10.

86. Ibid.

87. Hindemith, quoted in Hinton, *The Idea of Gebrauchsmusik* (1989), 114.

88. See Ornella Volta, introduction to Satie, *Musiques d'ameublement* (1999).

89. Ibid., ix.

90. Hans Lenneberg, "Speculating about Sociology and Social History," *The Journal of Musicology* 6, no. 4 (Autumn 1988): 415. For a more complete study, see Julia K. Wood, "'A Flowing Harmony': Music on the Thames in Restoration London," *Early Music* 23, no. 4, Music in Purcell's London I (November 1995): 553–81.

91. Rowen, "Some 18th-Century Classifications of Musical Style" (1947), 90.

92. Ibid.

93. Ibid. The term *table music* is also used, differently, to designate another genre: "the 'table-book' or 'table-music,' so-called because the singers sat round the table and all sang from the same copy." Cf. H. Elliot Button, "Music Printing in the Year 1603," *The Musical Times* 64, no. 965 (July 1, 1923): 472. The principle is that of the mirror canon, used by Mozart in the violin duets sometimes referred to as "Table Music for Two," written so that the second part can be read upside down, the two players seated on both sides of table.

94. Kant, *Kritik der Urteilskraft*, §44. See also Arden Reed, "The Debt of Disinterest: Kant's Critique of Music," *MLN: Modern Language Notes* 95, no. 3, German issue (April 1980): 568: "To determine the place of music in the *Critique of Judgment* assuming that this is possible, that the Critique is not itself a piece of music—we would do well to begin with §51, in which Kant classifies the fine arts into three categories: 'the arts of speech' (rhetoric and poetry), 'the formative arts' (sculpture, architecture, and painting), and 'the art of the play of sensations (as external sensible impressions)' (music and the 'art of color'—which two he goes on to combine under the name 'art of tone [Tonkunst]')."

95. Derrida, "Economimesis" (1975), 62.

96. As Stephen Hinton remarked, Kant was less interested in the production of fine arts than in the faculty of judging it, demonstrating how its reception—rather than the artwork itself—"emancipates itself from any practical connections." Hinton, *The Idea of Gebrauchsmusik* (1989), 29.

97. Following Jacques Derrida's analysis of Kant (especially of §43 and §44 of the *Critique of Judgment*), one can recognize that mercenary arts and fine arts do not stand in opposition to each other but bear a hierarchical relationship to each other: "Art, strictly speaking, is liberal or free [*freie*], its production must not enter into the economic circle of commerce, of offer and demand; it must not be exchanged. Liberal art and mercenary art therefore do not form a couple of opposite terms. One is higher than the other, more 'art' than the other; it has more value for not having any economic value. If art, in the literal sense, is 'production of freedom,' liberal art better conforms to its essence." Derrida, "Economimesis" (1975), 5.

98. Blainville, *L'Esprit de l'Art Musical* (1754) pp. 103 f. 86, quoted in Rowen "Some 18th-Century Classifications of Musical Style" (1947), 94–95.

99. Ibid.

100. Fernand Léger, "Satie Inconnu," in Myers, ed., *La Revue Musicale*, special issue "Erik Satie: Son Temps et ses Amis" (1952): 137–38. "Nous déjeûnions, des amis et lui dans un restaurant. Obligés de subir une musique tapageuse, insupportable nous quittons la salle et Satie nous dit: 'Il y a tout de même à réaliser une musique d'ameublement, c'est-à-dire une musique qui ferait partie des bruits ambiant, qui en tiendrait compte."

101. Such an objective, after all, is part of the Western musical heritage. As the priest and organist Adriano Banchieri (1567–1634) recommended, for instance, "[the] Masses, Psalms, Canticles, Motets, and Concerti to be performed with the Organ must be in the affettuoso, devout, attractive, and recitativo styles, imitating the words and employing gravity in concerting them," and "while singing the Dixit verses as cantus firmus, to have one voice sing at the same time Donec ponam, another Virgam, the third Tecum principio, and so on, successively, would make, alas, great confusion." It was the rule to "avoid the lengthy and confused pieces, so that the devout faithful may participate in the Divine Offices with souls that are satisfied and consoled." Adriano Banchieri, Conclusioni nel suono dell' organo (Bologna, 1609), Sesta et Settima Conclusioni., in *Reading in the History of Music in Performance*, selected, translated, and edited by Carol MacClintock (Bloomington: Indiana University Press, 1979), 129–30.

102. Fernand Léger, "Notes on the Mechanical Element" (1923) in Léger, *Functions of Painting*. Ten years earlier, Fernand Léger remembered, while visiting the Paris Air Show with Constantin Brancusi and Marcel Duchamp in 1912, Duchamp exclaimed: "Painting is finished! Who can do better than this propeller? Tell me, can you do that?" Cited in Dora Vallier, "La Vie fait l'oeuvre de Léger: Propos de l'artiste recueilles par Dora Vallier," *Cahiers d'Art* (Paris, 1954)L, 1401; cited in Eric Michaud, "Art War, Competition: The Three Battles Of Fernand Léger," in Dorothy Kosinki, ed., *Fernand Léger, 1911–1924 / The Rhythm of Modern Life* (Munich: Prestel, 1994), 57–63.

103. Satie, *Correspondance Presque complète*, 396. "La 'Musique d'Ameublement' est foncièrement industrielle. L'habitude—l'usage—est de faire de la musique dans des occasions ou la musique n'a rien à faire. Là, on joue des «Valses», des «Fantaisies» d'Opéras, & autres choses semblables, écrites pour un autre objet. / Nous, nous voulons établir une musique faite pour satisfaire les besoins 'utiles.' L'Art n'entre pas dans ces besoins. La «Musique d'Ameublement» crée de la vibration; elle n'a pas d'autre but; elle remplit le même rôle que la lumière, la chaleur—& le confort sous toutes ses formes."

104. Adorno, "Music in the Background" (1934), *Essays on Music*, 507.

105. Ibid.

106. Satie, *Correspondance Presque complète*, 396.

107. Ibid.

108. Ibid.

109. Ibid.

110. See Amedée Ozenfant, letter to Valentine Hugo, 3 Juillet 1956, IMEC, Fonds Satie, SAT 5. 66 and Ornella Volta, introduction to Satie, *Musiques d'ameublement pour petit ensemble*, (Editions Salabert, 1999), VI. This association with fashion will resurface in the mention of Satie's *Musiques d'ameublement* in a column in the first French issue of *Vogue*: R. F., "Conseils d'été," *Vogue* (June 15, 1920), 15 (Reference signaled by Davies, *Erik Satie* [2007], 128.

111. "Premier essai de Musique d'Ameublement (Sons industriels) / / Divertissement mobilier organisé par le groupe des musiciens ' Nouveaux Jeunes' pour JOVE, couturier décorateur. / / La Musique d'Ameublement pour soirées, réunions, etc... / Ce qu'est la Musique d'Ameublement ? / Un plaisir / La Musique d'Ameublement remplace / Les Valses / Les fantaisies sur les opéras" etc ... / Ne pas confondre ! C'est autre chose !!! / Plus de "fausse musique" : / du meuble musical / La Musique d'Ameublement complète le Mobilier; / Elle permet tout; / Elle vaut de l'or; / Elle est nouvelle; / Elle ne dérange pas les habitudes; / Elle ne fatigue pas; / Elle est française; / Elle est inusable; / Elle n'ennuie pas. / L'adopter c'est faire mieux ! / Ecoutez sans vous gêner. / Confection sur mesure." Manuscript reproduced in Satie, *Musiques d'ameublement* (1999), ii.

112. Le Corbusier, quoted in Eliel, ed., *L'Esprit nouveau* (2001), 76. Since 1915, Ozenfant had already organized several exhibitions there (including Picasso, La Fresnaye, Lhote, Herbin, Severini, Lipchitz), and in May 1916 Satie participated in a concert given at that same location. See Satie, *Correspondance presque complète*, 225.

113. Amadée Ozenfant, *Mémoires, 1886–1962* (Paris: Seghers, 1968), 93; partially cited in Susan L. Ball, *Ozenfant and Purism: The Evolution of a Style, 1915–1930* (Ann Arbor, Mich.: UMI Research Press, 1981), 31.

114. See Tyler, "Commerce and Poetry Hand in Hand" (1992), 75.

115. Indeed, Ornella Volta believes that Satie has planed to exhibit his scores on the wall of Jove: "Il allait bientôt mettre soigneusement au net ces deux partitions sur deux grandes feuilles de bristol afin de les exposer (comme ses amis artistes le faisaient avec leurs tableaux), et sans doute les proposer à la vente, dans la maison de couture et de décoration Jove, dont l'éminence grise était le peintre et théoricien «puriste», Amédée Ozenfant, qui avait accepté de faire exécuter ces «divertissements mobiliers» dans une séance publique de démonstration. Cette séance avait été prévue pour le printemps 1918. Les bombardements de Paris à cette date conseillèrent cependant la Maison Jove de se transporter, jusqu'à la fin de la guerre, à Bordeaux et de remettre le lancement des «divertissements mobiliers» à des temps meilleurs." Volta, introduction to Satie, *Musiques d'ameublement*, vi.

116. Satie, *Écrits*, 165.

117. Ibid.

118. Higgins, "Boredom and Danger" (1966), in *A Dialectic of Centuries* (1978), 43. See also Higgins's remarks on this matter, quoted by Sayre, *The Object of Performance: The American Avant-Garde since 1970*, 111–12.

119. The edition of the score I am referring to is Erik Satie, *Gymnopedies, Gnossiennes and Other Works for Piano* (New York: Dover, 1989), reproduced from the 1913 E. Demets edition. The reference to the song "Le bon roi Dagobert," dating

from the late eighteenth century and mocking the king, could also be referencing the *Le bon Roi Dagobert. Air avec douze variations précédé d'un Prélude ou introduction*, written by Louis Adam (1758–1848) (the father of Adolphe-Charles), which was in fashion in the nineteenth century. Nancy Perloff noted this quote in the margins of her study *Art and the Everyday: Popular Entertainment and the Circle of Erik Satie* (1991) note 15, p. 166: "Examples of Satie's piano pieces with folk song quotations include *Vieux Sequins et vieilles cuirasses* (1914) [*sic*] which paraphrases 'Malbrouck s'en va t'en guerre' and 'Le Roi Dagobert,' and 'Sur un vaisseau' from Descriptions automatiques (1913) which incorporates 'Maman les petits bateaux.' Satie quotes 'Au claire de la lune, mon ami Pierrot' (which was also used by Debussy in his early song Pierrot' [1881]) in 'The Flirt' from *Sports et divertissements*."

120. "Un tout petit enfant dort dans son tout petit lit. Son très vieux grand-père lui fait journellement une sorte d'étrange tout petit cours d'Histoire générale, puisée dans ses vagues souvenirs. / Souvent il lui parle du célèbre roi. Dagobert, de Monsieur le Duc de Marlborough et du grand général romain Marius. En rêve, le tout petit enfant voit ces héros combattant les Cimbres, à la journée de Mons-en-Puelle" (1304).

121. Musicologist Alan Gillmor suggests that this is the "reactionary, ultraroyalist Comte d'Artois, crowned King of France as Charles X in 1825 . . . the musical reference to the dissolute and by most accounts intellectually rather undernourished monarch takes on a deliciously satirical overtone in the context of the song's ["Le bon roi Dagobert"] opening verse: 'The good king Dagobert had his pants on inside out, The great Saint Eloi said to him: O my king, Your majesty is badly trousered. It's true, replied the king, I'm going to put them on again right side out.'" Alan M. Gillmor, "Musico-poetic form in Satie's 'Humoristic' Piano Suites (1913–1914)," *Canadian University Music Review* (January 1, 1987).

122. Higgins, "Boredom and Danger" (1966), in *A Dialectic of Centuries* (1978), 43.

123. Ibid.

124. As Brian Eno put it sixty years later describing his *Music for Airports*. Liner notes to Brian Eno's *Music for Airports / Ambient 1*, PVC 7908 (AMB 001), released 1978.

125. It does not seem necessary to translate the French word *riche* as "very splendid" (see ed. Dalabert)—it loses a possible double entendre.

126. Walter Gropius, "Programme of the Staatliches Bauhaus in Weimar" (1919), translated in Ulrich Conrads, ed., *Programs and Manifestoes on 20th-Century Architecture*, 49.

127. Satie, *Écrits*, 190. Draft for an advertising prospectus sent to Jean Cocteau in early March 1920.

128. See Orledge, *Satie the Composer* (1990), xxxv.

129. In *Dadaphone* (Dada, no. 7, March 1920): 4, quoted by Volta in introduction to Satie, *Musiques d'Ameublement*, viii.

130. Erik Satie, "Notes, brouillons et esquisses c. 1918–1919," Bibliothèque Nationale de France, Paris, Département de la Musique, Ref. Ms 9623 (2), pp. 26–27. Those sketches, appearing in a notebook, and separated by several blank pages from

notations for *Socrate*, contain a few bars of music surrounded by numerous possible titles (or ideas of titles) for furniture music written for flute, clarinet, and two violins, plus one alto and one cello; some of them realized. One can read: "Tenture Sonore / Ferait très bien dans un salon Louis XVI (fin de soirée) ~~pendant une réception de parents de province~~»; «Tapisserie en fer forgé pour l'arrivée des invités (~~réception~~ grande réception)»; «~~décoration pour vestibule~~ / Trépied à deux pieds / Soirée Intime (30 personnes)»; «carrelage phonique»; «papier phonique pour chambre d'ivrogne—très ordinaire / ameublement économique.» «Carrelage pour cabinet noir de luxe.» They are dated September 1917 by Ornella Volta, in introduction to Satie, *Musiques d'ameublement*, 1999.
    131. The words are Jean Wérnier's in Orledge, ed., *Satie Remembered*, 209.
    132. Gallez, "Satie's 'Entr'acte': A Model of Film Music" (1976), 36–50.
    133. Shattuck, *The Banquet Years* (1958), 170.
    134. Gallez, "Satie's 'Entr'acte': A Model of Film Music" (1976), 42.
    135. Ibid., 48.
    136. Armengaud, *Erik Satie*, 624.
    137. Gallez, "Satie's 'Entr'acte': A Model of Film Music" (1976), 42.
    138. Hanns Eisler, quoted by Graham McCann, in introduction to Adorno and Eisler, *Composing for the Films* (1947), xxviii.
    139. Hanns Eisler criticized as follow the conventions of such soundtracks: "Music must follow visual incidents and illustrate them either by directly imitating them or by using clichés that are associated with the mood and content of the picture." Quoted by Graham McCann, in introduction to Adorno and Eisler, *Composing for the Films* (1947), xvi.
    140. René Clair, "Picabia, Satie et la première *d'Entr'acte*," *Le Figaro littéraire* (June 1967), quoted in Patrick de Haas, *Cinéma intégral: de la peinture au cinéma dans les années vingt* (Bruxelles: Transéditions, 1985), 190.
    141. Richter, *Dada, Art and Anti-Art* (1965), 198. On this matter see also de Haas, *Cinema Integral*, ibid.
    142. "The Work of Art in the Age of Its Technological Reproducibility" (1936 version), section XVII, in Walter Benjamin, *Selected Writings* (vol. 3, 1935–38), Howard Eiland, Michael W. Jennings, eds. (Cambridge, Mass.: Belknap Press, 2002), 118.
    143. Cited in Dora Vallier, "La Vie fait l'oeuvre de Léger: Propos de l'artiste recueilles par Dora Vallier," *Cahiers d'Art* (Paris, 1954): 1401, cited and translated in Eric Michaud, "Art War, Competition: The Three Battles of Fernand Léger," in Dorothy Kosinski, ed., *Fernand Léger 1911–1924 / The Rhythm of Modern Life* (Munich: Prestel, 1994), 57–63.
    144. Mondrian, "The New Art—The New Life: The Culture of Pure Relationships" (1931), in Harry Holtzman and Martin S. James, eds., Piet Mondrian, *The New Art-The New Life: The Collected Writings of Piet Mondrian* (Boston: G. K. Hall, 1986), 252.
    145. Eric Hobsbawm, *Behind the Times: The Decline and Fall of the Twentieth-Century Avant-Gardes* (New York: Thames and Hudson, 1999), 30.
    146. In Hobsbawn's view (ibid.), Mondrian and Kandinsky shared "equally eccentric views about the world" (27) and wrote "often impenetrable manifestoes" (24); Yves

Klein "coloured all his canvases . . . in the manner of a house-painter" (26), and one must somehow overcome Warhol's "strange and disagreeable figure" (36).

147. For example, "much less could be communicated in the impoverished new languages of painting than in the old ones. This actually made it harder, or even impossible to 'express the times' in a communicable way." Ibid., 27.

148. Julian Stallabrass, "Money, Disembodied Art, and the Turing Test for Aesthetics," in Lolita Jablonskiene, Duncan McCorquodale, and Julian Stallabrass, eds., *Ground Control, Technology and Utopia* (Vilnius, Lithuania, London: Black Dog Publishing, 1997), 88.

149. Julian Stallabrass, "Shop until You Stop," in Christoph Grunenberg and Max Hollein, eds., *Shopping: A Century of Art and Consumer Culture* (Ostfildern-Ruit: Hatje Cantz, 2002), 22.

Chapter 2. Muzak Incorporated

1. Marshall McLuhan and Quentin Fiore, *The Medium Is the Massage: An Inventory of Effects* (New York: Bantam, 1967), n. p.

2. Buckminster Fuller, quoted in Frank Popper, *Art: Action and Participation*, translated by Stephen Bann (New York: New York University Press, 1975), 54–55.

3. Arseni Avraamov, "The Symphony of Sirens," (1923), translated from the Russian by Mel Gordon, in Kahn and Whitehead, eds., *Wireless Imagination: Sound, Radio, and the Avant-Garde* (1992), 245.

4. Husch, *Music of the Workplace* (1984), 57.

5. Lyrics from John Lennon, "How Do You Sleep," *Imagine*, Apple, EMI, 1971. The lyrics refer to the music of Paul McCartney.

6. Lucy Lippard, "Constellation by Harsh Daylight: The Whitney Annual," *Hudson Review* 21, no. 1 (spring 1968), quoted by Joseph Kosuth, "Art after Philosophy, Part I," *Studio International* 178, no. 915 (October 1969): 135: "formalist art is only art by virtue of its resemblance to earlier works of art. It's a mindless art. Or, as Lucy Lippard so succinctly described Jules Olitski's paintings: 'they're visual *Muzak*.'"

7. Lanza, *Elevator Music* (1994), 3.

8. "Rothko and Gottlieb's letter to the editor," the *New York Times*, June 13, 1943, sec. 2, X9, reprinted in Miguel López-Remiro, ed., *Mark Rothko: Writing on Art*, (New Haven, Conn.: Yale University Press, 2006), 36. (The letter was written in collaboration with Barnett Newman.)

9. Cage, "The Future of Music" (1974, revised text of a lecture given at the YMHA in New York), in Cage, *Empty Words: Writings '73–'78* (1980), 177.

10. Sterne, "Sounds Like the Mall of America" (1997), 22.

11. McLuhan and Fiore, *The Medium Is the Massage* (1967), n.p.

12. Bradshaw and Holbrook, "Must We Have Muzak Wherever We Go?" (2008), 25–43. The authors are respectively from the School of Business and Economics, University of Exeter, Exeter, UK, and the Graduate School of Business, Columbia University, New York, USA.

13. Ibid., 27.

14. Ibid., 40 (italics mine).

15. Ibid., 25.

16. Ibid., 40.

17. Umberto V. Muscio (president of the Muzak Division of Wrather Corp.), quoted in Richard Woodley, "Music by Muzak," (1971), 6. About Muscio's experience in the air-conditioning business, see also Haden-Guest, *The Paradise Program* (1973), 15: "What of Muscio himself before his connection with Muzak? He was, he says, with an air-conditioning firm . . . Muscio grins, understandingly. 'There *is* some sort of correlation . . . I mean, both Muzak and air-conditioning are part of the *Environment*.'" Such avoidance was already a rule of the BBC Music While You Work programming of functional music, for which, a memo stressed, "Artistic value must not be considered. The aim is to produce something which is rhythmically monotonous and repetitive; a 'sustaining' background of brisk, cheerful but unobtrusive music. Slow sentimental numbers and selections are ruled out." See Korczynski and Jones, "Instrumental Music? The Social Origins of Broadcast Music in British Factories" (2006).

18. Woodley, "Music by Muzak" (1971), 4.

19. Terminology used by Muzak Corp., "Why Muzak?": http://music.muzak.com/why_muzak/ (accessed November 23, 2009).

20. See Jean Baudrillard, "Design and Environment: Or, The Inflationary Curve of Political Economy," (1972) in *The Universitas Project: Solutions for a Post-Technological Society*, conceived and directed by Emilio Ambasz (New York: The Museum of Modern Art, 2006), p. 54.

21. Innumerable articles have been published on Muzak, background music, and functional music, mostly contributing to what David Huron accurately described in 1990 as a "dearth of published factual and critical literature . . . the pertinent analytic literature [being] surprisingly rarefied." See Huron, "Review of Stephen H. Barnes" (1990), 183–84.

22. Three informative studies present themselves as a comprehensive analysis of muzak (and related avatars): Husch, *Music of the Workplace* (1984); Barnes, *Muzak ®: The Hidden Message in Music* (1988); and, finally, Lanza, *Elevator Music* (1994).

23. See Muzak Corp. self-celebratory anniversary website: http://75.muzak.com/#/future/ (last accessed January 2010).

24. While not referenced on Muzak's commemorative website, the soundtrack to their "Future" comes from the track "Man Seeks the Future," in *Attilio Mineo Conducts / Man in Space with Sounds* [1962], Seattle World's Fair LP.

25. Here, the term *transcription* does not refer to any sort of arrangement or orchestration of the music. As Alexander Russo explained: "The term *transcription* encompassed a number of different but related technologies, practices, and aesthetic principles. Its primary use was to differentiate programs produced especially for radio broadcasts from commercially available phonograph records. While related to popular phonograph technology, transcriptions were more complicated and more expensive, and they possessed a higher level of sound quality. The individual

records were larger and rotated more slowly; sixteen inches across spun at 33 rpm, compared with phonographs' 10-inch diameter and 78-rpm speed." See "Defensive Transcriptions: Radio Networks, Sound-on-Disc Recording, and the Meaning of Live Broadcasting," *The Velvet Light Trap* 54 (Fall 2004): 5. Different types of transcription were recorded: "As the uses of the transcription came later to be classified in the jargon of the trade, the most important are: 1) 'Tailor made' transcriptions recording an entire program complete with sponsor's lugs. Such transcriptions may be made in advance of broadcast time, or the initial broadcast may be transcribed at the time of performance for subsequent rebroadcast. 2) 'Open end' transcriptions recording a complete program with blank spots for later insertion of announcements. 3) 'Spot commercials' recording a commercial plug for incessant re-use in the manner made notorious by the Pepsi-Cola jingle. 4) 'Library' transcriptions made without commercial plugs or blanks therefore, for use on sustaining programs." See Vern Countryman, "The Organized Musicians: II," *The University of Chicago Law Review* 16, no. 2 (winter 1949): 250.

26. Unlike commercial recordings, Muzak's ones "were made at 33-1/3 r.p.m., vertically engraved. These were the forerunners of the LP's that would not become commercially available until after World War II." Barnes, *Muzak: The Hidden Messages in Music* (1988), 67–68.

27. On this issue, see Anderson, "Buried under the Fecundity of His Own Creations" (2004), 232–69.

28. "A Tough Fight Looms," *Variety*, Wednesday, June 17, 1942, p. 41.

29. The AFM was the strongest union in the radio and recording fields, counting 231,202 members in early 1948: "practically every musician in the United States who plays for compensation is a member." See Lunde, "The American Federation of Musicians and the Recording Ban" (1948), 45.

30. James Petrillo, quoted in "Job Stealing," *Variety*, Wednesday, July 10, 1942, 39.

31. See Anderson, "Buried under the Fecundity of His Own Creations" (2004), 237–38, quoting "A.F. of M. Prohibits Making Recordings: President Petrillo Sets July 31st as Deadline for Members to Make Recordings and Transcriptions," *The International Musician* (July 1942): 1. In a nation at war, the strike was received with resistance. As Tim Anderson indicates, the actions of the AFM were perceived as potentially affecting the morale of the nation. In this context, researchers in industrial music were also promoting the idea according to which "[it] may well be that the future factory not employing music will be as out of place in the industrial picture as the crossbow in modern warfare" (Cardinell, *Music in Industry* [1944], 9). Even though Petrillo claimed that the AFM members would continue, "at the request of [their] commander-in-chief," to make recording for "the armed forces of the United States and its allies," the Director of the Office of War Information made a public appeal, urging Petrillo to "call off his ultimatum stopping union members from making phonograph records and radio transcriptions." James Petrillo quoted in "A.F.M. to Fight Canned Rivals," *Variety*, Wednesday, June 10, 1942, 27, and "Pass Up Fight for U.S's Sake," *Variety*, July 29, 1942 (front page).

32. A particularly interesting source in this regard is Maurice Mermey, "The Vanishing Fiddler," *The North American Review* 227, no. 3 (March 1929): 301–7.

33. "Taking Liberties with Folks' Habits," AFM paid advertising in the "Film Reviews" section of *Variety*, Wednesday, November 6, 1929, 31.

34. John Philip Sousa, "The Menace of Mechanical Music," *Appleton's Magazine* 8, no. 3 (September 1906): 278–84.

35. "Shall we not expect that when the nation once more sounds its call to arms and the gallant regiment marches forth, there will be no majestic drum major, no serried ranks of sonorous trombones, no glittering array of brass, no rolling of drums? In their stead will be a huge phonograph, mounted on a 100 H. P. automobile, grinding out 'The Girl I left Behind Me,' 'Dixie,' and 'The Stars and Stripes Forever.'" John Philip Sousa, ibid., 282.

36. "A Tough Fight Looms," *Variety*, Wednesday, June 17, 1942, 41.

37. Charles Williams, "Mr. Petrillo's Hopeless War," *The Nation*, October 3, 1942, 291.

38. In 1930, reported Anders S. Lunde, "the AFM lodged an ineffectual complaint with the Federal Radio Commission, requesting that the radio use of records be controlled or eliminated." Lunde, "The American Federation of Musicians and the Recording Ban" (1948), 47.

39. Leiter, *The Musician and Petrillo* (1953), 67.

40. Ibid., 70–71.

41. Ibid., 71.

42. "Muzak Picks Boom for Ops," *Billboard*, March 2, 1946, 92–95. See also Barnes, *Muzak: The Hidden Messages in Music* (1988), 70: "In all but Chicago, Muzak and its franchise holders had signed agreements with the A.F. of M. locals guaranteeing not to sell its services in restaurants where its installation would mean the dismissal of musicians or the reduction in their playing time."

43. "Canned Music Service Cut Off by Hotels in Jurisdictional Fight," *Chicago Daily Tribune*, July 24, 1949, 2.

44. Ibid. This fight was not the first of its kind: "in 1944 Petrillo led the union in a campaign to employ musicians as platter turners, technicians who would specialize in operating record players at union wages." See Anderson, "Buried under the Fecundity of His Own Creations" (2004), 257.

45. "Petrillo 'Unfair' Howls Chicago Muzak Licensee," *Variety*, Tuesday, October 18, 1950, 6.

46. "Chi AFM Local Settles Fracas With Muzak Over Disk-Spinners' Union," *Variety*, Wednesday, August 2, 1950.

47. For more details on the early Muzak networks, see Lillian G. Genn in "Music by Muzak," *New York Times*, October 12, 1941, X7.

48. A good account of the early history of Muzak is provided in Sidney Hyman, *The Lives of William Benton* (Chicago: University of Chicago Press, 1969), 211–39.

49. Lawrence Lader, "Music That Nobody Hears," *Nation's Business* 38, no. 9 (September 1950): 60. Published by the Chamber of Commerce of the United States.

50. See Cardinell, Burris-Meyer, and Lewis, "Music as an Aid to Healing" (1947), 545. The meaning of "a good thing" (humanitarian purpose? scientific progress? financial operation? all of the above?) remains purposefully vague.

51. In her 1945 guide to music in industry, Barbara Elna Benson, who also refers to studies conducted by the War Production Board, mentions Fellows Gear Shaper, Jack and Heintz, and RCA Victor as the leaders in industrial broadcasting. See Benson, *Music and Sound Systems in Industry* (1945), 11. Her study reveals that the material used for broadcasting was coming from three major companies: Columbia, Decca, and RCA Victor (or affiliated to the last).

52. Lawrence Lader, "Music That Nobody Hears," *Nation's Business* 38, no. 9 (September 1950): 60. Published by the Chamber of Commerce of the United States.

53. Stanley Green, "Music to Hear, But Not to Listen To," *Saturday Review*, Special Issue: "Ten Years of Recording," September 28, 1957, 55.

54. The Melachrino Strings and Orchestra, *Music for Reading*, RCA, LPS 1002, c. 1958. Liner notes by Richard Gehman.

55. *More Music For Relaxation* (RCA Victor LPM-2278, 1961).

56. *The Living Strings: Music to Help You Stop Smoking* (RCA Camden, CAL-821, 1964).

57. *Background Music: Music Blended to Mix Graciously with Social Gatherings—Songs for Harmonizing* (Capitol Records T472).

58. The Mystic Moods Orchestra, *Erogenous* (Warner Bros. Records, BS 2786, 1974).

59. Liner notes by Richard Gehman for the Melachrino Strings and Orchestra, *Music for Reading*, c. 1958. It would be misleading to assume that music as a form of "interior design" faded along with the recognizable sounds of such records. As Adam Krims observed recently, music as a functional product is more than ever contributing to a general social dynamic, facilitating what he aptly calls the "design-intensive production of the self." Hence titles like *Bach for Relaxation* offer only the most obvious examples of how major music companies, bypassing the need for rerecording, repackage their catalogue "under 'lifestyle' labels." Today, these lifestyle labels constitute "some of the preeminent vehicles of classical recordings to the general public." From Bach to Beethoven and from Sviatoslav Richter to Yo-Yo Ma, any values attached to the independent greatness of the music and/or the performances are easily subsumed into these lifestyle labels and incorporated into the larger "function of classical recordings to characterize and design an interior space." See Krims, *Music and Urban Geography* (2007), 138, 146.

60. See Walter Benjamin's remarks in "The Work of Art in the Age of Reproducibility" (1936), 119–20.

61. *New York Times* advertisement, April 28, 1940, 151.

62. *New York Times* advertisement, June 12, 1963, 87.

63. Liner note MUZAK® *Reveille*, MUZAK H-1 (1) 35B AB284V1H9 (SYB-488/489), 1969.

64. Woodley, "Music by Muzak" (1971), 10.

65. Michel Foucault, "The Subject and Power," *Critical Inquiry* 8, no. 4 (Summer 1982): 784 (this part originally written in English by Foucault).

66. "Absenteeism Down 7% / Production Up 9%." Full-page Muzak advertisement, *Fortune* (September 1957): 63.

67. Rabinbach, "The Aesthetics of Production in the Third Reich" (1976), 51. The author quotes Charles Fourier, *Design for Utopia*, trans. Julia Franklin (New York 1971), 164.

68. Ibid.

69. Hugo Munsterberg, *Grundzuge der Psychotecbnik* (Leipzig 1914), quoted in Rabinbach, ibid., 52.

70. Rabinbach, *The Human Motor* (1990), 291.

71. Hugo Munsterberg, *Grundzuge der Psychotecbnik* (Leipzig 1914), quoted in Rabinbach, "The Aesthetics of Production in the Third Reich" (1976), 52.

72. Jones and Schumacher, "Muzak: On Functional Music and Power" (1992), 157.

73. Harry E. Houghton (president of Muzak Corp.) in James Francis Cooke, "Music Brings New Joy to Life and Work," *The Etude—Music Magazine*, Philadelphia (May 1946): 246.

74. Rabinbach, *The Human Motor* (1990), 291.

75. Hugo Munsterberg, *Grundzuge der Psychotecbnik* (1914), quoted in Rabinbach, "The Aesthetics of Production in the Third Reich" (1976), 52.

76. Rabinbach, "Science, Work, and Worktime" (1993), 53–54.

77. Ibid.

78. Wyatt and Langdon, *Fatigue and Boredom in Repetitive Work* (1937). The board included a member of the government, professors of psychology, and representatives of various industries.

79. Ibid., iii.

80. See Michel Foucault, "La naissance de la médecine sociale" (1977), *Dits et écrits*, vol. III (Paris: Gallimard, 1994), 214.

81. Cardinell and Burris-Meyer, "Music in Industry Today" (1947), 548. The full quote reads: "Music in industry can only operate through the psycho-physical responses of the person who hears it. Its primary objective must be limited, therefore, to what is possible in that field, i.e., *the establishment and maintenance of a desired emotional relationship between the man, his work, and his environment.*"

82. Wyatt and Langdon, *Fatigue and Boredom in Repetitive Work* (1937), iii.

83. Ibid., 65.

84. Ibid.

85. Ibid., 31.

86. Ibid.

87. Ibid., 34–35.

88. Ibid.

89. Ibid., 43.

90. Ibid.

91. Ibid., 34. Workers were not only questioned ("Is there any other job in the factory which you would like? Why?"), but subjected to batteries of test to determine their intelligence, their ability to "think of other things while they work" (tying knots in pieces of string as fast as they could while being asked questions); their "creativity"; or their perseverance (alternating between writing Ss for thirty seconds and inverted Ss for thirty seconds, and concluding by two minutes of writing S followed by an inverted S, etc.). Ibid., 32.

92. Ibid., 42.

93. Figures given by Soibelman, *Therapeutic and Industrial Uses of Music: A Review of the Literature* (1948), 176.

94. Beckett, *Music in War Plants* (1943), 10.

95. Emery R. Hayhurst, M.D., and Leonard Greenburg, Ph.D, "Industrial Hygiene," *American Journal of Public Health* (November 17, 1927): 1192.

96. Halpin, "Industrial Music and Morale" (1943), 118–23.

97. Ibid.

98. Ibid.

99. Beckett, *Music in War Plants* (1943), 11.

100. Ibid., 7.

101. Richard Freymann, "Music While You Work," *The Musical Times* 82, no. 1185 (November 1941): 397.

102. W. R. Anderson, "Round about Radio," *The Musical Times* 83, no. 1197 (November 1942): 336.

103. Korczynski and Jones, "Instrumental Music? The Social Origins of Broadcast Music in British Factories" (2006), 148. Numbers based on Public Record Office file LAB 76/7, the Welfare of Industrial Workers (War History), by M. E. Rayner, Official Histories (Civil) Manpower Section, particularly Appendix 2.

104. Wyatt and Langdon, *Fatigue and Boredom in Repetitive Work* (1937), 6.

105. Ibid., 9.

106. Ibid., 31.

107. Ibid., 9.

108. "The Boredom of Repetition Work," *The British Medical Journal* 1, no. 3982 (May 1, 1937): 924. (Review of Wyatt and Langdon, *Fatigue and Boredom in Repetitive Work*.)

109. Ibid., 925.

110. Beckett, *Music in War Plants*, 14.

111. "The Boredom of Repetition Work," (1937), 924.

112. Cardinell and Burris-Meyer, "Music in Industry Today" (1947), 548–49.

113. Cardinell, Burris-Meyer, and Lewis, "Music as an Aid to Healing" (1947), 545.

114. Ibid. Still, the authors ultimately admitted their limited comprehension of the phenomenon by stressing clearly that there existed no "basis that can be accepted as medically valid" to prove that music is a therapy. "No existing techniques,

for the use of music with patients," they recognized with visible reluctance, "have general medical acceptance beyond the admission that entertaining music for the convalescent is desirable."

115. Wyatt and Langdon, *Fatigue and Boredom in Repetitive Work* (1937), 39.
116. Ibid.
117. Beckett, *Music in War Plants* (1943), 14.
118. Ibid.
119. Ibid., 13.
120. Wyatt and Langdon, *Fatigue and Boredom in Repetitive Work* (1937), 42.
121. Beckett, *Music in War Plants* (1943), 56.
122. Ibid., 12.
123. Wurtzler, *Electric Sounds: Technological Change and the Rise of Corporate Media* (2007), 199.
124. Beckett, *Music in War Plants* (1943), 56.
125. Benson, *Music and Sound Systems in Industry* (1945), 25.
126. Ibid.
127. Cardinell, Burris-Meyer, and Lewis, "Music as an Aid to Healing" (1947), 545.
128. Ibid.
129. Jane Jarvis, "Notes on Muzak," in Hitchcock, ed., *The Phonograph and Our Musical Life* (1977), 17.
130. Hutchinson, BBC Memo, July 10, 1940. Quoted in Korczynski and Jones, "Instrumental Music?" (2006), 149.
131. Beckett, *Music in War Plants* (1943), 46.
132. Ibid.
133. Ibid.
134. See Selvin, "Programming Music for Industry" (1943), 131, and Cardinell and Burris-Meyer, "Music in Industry Today" (1947), 548.
135. Cardinell and Burris-Meyer, "Music in Industry Today" (1947), 549.
136. Sterne, "Sounds Like the Mall of America" (1997), 31.
137. Ibid.
138. Lanza, *Elevator Music* (1994), 5.
139. Ibid., 3.
140. "Muzak 60th Anniversary: A Billboard Advertising Supplement," *Billboard* (October 29, 1994): 92.
141. Ibid.
142. Joseph Lanza, foreword to *Elevator Music* (1994).
143. "Muzak 60th Anniversary: A Billboard Advertising Supplement" (1994), 98.
144. "Why Muzak?" Muzak Website FAQ Section: http://music.muzak.com/why_muzak/faq/ (last accessed December 2010).
145. Sterne, "Sounds Like the Mall of America" (1997), 30.
146. Michel Foucault, "The Ethics of the Concern for Self as a Practice of Freedom," interview conducted by Raul Fornet-Betancourt, Helmut Becker, and Alfredo

Gomez-Muller on January 20, 1984, first published in *Concordia* 6, [Valencia, Spain], translated by Phillis Aranov and Dan McGrawth, in Sylvère Lotringer, ed., *Foucault Live, Collected Interviews, 1961–1984* (New York: Semiotext(e), 1989, 1996), 433.

147. Michael Hardt and Antonio Negri, *Empire* (Cambridge, Mass.: Harvard University Press, 2000), 150.

148. Michel Foucault, "The Ethics of the Concern for Self as a Practice of Freedom" (1984), 433.

149. Sterne, "Sounds Like the Mall of America" (1997), 32.

150. Muzak promotional brochure: http://music.muzak.com/assets/pdf/The-Positive-Impact.pdf (last accessed November 23, 2010).

151. Barnes, *The Hidden Messages in Music* (1988), 135.

152. Rabinbach, "Science, Work, and Worktime" (1993), 49.

153. Groom, "The Condition of Muzak" (1996), 3.

154. Ibid. p. 8. The author refers to Joseph Lanza, *Elevator Music* (1994).

155. See Jones and Schumacher, "Muzak: On the Functional Music and Power" (1992), 156. The authors precisely trace and perfectly summarize the limitations of the general discourse on Muzak: "Muzak has traditionally been criticized from one of two positions: either on aesthetic and musical grounds, as a form of sonic banality, musical 'castration,' or 'wallpaper music,' or as an instance of cultural totalitarianism, reproducing an ideology of bureaucratic rationalism and perpetuating alienation and false consciousness. In striving to avoid both of the positions, out intentions here are not to critique muzak as *music* per se, nor to reduce muzak to an unambiguous reflection of a monolithic, 'dominant ideology'" (156–57).

156. The "Hawthorne effect" was demonstrated in a research project led between 1927 and 1932 at the Hawthorne Plant of the Western Electric Company in Cicero, Illinois. See Huron, "Review: *Muzak: The Hidden Messages in Music*" (1990), 183–84.

157. Groom, "The Condition of Muzak" (1996), 8.

158. Charles Rosen, "Popular Art," in *The Romantic Generation* (Cambridge, Mass.: Harvard University Press, 1995, 1998), 602.

159. In Italian the term *tormentone* means a "hit" that indeed torments the mind of the listener. For a fascinating study of this phenomenon, see Szendy, *Tubes: la philosophie dans le juke-box* (2008).

160. Vadim Prokhorov, "Can't Get It Out of My Head," *The Guardian*, June 22, 2006. The pioneering inquiry into the painful phenomenon of earworms has been conducted by a professor of marketing—Dr. Kellaris—specialized in the study of "affective, cognitive, and behavioral influences of music on consumers, including effects of music in advertisements and retail environments." As a marketing tool, "earworms" certainly appear to be both valuable (to sell a song, and/or a product associated with it) and rather dangerous (because an "earworm" possesses a strong irritating potential). Still, a major question remains: whether one wants to exterminate earworms or produce them, what causes them? At first, as many critics of Muzak have argued, Dr. Kellaris thought that "the answer could be found in certain properties of music that make some songs 'catchy' or 'sticky.'" However, this expert in marketing

came to the conclusion that "although many earworms seem to share some common traits (e.g., simplicity, repetitiveness, incongruity with listeners' expectations), virtually *any* song can become an earworm for some people." Interestingly, suggests Kellaris, it does not appear to be enough for a "catchy" tune to adhere to certain standards (say, a "simple" tune and a steady beat), it also needs to depart from them to "hit" us and get trapped in the ear. Still, while Kellaris recognized that there exists "some interesting, albeit speculative theories" about how songs become stuck in one's head, the most assertive answer to the question remains: "no one knows for certain." See James Kellaris, "Earworms Research" webpage, University of Cincinnati, College of Business, http://www.business.uc.edu/earworms/FAQs#1 (last accessed December 2009). See also Szendy, *Tubes: la philosophie dans le juke-box* (2008), 12.

161. *New Dimensions, Volume 2* (Muzak SLP 8732/8733 [SXB-629A/630B]).

162. Cardinell and Burris-Meyer, "Music in Industry Today" (1947), 548–49. Moreover, opposing the individualization of music and/or musical choices to their standardization does not seem to be a tenable position. As Adorno argued: "The necessary correlate of musical standardization is *pseudo-individualization*. By pseudo-individualization we mean endowing cultural mass production with the halo of free choice or open market on the basis of standardization itself. Standardization of song hits keeps the customers in line by doing their listening for them, as it were. Pseudo-individualization, for its part, keeps them in line by making them forget that what they listen to is already listened to for them, or 'pre-digested.' / The most drastic example of standardization of presumably individualized features is to be found in so-called improvisations. Even though jazz musicians still improvise in practice, their improvisations have become so 'normalized' as to enable a whole terminology to be developed to express the standard devices of individualization: a terminology which in turn is ballyhooed by jazz publicity agents to foster the myth of pioneer artisanship and at the same time flatter the fans by apparently allowing them to peep behind the curtain and get the inside story. This pseudo-individualization is prescribed by the standardization of the framework." "On popular Music" (1941), in *Essays on Music*. 445.

163. Sterne, "Sounds Like the Mall of America" (1997), 29.

164. Advertising (full-page), "Key Punch Production Highest in 11 Years," *Fortune* (October 1956): 91.

165. Advertising (full-page), "Paper Work or Paper Play?" *Fortune* (October 1962): 6.

166. Muzak promotional brochure: http://music.muzak.com/assets/pdf/The-Positive-Impact.pdf (last accessed November 23, 2009).

167. Advertising (full-page), "Key Punch Production Highest in 11 Years."

168. Muzak promotional brochure: http://music.muzak.com/assets/pdf/The-Positive-Impact.pdf (last accessed November 23, 2009). The company references R. E. Milliman, "Using Background Music to Affect Behavior of Supermarket Shoppers," *Journal of Marketing* 46 (1982): 86–91.

169. Milliman, "Using Background Music to Affect Behavior of Supermarket Shoppers" (1982), 87.

170. Ibid.
171. Ibid., 91.
172. Ibid., 90.
173. Ibid.
174. Catherine M. Windwer, "An Ascending Music Stimulus Program and Hyperactive Children," *Journal of Research in Music Education* 29, no. 3 (Autumn 1981): 176.
175. Ibid., 175.
176. Muzak's seventy-fifth anniversary website: http://75.muzak.com/#/1930s/ (last accessed December 2010). Italics mine.
177. Woodley, "Music by Muzak" (1971), 6.
178. Wokoun, *Vigilance with Background Music* (1963).
179. Dubé et al., "The Effects of Background Music" (1995), 305–19.
180. Respectively: Curtis Nels Dollins, "The Use of Background Music in a Psychiatric Hospital to Increase Group Conversational Frequency," MMEd. thesis, University of Kansas, 1956; and D. T. Sommer, "The Effect of Background Music on Frequency of Interaction in Group Psychotherapy," *Music Therapy* 7 (1957): 167–68.
181. Dubé et al., "The Effects of Background Music" (1995), 306.
182. Ibid., 314.
183. Ibid.
184. Ibid., 306.
185. Ibid., 307.
186. Ibid., 311. Such procedures, as Milliman pointed out, are more evidently concerned with the effects of music on attitudes than on behavior. For his part, Milliman discovered only "a weak relationship" between attitude measures (*smile*) and actual behavior (*buy*). Furthermore, he insists, many conclusions on behavioral change are simply derived from the observation that "a majority of corporations that provide music for their employees 'believed' that this improved worker morale and relieved job monotony," just as "[store] managers expressed the 'belief' that their customers bought more as a result of the background music." In the end, Milliman concludes, one is confronted by studies that had "examined attitudes or beliefs rather than behavior, although each concluded with generalizations about behavior." A similar disjunct was noticed in a 1966 study on the effects of music on employee attitude and productivity: while workers demonstrated a "highly favorable attitude toward music and thought they did more work with it, there was no change in measured productivity." In the end, it is certainly less essential to condemn the dominantly positivist rhetoric of marketing than to try to understand the context in which it has been shaped and, concurrently, why and how Muzak's image gained credentials beyond credibility. R. E. Milliman, "Using Background Music to Affect Behavior of Supermarket Shoppers," *Journal of Marketing* 46 (1982): 86–87. Richard I. Newman Jr. and Donald L. Hunt, "Effects of Music on Employee Attitude and Productivity in a Skateboard Factory," *Journal of Applied Psychology* 50, no. 6 (December 1966): 493.

187. Frank Adams, "Bomber Hits the Empire State Building," *New York Times*, Sunday, July 29, 1945, section 1, 25.

188. See "San Francisco's Assessor Tells Story of the Wreck of the Titanic from Which He Escapes after Thrilling Experience," *The Bulletin*, San Francisco, April 19, 1912.

189. Brian Eno, "Ambient Music," 1978 liner notes, also reprinted in Eno, *A Year with Swollen Appendices: Brian Eno's Diary* (1996), 298.

190. Ibid.

191. Ibid.

192. Ibid.

193. Ibid., 295.

194. Quoted (loosely) by Genesis P. Orridge, "Muzak: A Concept in Muzak Engineering," *Vague* 16/17 (1984): 60. This article contains some low-quality reproductions of Muzak's promotional material used as a source for the article. In 1975, Genesis P. Orridge's musical outlet Throbbing Gristle had responded to Muzak's aesthetic, with the experimental noise-oriented *Final Muzak*. In *The First Annual Report (or The First Annual Report of Throbbing Gristle)*, Spurt Records, Genetic Terrorists, Thirsty Ear (THI57105.2).

195. Ibid., 60.

196. Muzak's chief programmer is quoted by Richard Henderson in "The Pioneering Firm's 'Functional Music' Has Upped Production, Aided the War Effort and Been to the Moon: What's Next for the Ambient Champion?" in "Muzak 60th Anniversary: A Billboard Advertising Supplement," *Billboard* (October 29, 1994): 96.

197. Iannis Xenakis quoted by Le Corbusier in *Modulor 2 / 1955 / (Let the User Speak Next) / Continuation of 'The Modulor' 1948* (London: Faber and Faber, 1958), 326.

198. Sterne, "Sounds Like the Mall of America" (1997), 23.

199. Ibid., 30–31.

200. Ibid.

201. Gyorgy Kepes, introduction to Kepes, ed., *The Nature of Art and Motion*, Vision + Value Series (New York: George Braziller, 1965), vi–vii.

202. Griffiths, *Cage* (1981), 38.

203. Janet Kraynak, "Dependent Participation: Bruce Nauman's Environments," *Grey Room* 10 (Winter 2003): 24.

204. Cage "[Memoir]" (1966) in Kostelanetz, ed., *John Cage: An Anthology* (1970, 1991), 77.

Chapter 3. Muzak-Plus and the Art of Participation

1. Cage, "The Future of Music" (1974), in Cage, *Empty Words: Writings '73–'78* (1980), 177. See also Cage, foreword to *A Year from Monday* (1967), ix: "The reason I am less and less interested in music is not only that I find environmental sounds

and noises more useful aesthetically than the sounds produced by the world's musical cultures, but that, when you get right down to it, a composer is simply someone who tells other people what to do. I find this an unattractive way of getting things done."

2. In 1961, for example, Cage stated: "I can see perfectly that, if I liked vibraphone, the world would be more open to me. In the same way, if I liked Muzak, which I also don't, the world would be more open to me. I intend to work on it. The simplest thing for me to do in order to come to terms with both things would be to use them in my work, and this was, I believe, how so-called primitive people dealt with animals which frightened them." Cage in "Interview with Roger Reynolds" (1961), in Schwartz and Childs, *Contemporary Composers on Contemporary Music* (1967), 338. This interview was first published in *Generation Magazine* (Ann Arbor, Mich., 1962), before being reprinted in the 1962 catalogue of the composers' scores and compositions [Cage and White] *John Cage* (New York: Henmar Press and C. F. Peters Editions, 1962), and later in *The Musical Quarterly* 65, no. 4 (October 1979): 573–94, as "John Cage and Roger Reynolds: A Conversation."

3. In "Music for Dining," *Food Service Magazine / The Merchandising Journal of the Food Industry* (May 1957): n.p. (Muzak promotional material).

4. Cage, Shattuck, and Gillmor, "Erik Satie: A Conversation," (1973), 22.

5. Cage, "Interview with Roger Reynolds" (1961), in Schwartz and Childs, *Contemporary Composers on Contemporary Music* (1967), 338.

6. McLuhan and Fiore, *The Medium Is the Massage* (1967), n.p. Less than twenty years later, McLuhan and Cage's exaltation was turned into a lament by a composer: "With any other medium," reportedly said the composer Jacob Druckman to the *New York Times* about the nuisance of muzak, "you can turn your back or close your eyes, but there is no escape from music." See Will Crutchfield, "Music by Musak: Orchestrating the Workday," *New York Times*, September 1, 1984, 9.

7. Quoted in Michael MacDonald, "Empire and Communication: The Media Wars of Marshall McLuhan," *Media, Culture & Society* 28, no. 4 (2006): 505.

8. Cage, "McLuhan's Influence" (1967), in Kostelanetz, ed., *John Cage: An Anthology*, 170–71.

9. McLuhan, "The Invisible Environment" (1967), 165.

10. Ibid.

11. Letter from John Cage to Billy Klüver, June 31, 1965 (*sic*). This unpublished letter was shown in 2006 in the exhibition *9 Evenings Reconsidered: Art, Theatre and Engineering, 1966* (Catherine Morris, curator) at MIT's List Visual Art Center, Cambridge, Mass.

12. Cornelius Cardew, "John Cage—Ghost or Monster?" originally published in *The Listener*, BBC Publications, May 4, 1972, reprinted in *Leonardo Music Journal* 8, nos. 3–4 (1998).

13. Ibid.

14. McLuhan, "The Invisible Environment" (1967), 165.

15. Ibid.

16. Ibid.

17. Cage "[Memoir]" (1966) in Kostelanetz, ed., *John Cage: An Anthology* (1970, 1991), 77.

18. For an insight on Lev Termen's career, see for example Stephen Montague, "Rediscovering Leon Theremin," *Tempo* 177 (June 1991): 18–23.

19. Cage, "The Music of the Future: Credo" (1937), in Cage, *Silence* (1961), 4.

20. See promotional material for Lev Termen's Terpsiton (or Tersitone), illustrated in *Radio-Craft* (December 1936), reproduced in Bulat M. Galeyev, "L. S. Termen: Faustus of the Twentieth Century," *Leonardo* 24, no. 5 (1991): 573–79.

21. Cage, "The Music of the Future: Credo" (1937), in Cage, *Silence* (1961), 4.

22. Ibid.

23. Cage, Shattuck, and Gillmor, "Erik Satie: A Conversation" (1973), 22.

24. This was an early concern for Cage, as his 1937 appreciation of Schoenberg's dodecaphonic system suggests: "Schoenberg's method assigns to each material, in a group of equal materials, its function with respect to the group. (Harmony assigned to each material, in a group of unequal materials, its function with respect to the fundamental or most important material in the group.) Schoenberg's method is analogous to modern society, in which the emphasis is on the group and the integration of the individual in the group." Cage, "The Music of the Future: Credo" (1937), in Cage, *Silence* (1961), 5.

25. Radano, "Interpreting Muzak: Speculations on Musical Experience in Everyday Life" (1989), 457–58.

26. Kirby, *Happenings* (1965), 1.

27. Claes Oldenburg quoted in Goldberg, *Performance: Live Art 1909 to Present* (1979), 87.

28. Following Cornelius Cardew's clarification in "Notation: Interpretation, etc.," *Tempo*, New Series, no. 58 (Summer 1961): 21.

29. Cornelius Cardew, "John Cage—Ghost or Monster?" originally published in *The Listener*, BBC Publications (May 4, 1972), reprinted in *Leonardo Music Journal* 8, nos. 3–4, (1998).

30. Ibid.

31. Allan Kaprow, *Some Recent Happenings*, Great Bear Pamphlet, (New York: Something Else Press, 1966), 5.

32. Ibid.

33. Ibid.

34. Marinetti quoted in Goldberg, *Performance: Live Art 1909 to Present* (1979), 21.

35. Cage, "A Composer's Confessions" (1948), in Kostelanetz, ed., *John Cage, Writer / Selected Texts* (1993), 43.

36. Ibid.

37. Christopher Shultis's interpretation reads: "This 'single idea' became a process of making music that Cage learned from Ananda Coomeraswamy [*sic*]: 'I have for many years accepted, and I still do, the doctrine about Art, occidental and oriental, set forth by Ananda K. Coomeraswamy [*sic*] in his book *The Transformation of Nature*

in Art, that the function of art is to imitate Nature in her manner of operation.' Cage used the *I Ching* as a way of 'imitating nature in her manner of operation,' and by constructing his 4'33" through chance operations, he did indeed find a method of making a process parallel to the seductiveness of 'the color and shape and fragrance of a flower.'" Shultis, "Silencing the Sounded Self: John Cage and the Intentionality of Nonintention" (1995), 319 (Shultis quotes from Cage, *A Year from Monday*, 31).

38. Ananda K. Coomaraswamy, *The Transformation of Nature in Art* (Cambridge, Mass.: Harvard University Press, 1934; Dover, 1956), 15.

39. Gann, *No Such Thing as Silence* (2010), 132–33.

40. On this issue, see Barnes, *Muzak ®: The Hidden Messages in Music* (1988), 48–64.

41. The origin of the term is commonly attributed to the composer John Philip Sousa, who used it in his article "The Menace of Mechanical Music," *Appleton's Magazine* 8, no. 3 (September 1906): 278–84.

42. "He receives $46,000 a year in addition to a generous expense account, maintains a suite at the Waldorf, rides around in a huge bullet-proof car, employs six or seven bodyguards, four of whom are relatives." Charles Williams, "Mr. Petrillo's Hopeless War," *The Nation* (October 3, 1942): 291.

43. See Jack Gould, "Portrait of the Unpredictable Petrillo," *New York Times*, December 28, 1947, SM11: "'Canned music,' . . . in non-union parlance means any music not provided by musicians in the flesh." From this point of view, it is difficult to follow Douglas Kahn when he argues: "The fact that it was canned recalls the ready-mades of Marcel Duchamp, with whose work Cage was quite familiar." See "John Cage: Silence and Silencing," 571.

44. Petrillo first urged the 140,000 union members to refuse employment to make new recordings after July 31, 1942 (at midnight). The strike lasted until the fall of 1943. The second ban of the same nature lasted from December 31, 1947, to mid-December 1948. For a detailed analysis of the AFM strikes, see part I of Tim J. Anderson, *Making Easy Listening: Material Culture and Postwar American Recording* (Minneapolis: University of Minnesota Press, 2006). Since the late 1920s, at least, the AFM had campaigned to raise public awareness of the substitution of "Real Music" by "Canned Music." (See the leaflet titled "MR. EXHIBITOR!! Do you want your theatre called: FIRST CLASS?" published by the AFM in *Variety*, Wednesday, November 20, 1929.)

45. Cage, "A Composer's Confessions" (1948), in Kostelanetz, ed., *John Cage, Writer / Selected Texts* (1993), 43.

46. An early formulation of Kahn's argument appeared in "The Latest: Fluxus and Music," catalogue *In the Spirit of Fluxus*, curated by Elizabeth Armstrong and Joan Rothfuss, Walker Art Center, Minneapolis, 1993. It was developed in Douglas Kahn, "John Cage: Silence and Silencing" (1997). A modified version of this article was incorporated to Kahn's opus *Noise, Water, Meat: A History of Sound in the Arts* (1999), 161–99. Subsequent references to Kahn's argument are taken from *The Musical Quarterly*'s version.

47. Kahn, "John Cage: Silence and Silencing" (1997), 573.
48. Ibid., 557.
49. Ibid., 569 (emphasis mine).
50. Ibid., 589.
51. This expression comes from "MR. EXHIBITOR!! Do you want your theatre called: FIRST CLASS?" published by the AFM in *Variety*, Wednesday, November 20, 1929.
52. Hence, by "[silencing] the sound of a music intended as environmental" (i.e., Muzak), *Silent Prayer* would expose Cage's failure. As he presents himself as a "promulgator of musical noise," Cage—argues Kahn—is in fact "involved in the business of noise abatement." In this regard, says Kahn, *Silent Prayer* is one of the many "techniques" Cage elaborated "for eliminating, diminishing, or displacing the source of the noise, transforming the noise into something else, or canceling the noise by playing back its image, so to speak, in the negative." Kahn, "John Cage: Silence and Silencing" (1997), 576.
53. Ibid. As part of the composer's "repertoire" of silencing fantasies, Kahn refers to the speech given by the young Cage for the Southern California Oratorical Contest in 1927 ("Other People Think"), in which Cage fantasized about the birth of a Pan-American consciousness coming from the United States having "her industries halted, her business discontinued, her people speechless, a great pause in her world of affairs created, and finally to have everything stopped that runs, until everyone should hear the last wheel go around and the last echo fade away."
54. For a more recent formulation of this idea, see Bruce Mau and the Institute without Boundaries, *Massive Change* (London: Phaidon Press, 2004, 2005).
55. Vern Countryman, "The Organized Musicians: II," *The University of Chicago Law Review* 16, no. 2 (winter 1949): 266. "Elmer Davis, as Director of the Office of War Information, fanned the flames by injecting patriotism into the controversy. He announced that 'the elimination of records . . . for use in restaurants, canteens and soda parlors where members of the armed forces go for recreation, and for use in factories where war workers use juke boxes for organized relaxation' would seriously jeopardize morale 'in the critical months ahead-months which may well decide the fate of this country's war effort,' and that elimination of transcriptions would jeopardize the existence of 'several hundred' small radio stations and thus 'seriously interfere with the communication of war information and messages vital to the public security.'" Petrillo reassured the public, claiming that the AFM members would continue, "at the request of [their] commander-in-chief," to make recordings for "the armed forces of the United States and its allies," and the director of the Office of War Information made a public appeal, urging Petrillo to "call off his ultimatum stopping union members from making phonograph records and radio transcriptions." See James Petrillo quoted in "A.F.M. to Fight Canned Rivals," *Variety*, Wednesday, June 10, 1942, 27, and "Pass Up Fight for U.S's Sake," *Variety*, July 29, 1942 (front page).
56. Vern Countryman, "The Organized Musicians: II," 266. "After [the ban] had gone into effect, the only new records made in the United States were those for the armed services, government transcriptions and transcriptions of non-commercial

patriotic program." Lunde, "The American Federation of Musicians and the Recording Ban," 48.

57. Ibid., 266, footnote 250.

58. Ibid., 281–82. Bootleg activities and imports also played a part in the resistance of the disc business.

59. Miles Davis and Quincy Troupe, *Miles: The Autobiography* (London: Simon and Schuster, 1989), 108.

60. Kahn, "John Cage: Silence and Silencing" (1997), 589.

61. B. H. Haggin, "Records," *The Nation* (September 11, 1943): 305.

62. Cage, "A Composer's Confessions" (1948), in Kostelanetz, ed., *John Cage, Writer / Selected Texts* (1993), 42.

63. Kahn, "John Cage: Silence and Silencing" (1997), 569. Fundamentally, such criticism only reveals what the artist's responsibility in modern society should be according to its author. If Cage is guilty of anything in this regard, it is of not fulfilling Kahn's expectations.

64. Branden W. Joseph, "'A Therapeutic Value for City Dwellers': The Development of John Cage's Early Avant-Garde Aesthetic Position," in D. W. Patterson, ed., *John Cage: Music, Philosophy, and Intention, 1933–1950* (2002), 155.

65. John Cage, "The East and the West" (1946), in Kostelanetz, ed., *John Cage, Writer / Selected Texts* (1993), 25.

66. David Patterson, "Cage and Asia: History and Sources," in David Nicholls, ed., *The Cambridge Companion to John Cage* (2002), 41.

67. Ibid., 59.

68. Cage, "A Composer's Confessions" (1948), in Kostelanetz, ed., *John Cage, Writer / Selected Texts* (1993), 40.

69. Theoretically, Cage's attitude toward recorded music was radical and straightforward. Throughout his life, he would never miss an opportunity to criticize phonograph recording as falsifying our relationship to music by both substituting itself for "live" music and turning music into a fetish commodity. "Record collections," as he made it clear—"that is not music." "To imagine you own any piece of music," he stressed in 1950, "is to miss the whole point." On the question of live music, Cage was not even inclined to admit, as did Adorno, that while the phonograph petrifies music by removing it from the realm of live production, the technology justified itself—beyond "any aesthetic objection to its reification"—for it "rescues the ephemeral and perishing art as the only one alive" ("Lecture on Nothing," *Silence*, 125). However, as Cage explained in his "Composer's Confessions," he became interested in subverting the technology by using "recording equipment for creative rather than the customary reproducing purposes." Yet Cage was not a fanatic, and he also admitting to using recording more conventionally when necessary. In the late 1930s, when he was giving lectures on modern art, he would indeed illustrate them the lectures at the piano "when the music was easy to play," but if not, he said, "I used recordings." Last but not least, he advertised—albeit apologetically—the availability of a recording of his piece *Three Dances* (1944–45) ("A Composer's Confessions," 29, 40).

168   NOTES TO CHAPTER 3

In 1950, Cage used the following metaphor: "A lady from Texas said: I live in Texas. We have no music in Texas. The reason they've no music in Texas is because they have recordings. Remove the records from Texas and someone will learn to sing." John Cage, "Lecture on Nothing," (1950), in *Silence*, 125. And in the early 1980s: "[A recording] merely destroys one's need for real music. It substitutes artificial music for real music, and it makes people think that they're engaging in a musical activity when they're actually not. And it has completely distorted and turned upside down the function of music in anyone's experience." John Cage interviewed in Peter Greenaway, *American [Four American] Composers: John Cage, Philip Glass, Meredith Monk, Robert Ashley* (New York: Mystic Fire Video, 1991).

Theodor W. Adorno, "The Form of the Phonograph Record," (1934) translated by Thomas Y. Levin, *October* 55 (winter 1990): 59. About Cage discography, Robert Haskins mentions: "The first releases of Cage's music were made by the composer himself or by individuals in his circle, including Maro Ajemian, the contralto Arline Carmen, and the astonishingly indefinable David Tudor. The earliest release appeared around 1947 on the Disc Company of America 607 (3058A): a shellac 78-rpm record containing Ajemian's performances of two movements from *Amores* (1943). During the 1950s, the available repertoire widened to include the aforementioned Dial recording of Sonatas and Interludes; the masterful *Three Dances* for two prepared pianos (1944–45), performed by Ajemian and William Masselos and released as Disc Company of America 643–648 (three mono 78 rpm shellac phonodiscs) in 1950; and a release by the New Music String Quartet performing his String Quartet in Four Parts (1949—50) on Columbia (ML 4495) in 1953." Robert Haskins, "John Cage and Recorded Sound: A Discographical Essay," *Notes* 67, no. 2 (December 2010): 383.

70. Pritchett, "What Silence Taught John Cage," in Julia Robinson (curator) *The Anarchy of Silence: John Cage and Experimental Art* (2009),170.

71. Kahn, "John Cage: Silence and Silencing" (1997), 574.

72. Or, as Brandon LaBelle writes, by attempting to "wipe away Muzak's insidious presence in the spaces of everyday life—for Muzak serves the machinery of the status quo built upon consumer society." LaBelle, *Background Noise: Perspectives on Sound Art* (2006), 10.

73. "How can a silent piece open with any idea at all?" writes Gann in *No Such Thing as Silence* (2010), 141.

74. Pritchett, "What Silence Taught John Cage" in Julia Robinson (curator), *The Anarchy of Silence: John Cage and Experimental Art* (2009), 170.

75. Cage, "Lecture on Nothing" (1950) in Cage, *Silence* (1961), 117.

76. Elizabeth Hellmuth Margulis, "Moved by Nothing: Listening to Musical Silence," *Journal of Music Theory* 51, no. 2 (fall 2007): 246.

77. See for instance, Shultis, "Silencing the Sounded Self: John Cage and the Intentionality of Nonintention" (1995), 318–19: "the idea of a 'silent piece' was conceived earlier than 1952 . . . [it] was first publicly mentioned in an address entitled 'A Composer's Confessions.'" Also Joseph, "'A Therapeutic Value for City

Dwellers': The Development of John Cage's Early Avant-Garde Aesthetic Position," 155. In "A Composer's Confessions," "[Cage] famously announced his intention to compose a *silent piece* and a work scored exclusively for radios [realized respectively as *4'33"* and *Imaginary Landscape No 4.*]."

78. Elizabeth Hellmuth Margulis, "Silences in Music Are Musical Not Silent: An Exploratory Study of Context Effects on the Experience of Musical Pauses," *Music Perception: An Interdisciplinary Journal* 24, no. 5 (June 2007): 485. "The same acoustic silence, embedded in two different excerpts, can be perceived dramatically differently. Impressions of the music that preceded the silence seep into the gap, as do expectations about what may follow. These impressions and expectations can cause two identical acoustic silences to seem like they occupy different lengths of time, or carry different amounts of musical tension, or function differently in other ways."

79. Husch, *Music of the Workplace* (1984), 72.

80. Ibid.

81. Ibid., 64.

82. Roy Lichtenstein in "What is Pop Art, Part I," interviews with G. R. Swenson (November 1963) reprinted in Steven H. Madoff, ed., *Pop Art: A Critical History* (Berkeley: University of California Press, 1997), 107.

83. Cage "[Letter to Paul Henry Lang] (1956)," in Kostelanetz, ed., *John Cage: An Anthology* (1970, 1991), 118.

84. Cage answering Daniel Charles in Charles, *For the Birds* (1981), 137.

85. Bertolt Brecht, "The Radio as an Apparatus of Communication" (1932). Excerpt from *Brecht on Theatre*, translated and edited by Jon Willett (New York: Hill and Wang, 1964). ["Der Rundfunk als Kommunikationsapparat" in Blätter des Hessischen Landestheaters, Darmstadt, No. 16, July 1932], reprinted in John Hanhardt, ed., *Video Culture: A Critical Investigation* (Rochester, N.Y.: Visual Studies Workshop), 53–54.

86. Ibid.

87. See supra note 69. Recognizing, as does Yasunao Tone, that Cage is the most recorded of modern composers does not affect much the position of the composer regarding the technology of recording. Yasunao Tone, "John Cage and Recording," *Leonardo Music Journal* 13 (2003): 11.

88. Toop, *Ocean of Sound: Ether Talk, Ambient Sound and Imaginary Worlds* (1995), 140.

89. *Variations IV* (LP), Everest 3132, US, 1966.

90. Cage, "Composition as Process / II. Indeterminacy" (1958), in Cage, *Silence* (1961), 40.

91. Brian Eno, "The Studio as Compositional Tool," (1979) reprinted in Cox and Warner, *Audio Culture: Readings in Modern Music* (2004), 127.

92. Ibid.

93. As Eno explained: "On my record *On Land*, some of the pieces are very directly based on places that I know or knew as a child, and some of the sounds on the record are attempts at imitating precise sounds of those places. When I make this

music, the first consideration is 'Where is this music?' I say, 'What's the temperature in this piece?' because sound behaves differently in different temperatures. 'What's the humidity?' because sound behaves differently in different humidities. 'Is it an open place or does it have walls? Does it have a ceiling? Is the ceiling right on top or is it a long way away? Are the walls made of stone or wood, or are they some other material? Is the place stable or do I feel like I am not quite secure in it?' All of these things I can specify (in the studio) with reverberation." Eno quoted by Mark Prendergast, "Brian Eno: 'A fervent nostalgia for the future'—Thoughts, Words, Music and Art," *Sound on Sound* 4, no 3 (January 1989): n.p.

94. Cage, "Composition as Process / II. Indeterminacy" (1958), in Cage, *Silence* (1961), 40.

95. Ibid.

96. Ibid.

97. Reinbert De Leeuw, *Vexations*, Philips PH 410 435–1, 1983.

98. Jean Stein and George Plimpton, *Edie: American Girl* (New York: Knopf, 1982), 235.

99. Ibid.

100. Cage in Kostelanetz, *Conversing with Cage* (1988), 223.

101. Bryars, "Vexations and Its Performers" (1979), 12–20.

102. Ibid.

103. See Gilles Deleuze, *Différence et Répétition* (Paris: Presses Universitaires de France, 1968), 97, translated by Paul Patton as *Difference and Repetition* (New York: Columbia University Press, 1994), 90.

104. Cage, Shattuck, and Gillmor, "Erik Satie: A Conversation" (1973) and also Cage in Kostelanetz, *Conversing with Cage* (1988), 223.

105. Higgins, "Boredom and Danger" (1966), in *A Dialectic of Centuries*, 44.

106. Branden W. Joseph, "The Play of Repetition: Andy Warhol's *Sleep*," *Grey Room* 19 (Spring 2005):, 25.

107. Cage in Kostelanetz, *Conversing with Cage* (1988), 223.

108. Griffiths, *Cage* (1981), 38.

109. Ibid.

110. It is probable that Cage had several pieces of Satie's furniture music performed simultaneously, as he expressed this idea more than once. He intended to use them (simultaneously) in 1972, for the ballet *Un jour ou deux* at the Opéra de Paris, but was not granted the permission. Again in 1985, in his notes for the *First Meeting of the Satie Society*, Cage writes: "Throughout this meeting some music of Satie is being played in another part of the same building, not a series of short pieces but long works: an excerpt from *Vexations* for instance, or one or several or all of the *Musique d'Ameublement* played simultaneously, or the *Socrate* in the two piano arrangement by the author and Arthur Maddox." I am grateful to Ornella Volta for sharing with me Cage's original typescript of this text, kept in her collection.

111. John Dinwiddie, "Mewantemooseicday: John Cage in Davis, 1969," *Source: Music of the Avant Garde* 7 (January 1970): 24.

112. In June 1977, in preparation for the *The Phonograph and Our Musical Life* symposium scheduled in December 1977, Cage wrote to Wiley Hitchcock: "Some years ago at Davis in California (1969) I presented a piece called *33 1/3*. The lobby was filled with musicians (live) playing Satie's Musique d'A . . . When a person entered the hall, he saw it was empty except for 12 play backs, stacks of LP's, 12 lg. speakers, 12 assistants standing at the playback stations and whatever other members of the audience there were already assembled. The fact that he cd. play and/or stop a record finally dawned on each person + if he had trouble with the machine, the asst. would help." (Letter to H. Wiley Hitchcock, June 16, 1977, Collection, Northwestern University). And again, to Norman O. Brown: "Do you remember in Davis the piece called *33 and 1/3*? The audience entered a room empty of chairs but with stations from which records could be played, but by them, not by other 'performers.' Outside in the lobby, live musicians were playing the Furniture Music of Satie." Letter to Norman O. and Beth Brown, October 28, 1977, from New York Collection, Northwestern University.

113. John Cage quoted by Wiley Hitchcock, "'Response to *Address* by John Cage," in Hitchcock, ed., *The Phonograph and Our Musical Life* (1977), 1.

114. Ibid., 5.

115. Joan Peyser, "Commentary: 'The Phonograph and Our Musical Life,'" *The Musical Quarterly* 64, no. 2 (April 1978): 251.

116. Christian Marclay, "Extended Play" (1988), reprinted in Jennifer Gonzalez, Kim Gordon, and Matthew Higgs, *Christian Marclay* (New York: Phaidon Press, 2005), 132.

117. Ibid.

118. Maurice Blanchot, *La Communauté inavouable* (Paris: Les Editions de Minuit, 1983), 52–54. "'Sans projet': c'était là le trait, à la fois angoissant et fortuné, d'une forme de société incomparable qui ne se laissait pas saisir, qui n'était pas appelée à subsister, à s'installer, fût-ce à travers les multiples 'comités' par lesquels se simulait un ordre-désordonné, une spécialisation imprécise. Contrairement aux 'révolutions traditionnelles,' il ne s'agissait pas de seulement prendre le pouvoir pour le remplacer par un autre, ni de prendre la Bastille, le Palais d'hiver, l'Élysée ou l'Assemblée nationale, objectifs sans importance, et pas même de renverser un ancien monde, mais de laisser se manifester, en dehors de tout intérêt utilitaire, une possibilité d'être-ensemble qui rendait à tous le droit à l'égalité dans la fraternité par la liberté de parole qui soulevait chacun."

119. See Cage's detailed introduction to "Rhythm Etc.," in Cage, *A Year from Monday*, 120.

120. For a comprehensive inquiry on this point see Joseph, "John Cage and the Architecture of Silence," 80–104.

121. Cage's emphasis. See Cage, "Rhythm Etc.," in Cage, *A Year from Monday* (1967), 126.

122. Ibid.

123. Ibid.

124. The statement is preceded and followed by empty spaces that Cage would translate as silences when giving the text as a lecture. Ibid., 120.

125. See Griffiths, *Cage* (1981), 38.

126. Cage, "The Future of Music" (1974), in Cage, *Empty Words: Writings '73–'78* (1980), 183.

127. "Why is it necessary to give the sounds of knives and fork consideration? Satie says so. He is right. Otherwise, the music will have to have walls to defend itself . . . It is evidently a question of bringing one's intended actions into relation with the ambient unintended ones. The common denominator is zero, where the heart beat no one means to circulate his blood." Cage, "Erik Satie" (1958), in Cage, *Silence* (1961), 76.

128. See Curtis L. Carter, Jack W. Burnham, Edward Lucie-Smith, *Richard Lippold: Sculpture*, published by Patrick and Beatrice Haggerty Museum of Art, Marquette University, Milwaukee, Wisconsin, exhibition catalogue, November 30, 1990–February 17, 1991.

129. Letter from Walter Gropius to Richard Lippold, October 13, 1960. *Richard Lippold papers, 1944–1977*, reels D342, Frame 636, Archives of American Art.

130. Richard Lippold, "Projects for Pan Am and Philharmonic," *Art in America* 2 (1962): 55.

131. Ibid.

132. The undated budget, inscribed "Info from John Cage" at the top is part of *Richard Lippold papers, 1944–1977*, reels D342, Frame 0027, Archives of American Art. Another similar set of notes is preserved at the New York Public Library for the Performing Arts under the title "Unrealized project for the Lippold room at Grand Central Building," NYC—Ref. JPB 95–3 Folder 1069.

133. Letter from Richard Lippold to James D. Landauer [president of Grand Central Building, Inc.], August 11, 1962, Richard Lippold papers, 1944–1977, reels D342, Frame 643, Archives of American Art.

134. Raymond Ericson, "Music World: No Sound," *New York Times*, August 12, 1962, X9.

135. Ibid.

136. Ibid.

137. Among things that could still be done, as one may remember from the introduction to this study, Cage later mentioned: "The use of photoelectric eyes to scan the principal entrances and exits at Grand Central bringing about pulverization of Muzak." Cage, "Diary: How to Improve the World (You Will Only Make Matters Worse) Continued 1973–1982," in Cage, *X: Writings '79–'82* (1983), 165.

138. Jill Johnston, "Billy Kluver" [*sic*], *Village Voice*, August 12, 1965, n.p.

139. Fetterman, *John Cage's Theatre Pieces: Notations and Performances* (1996), 130. Leta E. Miller, "Cage, Cunningham, and Collaborators: The Odyssey of *Variations V*," *The Musical Quarterly* 85, no. 3 (Fall 2001): 545–56.

140. Merce Cunningham, "A Collaborative Process between Music and Dance" (1982), in Kostelanetz, ed., *Merce Cunningham: Dancing in Space and Time* (1998),

146–147. For a study of *Variations V*, see also Marcella Lista, "Expanded Body: *Variations V* et la conversion des arts à l'ère électronique," *Les Cahiers du Mnam* 74 (Winter 2000–2001): 99–119.

141. Merce Cunningham, ibid.

142. Ibid.

143. Cage, "Happy New Ears" (1963), in Cage, *A Year from Monday* (1967), 30.

144. Richard Shiff, "Art and Life: A Metaphoric Relationship," *Critical Inquiry* 5, no. 1 (Autumn 1978):118.

145. On the seminal untitled event organized by Cage at Black Mountain College in 1952, see Cage, *Silence* (1961), x, and also Merce Cunningham, "A Collaborative Process between Music and Dance" (1982), in Kostelanetz, ed., *Merce Cunningham: Dancing in Space and Time* (1998), 141.

146. Cage, "Conversation with John Cage (Summer 1966)," in Kostelanetz, ed., *John Cage: An Anthology* (1970, 1991), 26. Cage had made a similar statement in 1965 during an interview with Michael Kirby and Richard Schechner: "I think what we're doing is something else and not that. So when I go to a Happening that seems to me to have intention in it I go away saying that I'm not interested. I also did not like to be told, in the Eighteen Happenings in Six Parts, to move from on room to another. Though I don't actively engage in politics I do as an artist have some awareness of art's political content, and it doesn't include policemen. . . . It is not during organized or policed moments that these things [awareness, curiosity . . .] happen." In John Cage, Michael Kirby, and Richard Schechner, "An Interview with John Cage," *The Tulane Drama Review* 10, no. 2 (Winter 1965): 69–70.

147. John Cage, Michael Kirby, Richard Schechner, "An Interview with John Cage" (1965). Cage refers to the fact that Oldenburg requested the audience "to stand in the side of the theater in the aisles and not occupy the seats." Claes Oldenburg, "Moviehouse (1965)," *Raw Notes* (Halifax: Press of the Nova Scotia College of Art and Design, 1973, 2005), 68. Apparently, Oldenburg himself would not object to Cage's reaction, as he wrote in subsequent theoretical notes on happenings: "The artist is a lunatic authoritarian and sadist and he must go (self-destruction)" (*Raw Notes*, 218.)

148. In 1966, after Cage had severely criticized Kaprow's aesthetic, the latter nuanced the general understanding of Cage's influence on his work as follows: "Now, speaking personally, my studies with Cage followed a direction I had begun to take a few years before when I was concerned with the implication that Action painting . . . led not to more painting, but to *more action*. I perceived that Cage could help, especially in the area of noisemaking which I was using in my Assemblages and Environments then. Needless to say, he did not discourage me, and I did my first happening in his classroom. Yet I possibly learned things which Cage was not inclined to teach, although I was quite satisfied. This is reason enough to relieve him of any responsibility for my different interests." In Allan Kaprow, "On Happenings," *The Tulane Drama Review* 10, no. 4 (Summer 1966): 282.

149. Cage, Kirby, and Schechner, "An Interview with John Cage," *The Tulane Drama Review* (Winter 1965), 69–70.

150. Kaprow, "The Right Living" (1987), in Kaprow, *Essays on the Blurring of Art and Life* (1993), 225.

151. "Communication Programming," originally appeared untitled in the *Great Bear Pamphlet Manifestos* (New York: Something Else Press, 1966), 21–23. It has been reprinted in the exhibition catalogue *Allan Kaprow*, Pasadena Art Museum, September–October 1967, 12–14, and under the title "Manifesto" in Kaprow, *Essays on the Blurring of Art and Life* (1993), 83.

152. As Kaprow's *Words* (1961) is described by the artist in Allan Kaprow, *Assemblage, Environments & Happenings* (1966).

153. Kultermann, *Art and Life* (1971), 106–7.

154. On this issue, see Jean-Luc Nancy, *La communauté désœuvrée* (Paris: Christian Bourgois, 1983), translated by Peter Connor, Lisa Garbus, Michael Holland, and Simona Sawhney as *The Inoperative Community* (Minneapolis: University of Minnesota Press, 1991).

155. Italo Calvino, "On Fourier I: The Society of Love," in *The Literature Machine: Essays* (London: Picador, 1987), 215.

156. Claire Bishop, "Antagonism and Relational Aesthetics," *October* 110 (Fall 2004): 60.

157. Cardinell and Burris-Meyer, "Music in Industry Today" (1947), 548.

158. Louis Adamic (Faculty, 1935, 1937) quoted in Marvin Lane, ed., *Black Mountain College / Sprouted Seeds: An Anthology of Personal Accounts* (Knoxville: University of Tennessee Press, 1990), 59.

159. Husch, *Music of the Workplace* (1984), 157.

160. Clement Greenberg, "Avant-Garde Attitudes: New Art in the Sixties" (1968), in Clement Greenberg, *The Collected Essays and Criticism, Volume 4, Modernism with a Vengeance, 1957–1969*, edited by John O'Brian (Chicago: University of Chicago Press, 1993), 292.

161. "In the late sixties and early seventies in New York there was somewhat of a 'junta' atmosphere in the art world. The Greenberg gang was attempting with great success to initiate an Official History gestalt, and there wasn't much generosity toward us 'novelty' artists that didn't happen to fit into the prescribed historical continuum. Fortunately, there were very few younger artists that did fit into his historical continuum, which is what collapsed the movement—in spite of the tremendous appeal of Greenberg's brand of formalism to academics and other upper middle class professionals. Exponents of the 'party line' had saturated all aspects of the art establishment." Joseph Kosuth, "1975," *The Fox* no. 2 (1975): 87–96, also reprinted in Alexander Alberro and Blake Stimson, eds., *Conceptual Art: A Critical Anthology*, (Cambridge, Mass.: MIT Press, 1999), 336.

162. Brian O'Doherty, "New York: 9 Armored Nights," *Art and Artists* 1, no. 9 (December 1966), 14–17, reprinted in Morris (curator), *9 Evenings Reconsidered: Art, Theatre and Engineering* (2006), 75–79.

163. Michelle Kuo, "9 Evenings in Reverse," in Morris (curator), *9 Evenings Reconsidered: Art, Theatre and Engineering* (2006), p. 43, note 35 (emphasis mine).

164. Despite the apparent disaster of *Nine Evenings*, wrote O'Doherty, "the impact of the affair has been enormous and its after-life, in film and still photos, begins to qualify and change what actually took place. These records tend to be more impressive imaginatively than the events themselves; the historical audience, seeking text-book photos, will regret they were not there. The actual audience often regretted that they were." O'Doherty, "New York: 9 Armored Nights." In the mid-1960s, thus, the dreadful yet unclear notion of "participation" was about to solidify into an "Official History gestalt" of its own.

165. Lucy Lippard, "Total Theatre?"*Art International* 11, no. 1 (January 20, 1967): 40–43. reprinted in [E.A.T / Billy Klüver] *E.A.T. Clippings (April 1960–July 1969)* 1, no. 1 (1969): 6–7.

166. Ibid.

167. Billy Klüver (interview), "Billy Klüver: The Engineer as a Work of Art," from Douglas Davis, "Feature: Art and Technology," *Art in America* (January–February 1968): 40–42.

168. Ibid.

169. Anonymous, *The Village Voice* 12, no. 1 (October 20, 1966): 13. See also John Gruen, "Nine Evenings: First a Bore," *World Journal Tribunal*, October 14, 1966. Clive Barnes, "Happening: Ineffable Night at Armory; John Cage's Electronic Music Is Presented; Program Gives Lesson on Man's Conformity," *New York Times*, October 17, 1966, 48.

170. Jean Baudrillard, "Design and Environment: Or, The Inflationary Curve of Political Economy" (1972), in *The Universitas Project: Solutions for a Post-Technological Society*, conceived and directed by Emilio Ambasz, the Museum of Modern Art, New York, 2006, p. 53.

171. "The City of the Future: HP-talk with Constant about New Babylon," originally published in Dutch in *Haagse Post*, August 6, 1966, translated in Martin van Schaik and Otakar Macel, eds, *Exit Utopia: Architectural Provocation 1956–1976* (Munich: IHAAU-TU Delft, Prestel, 2005), 11.

172. Ibid.

173. Ibid.

174. See Peter Galison, "The Ontology of the Enemy: Norbert Wiener and the Cybernetic Vision," *Critical Inquiry* 21, no. 1 (Autumn 1994): 228–66.

175. "The City of the Future: HP-talk with Constant about New Babylon," 11.

176. Patricia Sibbert, "Presenting John Cage's Electric Music Machine," *Champaign-Urbana Courier*, September 29, 1967, 21, quoted in Stephen Husarik, "John Cage and LeJaren Hiller: HPSCHD, 1969," *American Music* 1, no. 2 (Summer 1983), note 7.

177. Charles Junkerman, "Modeling Anarchy: The Example of John Cage's Musicircus," *Chicago Review* 38, no. 4 (1992): 153.

178. Again, I refer here to Claes Oldenburg's blunt statement: "The artist is a lunatic authoritarian and sadist and he must go (self-destruction)." See Claes Oldenburg, *Raw Notes*, 218.

179. See Charles, *Gloses sur John Cage* (1978), 156. "On pourrait—certes—rejeter dans l'inoffensif, dans l'utopie, le projet naïf d'une célébration collective de la chute du principe d'autorité. Mais il est plus difficile de se soustraire au *fait* que cette utopie prenne corps."

180. Ibid.

181. Cage, *Empty Words: Writings '73–'78* (1980), 178. See also Junkerman, "Modeling Anarchy" (1993), 153.

182. Patricia Sibbert, "Presenting John Cage's Electric Music Machine," note 7.

183. Steve Yahn, "John Cage: A Mixed Bag," *Focus on the Arts at Illinois* 1 (November 1976): 1; as quoted in Stephen Husarik, "John Cage and LeJaren Hiller: HPSCHD, 1969," note 8.

184. Ibid.

185. Ibid.

Conclusion

1. I refer here to the titles given by the composer to a series of notes and reflection, such as *Diary: How to Improve the World (You Will Only Make Matters Worse) Continued 1968*. Originally published in *S.M.S.* magazine, no. 4, August, 1968.

2. Herbert Marcuse, "Art in the One-Dimensional Society," *Arts Magazine* 41, no.7 (May 1967): 26.

3. Ibid.

4. Frederic Rzewski, "Little Bangs: A Theory of Improvisation," reprinted in Cox and Warner, eds., *Audio Culture: Readings in Modern Music* (2004), 271.

5. Ibid.

6. Ibid.

7. Ornette Coleman quoted in Martin Williams's liner notes to *Free Jazz: A Collective Improvisation by the Ornette Coleman Double Quartet*, Atlantic, SD 1364, 1961.

8. Alain Touraine, *Can We Live Together? Equality and Difference* (Stanford, Calif.: Stanford University Press, 2000), 20.

9. Ibid.

10. Roland Barthes, *Comment vivre ensemble?* Cours et séminaires au Collège de France (1976–77), edited, annotated, and introduced by Claude Coste, Series "Les cours et séminaires au Collège de France de Roland Barthes," dir. Eric Marty, Seuil, IMEC, coll. "Traces écrites," 2002, 69.

11. Alain Touraine, "Society as Utopia," in Roland Schaer, Gregory Claeys, and Lyman Tower Sargent, eds., *Utopia: The Search for the Ideal Society in the Western World* (New York: Oxford University Press, in association with the New York Public Library, 2000), 18. Emphasis mine.

12. See Touraine, *Can We Live Together? Equality and Difference*, 109.

13. As Pierre Bourdieu and Loïc Wacquant argued, it is through increased individual participation in a globalized economy that a certain communitarian ideal is threatened the most: "Thus the absolute reign of [neoliberal] flexibility is es-

tablished, with employees being hiring on fixed-term contracts or on a temporary basis and repeated corporate restructurings and, within the firm itself, competition among autonomous divisions as well as among teams forced to perform multiple functions. Finally, this competition is extended to individuals themselves, through the individualisation of the wage relationship: establishment of individual performance objectives, individual performance evaluations, permanent evaluation, individual salary increases or granting of bonuses as a function of competence and of individual merit; individualized career paths; strategies of 'delegating responsibility' tending to ensure the self-exploitation of staff who, simple wage labourers in relations of strong hierarchical dependence, are at the same time held responsible for their sales, their products, their branch, their store, etc. as though they were independent contractors. This pressure toward 'self-control' extends workers' 'involvement' according to the techniques of 'participative management' considerably beyond management level. All of these are techniques of rational domination that impose over-involvement in work (and not only among management) and work under emergency or high-stress conditions. And they converge to weaken or abolish collective standards or solidarities." See Pierre Bourdieu and Loïc Wacquant, "Neoliberal Newspeak: Notes on the New Planetary Vulgate," *Radical Philosophy* 108 (January 2001).

14. http://www.muzak.com (Last accessed July 2011).
15. http://www.muzak.com (Last accessed July 2011).
16. Touraine, "Society as Utopia," 18. Emphasis mine.
17. Ibid., 24. Italics mine.
18. Ibid. Italics mine.
19. Cage, *A Year from Monday* (1967), 66.
20. Touraine, "Society as Utopia," 24.
21. Cage and Charles, *For the Birds* (1981), 233–34.
22. Ibid.
23. Nyman, "Cage/Cardew" (1973), 37.
24. Jacques Attali, *Noise: The Political Economy of Music* (1977), excerpted chapter in Cox and Warner, eds., *Audio Culture: Readings in Modern Music* (2004), 7.
25. Barthes, *Comment vivre ensemble?*, 39.
26. Ibid., 69.
27. Billy Klüver (interview), "Billy Klüver: The Engineer as a Work of Art," from Douglas Davis, "Feature: Art and Technology," *Art in America* (January–February 1968), 40–42.
28. Cornelius Cardew, "John Cage—Ghost or Monster?" originally published in *The Listener*, BBC Publications, May 4, 1972, reprinted in *Leonardo Music Journal* 8, nos. 3–4 (1998).
29. Ibid.
30. Nyman, "Cage/Cardew" (1973), 34.
31. Julian Stallabrass, "Off Their Trolleys?" *New Statesman* (November 15, 2004): 38.
32. Ibid.

33. Confronting Cage's view, according to which "the very life we're living . . . is so excellent once one gets one's mind and one's desire out of its way and lets it act of its own accord," Yvonne Rainer answered: "Let's not come down too heavily on the goofy naiveté of such a utterance, on its invocation of J. J. Rousseau, on Cage's adherence to the messianic ideas of Bucky Fuller some years back, with their total ignoring of worldwide struggles for liberation and the realities of imperialist politics, on the suppression of the question, 'Whose life is so excellent and at what cost to others?'" Rainer, "Looking Myself in the Mouth" (1981), 67.

34. See Kahn, "John Cage: Silence and Silencing" (1997), 557.

35. Barnett Newman, "'Frontiers of Space' Interview with Dorothy Gees Seckler," *Art in America* 50, no. 2 (Summer 1962): 83–87, reprinted in Barnett Newman, *Selected Writings and Interviews*, ed. John P. O'Neill (New York: Knopf, 1990), 251.

36. Barnett Newman, quoted in A. J. Liebling, "Two Aesthetes Offer Themselves as Candidates to Provide Own Ticket for Intellectuals," *New York World Telegram*, November 4, 1933, reproduced in Harold Rosenberg, *Barnett Newman* (New York: Abrams, 1978, 1994), 231: "We must spread culture through society. Only a society entirely composed of artists would be really worth living in. That is our aim, which is not dictated by expediency."

37. For a contrasting analysis of John Cage's and Joseph Beuys's views of a modern *Gesamtkunstwerk*, see Eric Michaud, "De Fluxus a Beuys: La fascination du politique," in *L'oeuvre d'art totale* (Paris: CNRS, 1995), 291.

38. John Cage, "Happy New Ears" (1963), in Cage, *A Year from Monday* (1967), 33.

39. Hence, Cage formulated the principle of "a music in which I would not express my feelings or my ideas but in which the sounds themselves would change me . . . They would change in particular my likes and dislikes." See Hans G. Helms, interview with John Cage (1972), "Reflections of a Progressive Composer on a Damaged Society," *October* 82 (Autumn 1997): 79.

40. Richard Shiff, "Art and Life: A Metaphoric Relationship," *Critical Inquiry* 5, no. 1 (Autumn 1978): 107.

41. I take the license to expand Richard Shiff's conclusion about Newman to the philosophy of John Cage. See Richard Shiff's introduction to Barnett Newman, *Selected Writings and Interviews*, xxvi.

42. Kostelanetz, "Environmental Abundance" (1969), in Kostelanetz, ed., *John Cage: An Anthology*, 175.

43. Cage, "Political/Social Ends? (1969)," in Kostelanetz, ed. *John Cage, Writer: Selected Texts* (1993), 115.

44. Cage in Charles, *For the Birds* (1981), 53.

45. Cage, "The Future of Music" (1974) in Cage, *Empty Words* (1980), 182. Cage refers to Mary Caroline Richards, *The Crossing Point: Selected Talks and Writings* (Middletown, Conn.: Wesleyan, 1973).

46. Richard Taruskin, "Letter to the editor," *New York Times*, September 27, 1992, H4.

47. Cage, "The Future of Music" (1974), in Cage, *Empty Words* (1980), 183.

48. Britta B. Wheeler, "The Institutionalization of an American Avant-Garde: Performance Art as Democratic Culture, 1970–2000," *Sociological Perspectives* 46, no. 4, Media, Popular Culture, and the Arts (Winter 2003): 491–512.

49. Ibid. Italics mine.

50. John Cage in interview (conducted in 1972) transcribed in Hans G. Helms, "Reflections of a Progressive Composer on a Damaged Society," *October* 82 (Autumn 1997): 89.

51. Jacques Derrida, "The Spirit of the Revolution," in Jacques Derrida and Elisabeth Roudinesco, *For What Tomorrow . . . A Dialogue,* translated by Jeff Fort (Stanford: Stanford University Press, 2004), 83.

52. Ibid.

References

The following section does not constitute an exhaustive bibliography. It only provides the full citations of the abbreviated references found in the endnotes. Documents (archival material, LPs, CDs, articles or books) that have been cited in full in the endnotes are not repeated here.

Adlington, Robert, ed. *Sound Commitments: Avant-Garde Music and the Sixties*. Oxford: Oxford University Press, 2009.

Adorno, Theodor W. *Essays on Music*. Selection, introduction, commentary, and notes by Richard Leppert, new translation by Susan H. Gillespie. Berkeley: University of California Press, 2002.

———, and Hanns Eisler. *Composing for the Films* (1947), republished with an introduction by Graham McCann, London: Continuum, Athlone Press, 2005.

Anderson, Tim J. "Buried under the Fecundity of His Own Creations: Reconsidering the Recording Bans of the American Federation of Musicians, 1942–1944 and 1948." *American Music* 22, no. 2 (Summer 2004): 231–69.

———. *Making Easy Listening: Material Culture and Postwar American Recording*. Minneapolis: University of Minnesota Press, 2006.

Arceneaux, Noah. "A Sales Floor in the Sky: Philadelphia Department Stores and the Radio Boom of the 1920s." *Journal of Broadcasting and Electronic Media* 53, no. 1 (2009): 76–89.

Armengaud, Jean-Pierre. *Erik Satie*. Paris: Fayard, 2009.

Austin, William. "Satie before and after Cocteau." *The Musical Quarterly* 48, no. 2 (April 1962): 216–33.

Barnes, Stephen H. *Muzak ®: the Hidden Message in Music: A Social Psychology of Culture*. Vol. 9 from *Studies on the History of Interpretation in Music*. Lewiston, N.Y.: Edwin Mellen Press, 1988.

Beckett, Wheeler. *Music in War Plants*. Washington, D.C.: War Production Drive Headquarters, War Production Board, (August) 1943.

Benson, Barbara Elna. *Music and Sound Systems in Industry*. New York: McGraw-Hill, 1945.

Blickhan, Charles T. *Erik Satie: Musique d'ameublement.* Unpublished DMA dissertation, University of Illinois at Urbana-Champaign, 1976.

Bradshaw, Alan, and Morris B. Holbrook. "Must We Have Muzak Wherever We Go? A Critical Consideration of the Consumer Culture." *Consumption Markets & Culture* 11, no. 1 (March 2008): 25–43.

Bryars, Gavin. "Vexations and Its Performers" (written 1979). *Contact* 26 (Spring 1983): 12–20.

Cage, John. *Empty Words: Writings '73–'78.* London: Marion Boyars, 1980.

———. *M: Writings '67–'72.* Middletown, Conn.: Wesleyan University Press, 1973.

———. *X: Writings '79–'82.* Middletown, Conn.: Wesleyan University Press, 1983.

———. "Rhythm Etc." In Gyorgy Kepes, ed., *Module, Proportion, Symmetry, Rhythm.* New York: George Braziller, 1966.

———. *Silence.* Middletown, Conn.: Wesleyan University Press, 1961.

———. *A Year from Monday.* Middletown, Conn.: Wesleyan University Press, 1967, 1969.

———, Michael Kirby, and Richard Schechner. "An Interview with John Cage." *The Tulane Drama Review* 10, no. 2 (Winter 1965): 50–72.

———, and Robin White. *John Cage.* New York: Henmar Press, 1962.

———, Roger Shattuck, and Alan Gillmor. "Erik Satie: A Conversation" (1973) (with Roger Shattuck and Alan Gillmor), *Contact: A Journal of Contemporary Music* 25 (Autumn 1982): 21–26.

Cardinell, R. L. *Music in Industry: The Nature and Development of Work Music.* New York: American Society of Composers, Authors and Publishers, 1944.

——— and Harold Burris-Meyer. "Music in Industry Today." *The Journal of Acoustical Society of America* 19, no. 4 (July 1947): 547–49.

———, Harold Burris-Meyer, and R. C. Lewis. "Music as an Aid to Healing." *The Journal of Acoustical Society of America* 19, no. 4 (July 1947): 544–46.

Charles, Daniel. *For the Birds: John Cage in Conversation with Daniel Charles.* Boston: Marion Boyars, 1981.

Charles, Daniel. *Gloses sur John Cage.* Paris: 10:18, 1978.

Cocteau Jean. *Le Rappel à l'ordre.* (Includes *Le coq et l'Arlequin* [1918], *Carte blanche* [1920], *Visites à Maurice Barrès* [1921], *Le secret professionnel* [1922], *D'un ordre considéré comme une anarchie* [1923], *Autour de "Thomas l'imposteur"* [1923], *Picasso* [1923]). Paris: Librairie Stock, Delamain et Boutelleau, 1926, 1948.

Cox, Christoph, and Daniel Warner, eds. *Audio Culture: Readings in Modern Music.* London: Continuum, 2004.

Dahlhaus, Carl. *The Idea of Absolute Music.* Translation of *Die Idee der absoluten Musik* (1978), introduced by Roger Lustig. Chicago: University of Chicago Press, 1989.

Davis, Mary E. *Erik Satie.* London: Reaktion Books, 2007.

Derrida, Jacques. "Economimesis." In *Mimesis Desarticulations.* Paris: Aubier-Flammarion, Coll. La Philosophie en effet, 1975.

Dubé, Laurette, Jean-Charles Chebat, and Sylvie Morin. "The Effects of Background Music on Consumers' Desire to Affiliate in Buyer-Seller Interactions." *Psychology & Marketing* 12, no. 4 (July 1995): 305–19.

REFERENCES 183

Eliel, Carol S., ed. With essays by Françoise Ducros and Tag Gronberg. *L'Esprit nouveau: Purism in Paris, 1918–1925.* New York: Harry N. Abrams, 2001.

Emmerik, Paul van (in collaboration with Herbert Henck and András Wilheim). *A John Cage Compendium.* http://cagecomp.home.xs4all.nl (Last accessed August 2012).

Eno, Brian. *A Year with Swollen Appendices: Brian Eno's Diary.* London: Faber & Faber, 1996.

Fetterman, William. *John Cage's Theatre Pieces: Notations and Performances.* Amsterdam: Harwood Academic, 1996.

Gallez, Douglas W. "Satie's Entr'acte: A Model of Film Music." *Cinema Journal* 16, no. 1 (Autumn 1976): 36–50.

Gann, Kyle. *No Such Thing as Silence: John Cage's 4'33".* New Haven, Conn.: Yale University Press, 2010.

Gillmor, Alan M. *Erik Satie.* Boston: Twayne, 1988.

Goldberg, RoseLee. *Performance: Live Art 1909 to Present.* London: Thames and Hudson, 1979.

Griffiths, Paul. *Cage.* London: Oxford University Press, 1981.

Groom, Nick. "The Condition of Muzak." *Popular Music and Society* 20, no. 3 (Autumn 1996): 1–17.

Haden-Guest, Anthony. *The Paradise Program: Travel through Muzak, Hilton, Coca-Cola, Texaco, Walt Disney and other World Empires.* New York: Morrow, 1973.

Halpin, Dan D. (RCA Victor Division, Radio Corporation of America), "Industrial Music and Morale." *The Journal of the Acoustical Society of America* 15, no. 2 (October 1943): 118–23.

Haskins, Rob. "Composition (Not Philosophy): James Pritchett's The Music of John Cage." *Perspectives of New Music* 34, no. 2 (Summer 1996): 216–23.

Heimbecker, Sara. "HPSCHD, Gesamtkunstwerk, and Utopia." *American Music* 26, no. 4 (Winter 2008): 474–98.

Herwitz, Daniel A. "The Security of the Obvious: On John Cage's Musical Radicalism." *Critical Inquiry* 14, no. 4 (Summer 1988): 784–804.

Higgins, Dick. *A Dialectic of Centuries: Notes toward a Theory of the New Arts.* New York: Printed Editions, 1978.

Hinton, Stephen. *The Idea of Gebrauchsmusik: A Study of Musical Aesthetics in the Weimar Republic (1919–1933) with Particular Reference to the Work of Paul Hindemith.* London: Garland, 1989.

Hitchcock, Wiley, ed. *The Phonograph and Our Musical Life.* Proceedings of a centennial conference, December 7–10, 1977, Institute for Studies in American Music, Department of Music, School of Performing Arts, Brooklyn College of the City University of New York, 1980.

Huron, David. "Review of Stephen H. Barnes, *Muzak ®: The Hidden Messages in Music: A Social Psychology of Culture* (1988)," *Psychology of Music* 18, no. 2 (1990): 183–84.

Husarik, Stephen. "John Cage and LeJaren Hiller: HPSCHD, 1969." *American Music* 1, no. 2 (Summer 1983): 1–21.

Husch, Jerri Ann. *Music of the Workplace: A Study of Muzak Culture (Social Change Ideology, Technology)*. PhD dissertation, University of Massachusetts, May 1984.

Jones, Simon C., and Thomas G. Schumacher. "Muzak: On Functional Music and Power." *Critical Studies in Mass Communication* 9, no. 2 (1992): 156–69.

Joseph, Branden W. "John Cage and the Architecture of Silence." *October* 81 (Summer 1997): 80–104.

———. "'A Therapeutic Value for City Dwellers': The Development of John Cage's Early Avant-Garde Aesthetic Position." In David W. Patterson, ed., *John Cage: Music, Philosophy, and Intention, 1933–1950*. New York: Routledge, 2002.

———. "The Tower and the Line: Toward a Genealogy of Minimalism." *Grey Room* 27 (Spring 2007): 58–81.

Junkerman, Charles. "Modeling Anarchy: The Example of John Cage's Musicircus." *Chicago Review* 38, no. 4 (1993): 153–68.

Kahn, Douglas. *Noise, Water, Meat: A History of Sound in the Arts*. Cambridge, Mass.: MIT Press, 1999.

———. "John Cage: Silence and Silencing." *The Musical Quarterly* 81, no. 4 (Winter 1997): 556–98.

Kahn, Douglas, and Gregory Whitehead, eds. *Wireless Imagination: Sound, Radio, and the Avant-Garde.*, Cambridge, Mass.: MIT Press, 1992, 1994.

Kaprow, Allan. *Assemblage, Environments & Happenings*. Text and design by Allan Kaprow; with a selection of scenarios by: 9 Japanese of the Gutai Group, Jean-Jacques Lebel, Wolf Vostell, George Brecht, Kenneth Dewey, Milan Knížák, Allan Kaprow. New York: Abrams, 1966.

———. *Essays on the Blurring of Art and Life*. Expanded edition. Jeff Kelley, ed. Berkeley: University of California Press, 2003.

Kim, Rebecca Y. *In No Uncertain Musical Terms: The Cultural Politics of John Cage's Indeterminacy*. PhD dissertation, Columbia University, Department of Music, 2008.

Kirby, Michael. *Happenings*. New York: E. P. Dutton, 1965.

Klein, Lothar. "Twentieth Century Analysis: Essays in Miniature." *Music Educators Journal* 53, no. 4 (December 1966): 54–55

Korczynski, Marek, and Keith Jones. "Instrumental Music? The Social Origins of Broadcast Music in British Factories." *Popular Music* 25, no. 2 (2006): 145–64.

Kostelanetz, Richard, ed. *Conversing with Cage*. New York: Limelight Editions, 1988.

———. *John Cage: An Anthology* (1970). New York: Da Capo Press, 1991.

———. *John Cage, Writer / Selected Texts*. New York: Cooper Square Press, 1993, 2000.

———. *Merce Cunningham: Dancing in Space and Time*. Cambridge, Massachusetts: Da Capo Press, 1998.

———. *The Theatre of Mixed Means*. New York: RK Editions, 1980.

Krims, Adam. *Music and Urban Geography*. New York: Routledge, 2007.

Kultermann, Udo. *Art and Life*. Translated by William Gabriel. New York: Praeger, 1971.

LaBelle, Brandon. *Background Noise: Perspectives on Sound Art*. New York: Continuum, 2006.

Lanza, Joseph. *Elevator Music: A Surreal History of Muzak, Easy-Listening, and Other Moodsong.* New York: St. Martin's Press, 1994.

Léger, Fernand. *Fonctions de la peinture.* Paris: Gonthier, 1965. Translated by Alexandra Anderson as *Functions of Painting.* Edward F. Fry, ed., with a preface by George L. K. Morris. New York: Viking Press, 1973.

Leiter, Robert D. *The Musician and Petrillo.* New York: Bookman Associates, 1953.

Lunde, Anders S. "The American Federation of Musicians and the Recording Ban." *The Public Opinion Quarterly* 12, no. 1 (Spring 1948): 45–56.

McLuhan, Marshall. "The Invisible Environment: The Future of an Erosion." *Perspecta* 11 (1967): 163–67.

———, and Quentin Fiore. *The Medium Is the Massage: An Inventory of Effects.* New York: Bantam, 1967.

Mellers, Wilfrid H. "Erik Satie and the 'Problem' of Contemporary Music." *Music & Letters* 23, no. 3 (July 1942): 210–27.

———. "Satie et le musique 'fonctionnelle." In Rollo H. Myers, ed., *La Revue musicale, Erik Satie, son temps et ses amis.* Special issue dedicated to Erik Satie, no. 214 (June 1952).

Milhaud, Darius. *Notes sans musique.* Paris: Julliard, 1949 (first edition); revised and augmented 1963. Translated by Donald Evans as *Notes without Music.* London: Calder and Boyars, 1967.

Morris, Catherine (curator) et al. *9 Evenings Reconsidered: Art, Theatre and Engineering, 1966.* Cambridge, Mass.: MIT, List Visual Art Center, 2006.

Myers, Rollo H. *Erik Satie.* London: Dobson, 1948; unabridged, slightly corrected reprint New York: Dover, 1968.

———, ed. *La Revue musicale—"Erik Satie, son temps et ses amis."* Special issue dedicated to Erik Satie, no. 214 (June 1952).

———. "The Strange Case of Erik Satie." *The Musical Times* 86, no. 1229 (July 1945): 201–3.

Nicholls, David, ed. *The Cambridge Companion to John Cage.* Cambridge: Cambridge University Press, 2002. Texts by David Nicholls, Christopher Shultis, David W. Patterson, David W. Bernstein, Kathan Brown, William Brooks, Leta E. Miller, John Holzaepfel, Alastair Williams, Kyle Gann.

Nyman, Michael. *Experimental Music: Cage and Beyond.* Cambridge: Cambridge University Press; second edition (1999).

———. "Cage and Satie." *The Musical Times* 114, no. 1570 (December 1973): 1227–29.

———. "Cage/Cardew." *Tempo.* New Series, no. 107 (December 1973): 32–38.

Orledge, Robert. *Satie the Composer.* Cambridge: Cambridge University Press, 1990.

———, ed. *Satie Remembered.* Compiled and edited by Robert Orledge, with translations from the French by Roger Nichols. Portland, Ore.: Amadeus Press, 1995.

Pasler, Jann. "New Music as Confrontation: The Musical Sources of Jean Cocteau's Identity." *The Musical Quarterly* 75, no. 3 (Autumn 1991): 255–78.

Patterson, D. W. (ed.). *John Cage: Music, Philosophy, and Intention, 1933–1950.* New York: Routledge, 2002.

Perloff, Nancy. *Art and the Everyday: Popular Entertainment and the Circle of Erik Satie.* Oxford: Clarendon Press, 1991.

Pritchett, James. *The Music of John Cage.* Cambridge: Cambridge University Press, 1993.

———. "What Silence Taught John Cage: The Story of 4'33"." In Robinson et al., *The Anarchy of Silence: John Cage and Experimental Art.* Barcelona: Museu d'Art Contemporani de Barcelona, 2009.

Rabinbach, Anson G. "The Aesthetics of Production in the Third Reich." *Journal of Contemporary History* 11, no. 4, Special Issue: Theories of Fascism (October 1976): 43–74.

———. *The Human Motor: Energy, Fatigue, and the Origins of Modernity.* New York: Basic Books, 1990.

———. "Science, Work, and Worktime." In *International Labor and Working-Class History*, no. 43 (Spring 1993): 48–64.

Radano, Ronald M. "Interpreting Muzak: Speculations on Musical Experience in Everyday Life." *American Music* 7, no. 4 (Winter 1989): 448–60.

Rainer, Yvonne. "Looking Myself in the Mouth." *October* 17 (Summer 1981): 65–76.

Revill, David. *The Roaring Silence—John Cage: A Life.* New York: Arcade, 1992.

Robinson, Julia (curator). *The Anarchy of Silence: John Cage and Experimental Art.* Barcelona: Museu d'Art Contemporani de Barcelona, 2009, with contributions by Julia Robinson, Yve-Alain Bois, Liz Kotz, Branden W. Joseph et al.

Rowen, Ruth Halle. "Some 18th-Century Classifications of Musical Style." *The Musical Quarterly* 33, no. 1 (January 1947): 90–101.

Satie, Erik. *Les Cahiers d'un Mammifère: Chroniques et articles entre 1895 et 1924.* Introduced by Sebastien Arfouilloux, ed. Saint-Didier, Vaucluse, France: Editions l'Escalier, Collection Écrits d'Artistes, 2009.

———. *Correspondance presque complète.* Ornella Volta, ed. Paris: Fayard, Imec, 2000.

———. *Écrits.* Ornella Volta, ed. Paris: Champ libre, 1977, 1981.

———. *Musiques d'ameublement pour petit ensemble* (scores). Edited and introduced by Ornella Volta. Paris: Series "œuvres inédites et posthumes," coll. "Archives Erik Satie." Ed. Salabert, 1999. This edition contains reproduction of the manuscripts of *Carrelage Phonique* (1918), *Tapisserie en fer forgé* (1918), *Un Salon* (1920), *Tenture de Cabinet Préfectoral* (1923).

Sayre, Henry M. *The Object of Performance: The American Avant-Garde since 1970.* Chicago: University of Chicago Press, 1989.

Schwartz, Elliott, and Barney Childs. *Contemporary Composers on Contemporary Music.* New York: Holt, Rinehart, and Winston, 1967.

Selvin, Ben. "Programming Music for Industry." *The Journal of the Acoustical Society of America* 15, no. 2 (October 1943): 131–32.

Shattuck, Roger. *The Banquet Years; The Origins of the Avant Garde in France, 1885 to World War I: Alfred Jarry, Henri Rousseau, Erik Satie, Guillaume Apollinaire* (1958). New York: Vintage Books, 1968.

Shlomowitz, Matthew. "Cage's Place in the Reception of Satie." Online publication, part of his PhD at the University of California at San Diego, 1999. http://www.af.lu.se/~fogwall/article8.html.

Shultis, Christopher. *Silencing the Sounded Self: John Cage and the American Experimental Tradition*. Boston: Northeastern University Press, 1998.

———. "Silencing the Sounded Self: John Cage and the Intentionality of Nonintention." *The Musical Quarterly* 79, no. 2 (Summer 1995): 312–50.

Silverman, Kenneth. *Begin Again: A Biography of John Cage*. New York: Knopf, 2010.

Soibelman, Doris. *Therapeutic and Industrial Uses of Music: A Review of the Literature*. New York: Columbia University Press, 1948.

Sterne, Jonathan. "Sounds Like the Mall of America: Programmed Music and the Architectonics of Commercial Space." *Ethnomusicology* 41, no.1 (Winter 1997): 22–50.

Sundstrom, Eric D., and Mary Graehl. *Work Places: The Psychology of the Physical Environment in Offices and Factories*. New York: Cambridge University Press, Environment and Behavior Series, 1986.

Szendy, Peter. *Tubes: la philosophie dans le juke-box*. Paris: Éditions de Minuit, 2008.

Tamm, Eric. *Brian Eno, Electronic Musician: Progressive Rock and the Ambient Sound, 1973–1986*. PhD dissertation, University of California, Berkeley, 1987.

Templier, Pierre-Daniel. *Erik Satie*. Paris: Les Editions Rieder, 1932. Translated by Elena L. French and David S. French. Cambridge, Mass.: MIT Press, 1969.

Thompson, Emily. *The Soundscape of Modernity: Architectural Acoustics and the Culture of Listening in America, 1900–1933*. Cambridge, Mass.: MIT Press, 2002.

Toop, David. *Ocean of Sound: Ether Talk, Ambient Sound and Imaginary Worlds*. London: Serpent's Tail, 1995.

Tyler, Linda L. "Commerce and Poetry Hand in Hand: Music in American Department Stores, 1880–1930." *Journal of the American Musicological Society* 45, no. 1 (Spring 1992): 75–120.

Volta, Ornella. "Erik Satie." In Laurent Le Bon, ed., *Dada*. Exhibition catalogue, Centre Georges Pompidou. Paris: Editions du Centre Pompidou, 2005.

———. *Erik Satie: Bibliographie raisonnée*. France: Arcueil, Mairie d'Arcueil, 1995.

———. *Satie/Cocteau: les malentendus d'une entente*. Bordeaux, France: Editions Le Castor Astral, 1993.

———. *Satie: D'Esoterik Satie à Satierik*. Paris: Editions Seghers-Humour, 1979.

Wokoun, William. *Vigilance with Background Music*. Unclassified document, Aberdeen Proving Ground, Maryland, U.S. Army Human Engineering Laboratories, August 1963.

Woodley, Richard. "Music by Muzak." *Audience* 1, no. 5. (September–October 1971).

Wurtzler, Steve J. *Electric Sounds: Technological Change and the Rise of Corporate Media*. New York: Columbia University Press, 2007.

Wyatt, S., and J. N. Langdon (assisted by F. G. L. Stock). *Fatigue and Boredom in Repetitive Work*. London: His Majesty's Stationery Office (Report No. 77, Medical Research Council, Industrial Health Research Board), 1937.

Index

Note: Page numbers in *italics* refer to illustrations.

Acoustical Society of America, 68
Address (Cage, 1963), 107–108
Adorno, Theodore W., 12, 32–33, 42, 160n162, 168n69
Ambient works (Cage), 103
American Federation of Musicians (AFM): campaign against movies and recording, 154n44; Federal Radio Commission complaint, 154n38; strikes against recording companies, 50–52, 93–96, 153n31, 165n42, 165n44; wartime ban on recordings, 166–167n56, 166n55
American Journal of Public Health, 61
Anderson, Tim, 50
art: as anonymous activity, 139–140n13; art/life boundary blurring, 116–117; as connected to politics, 7–9; as life, 111, 172n127; Satie on, 33; as social reformation, 82–83
"artificial acoustic space," 103
Art of Noise (Russolo), 26
Attali, Jacques, 129
audience participation, 106–115
audio architecture, 6, 79–83
Auric, George, 25
Austin, William, 10
Avraamov, Arseni, 46

Bach, J. S., 30
Barthes, Roland, 127, 129

Baudrillard, Jean, 48
Bauhaus, 37–38
BBC "Music While You Work," 60–61, 62, 152n17
Benjamin, Walter, 42
Benson, Barbara Elna, 65, 155n51
Bertin, Pierre, 16
Besseler, Heinrich, 28–29
Big Country billboard, *100*
Bishop, Claire, 119
Black Mountain College, 120
Blainville, Charles-Henri, 31
Blanchot, Maurice, 109, 171n118
Bongard, Germaine, 35
Le bon roi Dagobert, 36–37, 148–149n119, 149n120–121
Boom Electric and Amplifier, 51–52
Bradshaw, Alan, 48
Brecht, Bertholt, 101
British Industrial Health Research Board, 56–58
British Medical Journal, 63
Brooks, William, 8
Brown, Norman O., 108
Burris-Meyer, Harold, 69–70

Cage, John, *115*; on American Federation of Musicians bans on recordings, 94; on Ananda Cooraswamy, 164–165n37; anarchism, 8, 124, 131, 173n146; anticapitalism, 98–99; art as social reformation, 42, 82–83; Asian influence, 93; compositional tool, 89; controversial nature,

84, 162–163n1; Eastern philosophies influence, 93, 96–97; elitism, 129–130; furniture music references, 2–9; goal, 131–132, 177n39; on Happenings, 117; ideal, 120, 125, 126–128; indeterminacy, 89; liberation of people and sounds, 132; music participation function, 92; *musique d'ameublement* (Satie) references, 2–9; on Muzak, 2, 163n2; Muzak-plus concept, 131–132; Muzak relationship, 4, 47, 84, 99–101, 106, 109; naiveté, 130–131, 177n33; paradoxical nature, 132; physical space and music performance, 102–103; on politics, 131; politics, 7–9; recorded music attitude, 98, 167–168n69; on recording music, 103; redefinition of art's function in society, 42; on repetition, 105; Satie, 2–9, 14, 136n18, 136n19; on Schoenberg, 164n24; self-discovery as purpose of music, 97; silence in music, 98–99, 169n78; on social functions of *musique d'ameublement* (furniture music), 4; on social functions of Muzak, 4; sociopolitical viewpoint, 127–131; on *Vexations* (Satie, 1893), 12, 139n2; on *Vexations* 1963 performance, 105; Vision + Value series (1966), 1

Calvino, Italo, 119
"canned music," 50, 93–94, 165n41. *See also* "functional music"
Capital Transit, 93
Cardew, Cornelius, 86, 89, 92, 129–130
Cardinall, H. M., 69–70
Carrelage phonique (Phonic tiling) (Satie, 1917), 19, 107–108
Cartridge Music (Cage, 1960), 1
Cassette, 107–108
chamber music, 30, 146n93
Charles, Daniel, 124
Cheap Imitation (Cage, 1969), 3
"Chez un 'bistrot'" ("At a 'Bar,'" Satie), 16
Cinéma (Gallez), 39–40
Clair, René, 39–40, 41, 94
Cocteau, Jean, 25–28; American jazz influence, 26; association with Muzak, 25, 144n63; on music as background for sounds of modern life, 25–26, 145n73, 145n74; nationalism, 15, 34; neoclassicism, 15; post-futurism, 25–28
Coleman, Ornette, 84, 127

communication programming, 118–119
communitarianism v. individuation, 128, 176–177n3
"A Composer's Confessions" (Cage lecture), 92–93, 97
Cooraswamy, Ananda, 93, 164–165n37
Le Coq et l'arlequin (Cocteau), 27–28
Le Corbusier, 15, 81–82, 109, 148n112
Correlage Phonique (Satie), 3
Cortot, Alfred, 21
"counterfeit music," 35
Critique of Judgment (Kritik der Urteilskraft) (Kant, 1790), 30–31, 146n94–96
The Crossing Point (Richards), 131
Cunningham, Merce, *115*, 116
cybernetics, 123–124

Dadaism, 15, 18
Dahlhaus, Carl, 28
Dans Macabre (Saint-Saëns), 19–20
Davis, Miles, 96
Debord, Guy, 85
Debussy, Claude, 14, 140n20
Decoder (Maeck), 4
De Leeuw, Reinbert, 103
Derrida, Jacques, 132

earworms, 70–75, 159–160n160
"The East in the West" (Cage, 1946), 96–97
18 Happenings in 6 Parts (Kaprow, 1959), 117, 119
Eisler, Hanns, 40, 150n139
Eno, Brian, 80–81, 102, 169–179n93
Entr'acte (Clair), 39–40, 94
"environmental music," 47

"Fatigue and Boredom in Repetitive Work," 56–58, 157n91
Federal Radio Commission, 50–52, 154n58
feedback, 120
Fifth Symphony (Beethoven), 12
film soundtracks, 39–41, 150n139
Fiore, Quentin, 47
Foster, Hal, 5
Foucault, Michel, 72
4'33" (Cage, 1952), 93
Fourrier, Charles, 56
Free Jazz (Coleman), 127
Fuller, Buckminster, 7, 9, 46, 83, 108
"functional music": aesthetic, 67–75;

content limitations, 65–66, 69; definition, 13; industrial broadcasting, 155n51; industrial psychology, 58, 61–62; playlist example, *65*; production and implementation, 69–70; separation of performer and audience, 18; tempo limitations, 67–68; therapeutic-economic connection, 62–64; utilization instructions, 69–70; volume limitations, 68; worker productivity, 61–62. *See also* "canned music"; industrial music

furniture music. *See musique d'ameublement* (furniture music) (Satie)

Galerie Barbazanges, 16, 19
Gallez, Douglas W., 39–40
Gann, Kyle, 93
Gatehill Cooperative Community, 120
Gebrauchmusik (utility music), 28–29
German instrumental music, 25
Gillmore, Alan, 3
The Globe (or Flight) (Lippold, 1963), *113*
Goldberg, RoseLee, 92
Gottlieb, Adolph, 47
Greenberg, Clement, 120–121, 122
Greusel, Louise, 112
Griffiths, Paul, 111
Groom, Nick, 72
Gropius, Walter, 112
Groupe des Six ("Les Six"), 14, 16

Happenings, 88–89, 92, 117–125
Hardt, Michael, 71
Heimbecker, Sarah, 7
Higgins, Dick, 36, 37
Hinton, Stephen, 13, 20–21, 28, 29
Hitchcock, Wiley, 107, 108
Hobsbawm, Eric, 42, 150–151n146
Hoffman, E. T. A., 28
Holbrook, Morris B., 48
Homage to New York (Tinguely and Klüver, 1960), 122
"How Much Is Worker Tension Costing Your Company?" 77
Hume, David, 104
Husch, Jerri, 99

idiorrhythmy *(idiorhythmie)*, 129
Imaginary Landscape No. 4 (Cage lecture topic), 93

individuation v. communitarianism, 128, 176–177n3
industrial music: aesthetic, 66–70; audio architecture, 79–83; as "functional music," 61–62; Muzak Corporation, 56, 67–69; origins, 24; pleasant work experience, 56–59; programming, 64–66; research, 60–61; Satie on, 33; scientific arguments, 75–79; standardization, 70–75; work management, 62–64, 119, 153n31; World War II plants, 68. *See also* "functional music"
industrial psychology, 57

Jacob, Max, 16
Johnston, Jill, 115
Jones, Simon, 57
Jorn, Asger (poster), *110*
Joseph, Branden W., 9
Jove, 35, 148n112
Junkerman, Charles, 124

Kahn, Douglas, 7, 94–95, 137n26, 155n53, 166n52
Kandinsky, Wassily, 6
Kant, Immanuel, 30–31, 146n94–96
Kaprow, Allan, 5, 92, 117–118, 119, 173n148
Kepes, Gyorgy, 1, 82–83, 109
Klein, Lothar, 2, 22
Klüver, Billy, 121, 129
Kraynak, Janet, 83
Krims, Adam, 155n59
Kultermann, Udo, 118–119
'Kunstreligion,' 28

Langdon, J. N., 49, 56–58, 62–64, 78, 157n91
Lanza, Joseph, 23, 70–71
Léger, Fernand, 15, 27, 31, 42, 147n100
Lenneberg, Hans, 30
L'esprit de l'art musical (Blainville, 1754), 31
Lichtenstein, Roy, 99–100
Lippold, Richard, 111–112, 114
Living Room Music (Cage, 1940), 17

Maeck, Klaus, 4
"Making Work Pleasant," 56–61
Mantovani, 53
Marclay, Christian, 108
Marcuse, Herbert, 126
Margulis, Elizabeth Hellman, 98, 169n78

Mathews, Max, 14, 112, 115
Matisse, Henri, 21–22, 142–143n45, 143n46, 143n49
Mauriat, Paul, 53
McLuhan, Marshall, 47, 83, 85–86
The Medium Is the Message: An Inventory of Effects (McLuhan and Fiore), 47
Melachrino, George, 53
Mellers, Wilfrid, 13, 139n11
"melodic surveillance," 72–75
Memoirs of an Amnesiac (Satie), 10
MEV (Musica Elettronica Viva), 126
"Mewantemooseicday," 106, 170n110, 171n112
Meyer, Mrs. Eugene, 20
Mignon (Thomas, 1866), 19–20, 141n22
Milhaud, Darius: association with Muzak, 24, 144n59; background music perception, 24; Cage interview, 3; on culture industry, 43; on "functional music," 18–19; *musique d'ameublement* (furniture music) (Satie), 16, 17, 140–141n29, 141n30
Milliman, R. E., 76–77, 161n186
modernism, 43
The Modular (Le Corbusier), 109
Module, Symmetry, Proportion, Rhythm (Cage), 1, 109
Mondrian, Piet, 42
"More Striking Proof that It Pays to RELIEVE WORKERS' TENSION WITH MUZAK," 59
Moviehouse (Oldenburg, 1965), 117, 119
movie soundtracks, 39–41, 150n139
Mumma, Gordon, *115*
Musica Elettronica Viva (MEV), 126
"Music by Muzak," 52, 53, *73*, 75. *See also* Muzak; Muzak Corporation
Music for Airport (Eno), 81
Music from the Ether (Thérémin), 87
Musicircuses (Cage), 107, 124
"Music While You Work" (BBC), 60–61, 62, 152n17
musique d'ameublement (furniture music) (Satie): associations with *Vexations* (Satie, 1893), 12, 139n7; audience as consumers, 16; audience reaction, 17–18; as "autonomous music," 20–21; as background for sounds of modern life, 25–30; basic principles, 20–21;

boredom factor, 36; Cage references, 2–9; composition, 12; as conservative, 32, 147n101; context intended, 16–17, 20; dilemmas, 41–43; failed premiere, 34–35, 148n115; first mention, 19, 139–140n40; as "functional music," 13, 139n11; Gebrauchmusik (utility music) association, 29; instrumentation, 17, 19; as intermission music, 16; marginality, 13; Matisse association, 21–22, 142–143n45, 143n46, 143n49; Milhaud collaboration, 16, 17, 140–141n29, 141n30; musician placement, 17, 20; Muzak association, 22–25, 41–43, 143n52; Muzak comparison, 84–85, 163n6; neoclassicism, 21; oblivion, 13; orchestration, 17; performance, 16–19; popular music recycling, 20; publication of scores, 142n41; publicity leaflet, 34; repetition element, 12; romantic generation music v., 28; three sets differentiated, 19–20; titular suggestions, 19
Muzak: architecture relationship, 79–83; arrangements, 70; "artist-engineers," 6; art relationship, 5–6; as "Audio Architecture," 48; buyer-seller interaction connection, 78–79; Cage relationship, 2, 4, 84, 106, 109, 163n2; catastrophic circumstances, 79–81, *80*; content limitations, 72–75; as corruption, 48; critical consensus, 47–48; criticisms, 4–7, 23; definition, 2; as desensitizing, 48; as environment in itself, 85–86; as functional device, 55–56; as "functional music," 48, 49; historical precedents, 30–33; homogenization, 70–77; impersonality, 48, 152n17; musical standardization, 75, 160n162; *musique d'ameublement* (furniture music) (Satie) comparison, 84–85, 163n6; Muzak-plus relationship, 3–4, 88–89; product v. corporation, 2; stylistic conformity, 70; as subliminal music, 4; therapeutic value claims, 78–79
Muzak Corporation: advertisements, *54, 56, 59, 67, 73, 77, 80*; commodification of music, 53, 155n59; evolution, 70–75; explained, 46–47; growth and expansion, 52–54; history, 46–47; image, 47; industrial psychology, 49; logo from 1957,

46; "Making Work Pleasant," 56–61; marketing strategy changes of 1980s, 70; Muscio on, 22; musicians, 53; musicians union v., 50–52; origins, 46; promotional material, 48–49; recorded (rather than performed) music, 50; research department, 69–70; residential music, 53; *Reveille* (1969 promotional LP), 53–57, *55*; scientific arguments, 75–79; transcription of music, 49–50, 152–153n25, 153n26; worker to consumer shift, 76; workplace music, 56–83; World War II, 52–53, 155n51

Muzak-plus: art as life, 110–114; audience-environment relationship, 110–114; audience reaction goal, 124–125; Cage's concept, 131–132; characteristics, 1–2, 114; concept, 109, 111; *feedback*, 120; implications suggested, 86; introduction, 83; liberation of people and sounds, 132; Muzak relationship, 3–4, 88–89; Pan Am building lobby sound environment, 111–114; paradoxical nature, 132; performer question, 125

Mystic Moods Orchestra, 53

Nam June Paik, 116
Nancy, Jean-Luc, 6
Nations Business, 53
Negri, Antonio, 71
New Babylon (Constant), 122–123, *123*
Newman, Barnett, 47
New York Times, 79, 104, 114
Niewenhuys, Constant, 122–123
Nine Evenings: Theatre and Engineering (Klüver and Rauschenberg, 1966), 121–122, *122*, 175n164
Notations (Cage, 1969), 3
"Notes, brouillons et esquisses" (Satie, 1918–1919), *39*
Nyman, Michael, 130

O'Doherty, Brian, 121
Office of War Information, 95–96
Official History gestalt, 121
Oldenburg, Claes, 117, 119, 175n178
Orledge, Robert, 12, 21, 24, 38
Orridge, Genesis P., 81, 162n194
Ozenfant, Amédée, 15, 148n112

Pagan Muzak (Rice, 1978), 108
Pan Am building lobby sound environment, 111–116, 172n132, 172n137
Papier phonique (Satie), 39, 149–150n130
Parade (Cocteau), 25–28
Patterson, David, 97
Petrillo, James, 50, 51–52, 93–96, 165n42–44
The Phonograph and Our Musical Life (Brooklyn College conference, 1977), 107–108
Picabia, Francis, 38, 39, 94
Pollack, Jackson, 127
post-Futurism, 25–26
Pritchett, James, 98
pseudo-individualization, 160n162

Rabinbach, Anson G., 57–58, 72
Radio Music (Cage), 101
Rainier, Yvonne, 7
Rauschenberg, Robert, 100, 121
"rearrangeable environments," 118–119
recording technologies: Cage on, 85–86, 102; Cage response, 102–103; Greenberg on, 121; Happenings, 121–122; mass market, 42; music aspect, 49–52; Muzak orchestration, 53; Satie-Muzak connection, 23; sonic community, 127. See also *Radio Music* (Cage); *Silent Prayer* (Cage); *33 1/3* (Cage)
Relâche (Picabia), 39, 94
required participation, 119, 121, 122
residential music, 53
"Rhythm, etc." (Cage, 1961), 109
Rice, Boyd, 108
Richards, M. C., 131
Richter, Hans, 41
Risveglio di un citta, per intonarumore (Russolo, 1913), 26
Rogers, Joel A., 26
Rosen, Charles, 74
Rosenquist, James, 100
Rosler, Martha, 133
Rothko, Mark, 47
Rowen, Ruth Halle, 30
Ruffian toujours, truand jamais (Always Wicked, Never a Crook, Jacob), 16
Russo, Alexander, 152–153n25
Russolo, Luigi, 26
Rzewski, Frederic, 126

Saint-Saëns, Camille, 20
"Un Salon" ("A Living Room/Lounge," Satie), 16
Satie, Erik: on art, 33; artistic circle variations, 15; Bauhaus alignment, 37; Cage references, 2–9, 107–108, 136n18–19; career paradoxes, 14; on Cocteau's nationalism, 34; on communists, 15; "counterfeit music," 35; criticism reactions, 14, 140n19; Debussy on, 14; as "father of Muzak," 10; film scores, 39–41, 94; "functional music" conception, 18; influence on Cage, 95; as innovator, 10; interpretive tendencies, 21–25; as inventor of Muzak, 2; as "musical analphabet," 10, 138–139n1; *musique d'ameublement* (furniture music) approval, 84; on *musique d'ameublement* (furniture music) concept, 32, 147n103; as Muzak inventor, 22; *Parade* (Cocteau) score, 27–29; personal characteristics, 14; politics, 15, 38; promotional slogans for *musique d'ameublement* (furniture music) (Satie), 33–34; sanctuary, 14–15; as "Les Six" father figure, 14
Sauget, Henri, 3
Schapiro, Meyer, 7
Schoenberg, Arnold, 164n24
Schumacher, Thomas, 57
Schwertsik, Kurt, 89
Seattle World's Fair Commemorative LP, 152n24
Selvin, Ben, 68–69
Shattuck, Roger, 3–4, 21, 40, 144n59
Shiff, Richard, 117
Silent Prayer (Cage), 92–99
situationism, 122
"Les Six." *See Groupe des Six* ("Les Six")
"Sons industriels" ("Industrial Sounds") (Satie, 1920), 19
Sousa, John Philip, 50, 93, 154n35, 165n41
Squier, George Owen, 46
Stallabrass, Julian, 42, 130
Sterne, Jonathan, 70, 82
Stevens Institute of Technology, 52
Surreal History of Muzak, Easy-Listening, and Other Moodsong (Lanza), 70–71
surrealism, 15
Symposium on Music and Industry, 68

Tafelmusik (Table Music) (Telemann, 1733), 30–31, 146n93
Tapisserie en fer forgé (Wrought-iron tapestry) (Satie, 1917), 3, 19, 37, *38*, 95, 107–108
Taruskin, Richard, 131–132
Taylorization, 57–58
technology. *See* recording technologies
Tenture de cabinet préfectoral (*Upholstery for a Governor's Office*) (Satie, 1923), 20, 95, 107–108, 142n13
Termen, Lev, 88, 116
Terpsiton, 116
Theremin, 116
Thérémin, Leon, 88
33 1/3 (Cage), 106–107, 171n112
Thomas, Ambrose, 19–20
Thoreau, Henry David, 128
"Time Out for Lunch," *67*
Tinguely, Jean, 122
Toop, David, 24
Touraine, Alain, 127–128
The Transformation of Nature in Art (Cooraswamy), 93
Tudor, David, 101, *115*, 116

Untitled (O'Hare) (Rosler), *133*
"useful music." *See* "functional music"

VanDerBeek, Stan, 116
Varèse, Edgard, 1, 3
Variations I (Cage, 1958), 89, *90*, *91*
Variations IV (Cage, 1963), 101
Variations V (Cage, 1965), 115–116, *115*, 124
Variations VII (Cage, 1966), 121
Variety, 50
"the Velvet Gentleman," 14
Vexations (Satie, 1893), 10, *11*, 103, 109
Vexations 1963 performance, 103–107
Vieux séquins et vielles cuirasses (*Old Sequins and Old Armor*) (Satie, 1913), *36*, 148–149n119, 149n120–121
Village Voice, 115, 122
Virilio, Paul, 7
Vision + Value series (Cage, 1966), 1
"visual Muzak," 112
"*Vive la revolution pasioné*" poster, *110*
Volta, Ornella, 15, 17, 27, 29

Wagner, Richard, 25
Warhol, Andy, 12, 100
War Production Board, 52, 155n51
White Light (Pollack), 127
"Wired for Sound by Muzak," *54*
Wokoun, William, 53, 56, 78

Wolff, Christian, 103–104
Words (Kaprow, 1962), 119
workplace music. *See* "functional music"; industrial music
World War II, 52–53, 61–62, 155n51
Wyatt, S., 49, 56–58, 62–64, 78, 157n91

HERVÉ VANEL teaches art history at The American University of Paris and is the the author of *Le parti commoniste, Roy Lichtenstein et L'art Pop,* Paris, Ed. Canné, 2013.

The University of Illinois Press
is a founding member of the
Association of American University Presses.

Composed in 10/13 ITC New Baskerville
by Lisa Connery
at the University of Illinois Press
Manufactured by Sheridan Books, Inc.

University of Illinois Press
1325 South Oak Street
Champaign, IL 61820-6903
www.press.uillinois.edu